JUN 0 7 2002

W9-BZU-179

TRUE BLUE

ALSO BY STEVE DELSOHN

Out of Bounds with Jim Brown

The Fire Inside: Firefighters Talk About Their Lives

Talking Irish: The Oral History of Notre Dame Football

TRUE BLUE

THE DRAMATIC HISTORY OF THE LOS ANGELES

DODGERS, TOLD BY THE MEN WHO LIVED IT

STEVE DELSOHN

WM

WILLIAM MORROW

75 Years of Publishing

An Imprint of HarperCollins*Publishers*

TRUE BLUE. Copyright © 2001 by Steve Delsohn. All rights reserved. Printed in the United States
of America. No part of this book may be used or reproduced in any manner whatsoever without
written permission except in the case of brief quotations embodied in critical articles and reviews.
For information address HarperCollins Publishers Inc.,
10 East 53rd Street, New York, NY 10022.

HarperCollins books may be purchased for educational, business, or sales promotional use. For
information please write: Special Markets Department, HarperCollins Publishers Inc.,
10 East 53rd Street, New York, NY 10022.

FIRST EDITION

Designed by Glen Edelstein

Library of Congress Cataloging-in-Publication Data

Delsohn, Steve.
    True Blue : the dramatic history of the Los Angeles Dodgers, told by the men
who lived it / by Steve Delsohn.
        p.   cm.
    ISBN 0-380-97755-9
    1. Los Angeles Dodgers (Baseball team)—History.   2. Baseball players—United
States—Anecdotes.   I. Title.
    GV875.L6 D45 2001
    796.357'64'0979494—dc21   00-061649
            01 02 03 04 05 QBF 10 9 8 7 6 5 4 3 2 1

To my father, Norman Delsohn,
who taught me to never give up

CONTENTS

PART III: THE SEVENTIES

PART IV: THE EIGHTIES

PART V: THE NINETIES

INTRODUCTION

SINCE 1957, WHEN THEY MADE THEIR SHOCKING EXODUS FROM BROOKLYN, THE Dodgers have created their own fabled history in Los Angeles. They have routinely drawn record crowds to Chavez Ravine. They have won nine pennants and five World Series championships, more than any team in that span except for the astounding New York Yankees.

Moreover, like the Yankees, the Dodgers are synonymous with baseball. Their classic uniforms and classic ballpark are known to baseball fans around the world. And yet, to *fully* understand the Dodgers, you have to begin at their birthplace. You have to return to Brooklyn.

Dating back to the 1850s, when the new game of baseball spread throughout America, Brooklyn was represented by several different teams. During the late 1880s, one of those teams was dubbed the Trolley Dodgers (which in populous, bustling Brooklyn at the time was what a person became if a person deemed it important to stay alive).

The Trolley Dodgers, or more simply the Dodgers, joined the National League in 1890. By the time the American League emerged in 1901, Brooklyn had won three pennants; there were 16 major league teams, and three of them made their home in New York City: the Dodgers, the Giants, and the Yankees.

Soon Gotham became "the capital of baseball," wrote documentary filmmaker Ken Burns. *The New Yorker*'s Roger Angell once told an interviewer that during the golden age of New York baseball—when city teams appeared in every World Series from 1949 through 1958—the so-called national pastime was "almost a private possession of New York City."

"You could walk through the city in October and the sounds of baseball were everywhere," Angell said. "From car radios, taverns, people (coming) out of taverns would say, 'Campy just hit one.' You were aware of a ribbon of baseball going on around you."

Among the three New York teams—Brooklyn's Dodgers, the Bronx's Yankees, and East Harlem's Giants—the Yankees were by far the most dominant, winning 18 World Series from 1923 to 1958 while the Dodgers and Giants won only three. Then again, as the great columnist Red Smith once put it, "Rooting for the Yankees is like rooting for U.S. Steel."

Meanwhile, in Brooklyn the Dodgers were worshiped. This feeling was partly due, wrote New York University professor Carl E. Prince, to the borough's second-class status in the city. "Brooklyn was not really thought to be part of New York City by 'genuine' New Yorkers," Prince explained. "There were the *New York Yankees* and the *New York Giants*, after all, but the *Bums* were the Brooklyn Dodgers."

Thus Brooklynites rallied around their beloved Dodgers as a source of local pride and identity. But according to Mark Reese, a Los Angeles film producer and the son of Brooklyn Hall of Famer Pee Wee Reese, there was another key reason for the close emotional ties between the Dodger players and their fans: "They played in this wonderful little ballpark, in this close-knit blue-collar area that was Brooklyn. There wasn't this division between the entertainers and regular folks. They were part of the same community."

That wonderful little ballpark was Ebbets Field, built in 1913 on a garbage dump called Pigtown in one of the poorest sections of the borough. Considered spacious and modern when it opened, it would later be viewed as too small and decayed by then–Dodger owner Walter O'Malley. His discontent would touch off a stunning chain of events that would leave the Brooklyn faithful devastated.

But all of that came during the 1950s. In 1916 and 1920, the Dodgers won two more pennants before losing the first two World Series they played in. Then, from 1922 to 1938, the most inglorious stretch in franchise history, they became known as the "daffiness boys" and the "bums."

The numbers were awful enough—ten sixth-place finishes in 17 years—but the Dodgers were noted for more than simply losing. They served as the laughingstock of baseball, with characters like Babe Herman, who had fly balls bounce off his head, and Walter "Boom-Boom" Beck, whose pitches first went *boom* when they were hit, and again when they slammed off the outfield walls.

As for their baserunning prowess? Well, this was a standard bit of Brooklyn shtick: "The Dodgers have three men on base." "Oh yeah? Which one?"

In 1938 the brilliant, when not boozing, Larry MacPhail took over as president and general manager. In 1939 he hired as manager his own feisty shortstop, Leo Durocher, and in 1941 Brooklyn won its first pennant in two decades. Then, after the villainous Yankees defeated the cherished Dodgers in the World Series, the Brooklyn *Eagle* ran its legendary headline: WAIT TILL NEXT YEAR.

In 1942, when MacPhail joined the army, Branch Rickey arrived in Brooklyn as the team's new general manager and part-owner. The silver-tongued "Mister Rickey" came via St. Louis, where he had built the Cardinals into a league power and transformed the entire game by creating the farm system in 1919.

Under Rickey in the late 1940s, Brooklyn established itself as the National League's best team with a formidable array of stars including the likes of Jackie Robinson, Duke Snider, Roy Campanella, Gil Hodges, Carl Furillo, Pee Wee Reese, and Carl Erskine. Simultaneously, Rickey set in stone what would later be dubbed the Dodger Way: Never rely on trades with other teams; build a strong minor league system and develop your own players; teach them to play fundamentally sound "Dodger baseball"; then, if they become stars in the big leagues, get rid of them one year too early rather than one year too late.

Of course, Rickey is still most revered for his historic encounter with Jackie Robinson. In 1947, when Rickey and Robinson broke the color line in major league baseball, life in America meant segregation. There were separate drinking fountains, separate schools, separate restaurants, separate platoons in the Armed Forces. Jackie Robinson could not cure all of that. But seven years before *Brown v. Board of Education*, Robinson was a powerful agent for change.

Naturally, he was met with vicious resistance. In May 1947 white fans mocked him by throwing black cats on the field at Cincinnati. He also got taunted that game by racist bench jockeys, thrown at by the Reds' pitchers when he batted, and spiked by their runners as he played at first base. Once when it looked like Robinson got spiked badly, time-out was called by captain Pee Wee Reese. The noisy crowd looked on as Reese, a white Southerner from nearby Kentucky, walked over from shortstop to check on his black teammate. Then Reese put his arm around Robinson's shoulder.

Robinson never forgot the simple and powerful gesture. And as Robinson, Rickey, and Reese spearheaded the "Great Experiment," the Dodgers became far more than Brooklyn's favorite team. They were a glimmer of hope in a nation with terribly backward race relations.

By 1950, the year the fabled Rickey left Brooklyn, one of his three fellow Dodger owners was Walter O'Malley. A New York–born graduate of Fordham Law, he had once been the Dodger attorney before buying his 25 percent of the club. Then, as the cunning O'Malley increased his power, he began to plot Rickey's departure.

Their ongoing feud was partly financial. Rickey, the baseball man, tended to spend lavishly in every area but players' salaries. O'Malley, the businessman, was strictly committed to the bottom line. But they also simply hated each other. Rickey didn't drink, had an enormous ego, and endlessly quoted Scripture. O'Malley loved Irish whiskey, had an enormous ego, and privately called Rickey that "psalm-singing fake."

In 1950 O'Malley saw a chance to force out his rival. When one of the four Dodger owners died in June, O'Malley smoothly secured his block of shares. Then, already owning 50 percent of the club, O'Malley offered Rickey $346,667 (exactly what Rickey had paid in 1943) for his 25 percent interest in the Dodgers.

Rickey knew he was out and had already lined up a job with the Pittsburgh Pirates. But rather than accept the rock-bottom offer, he produced an offer from William Zeckendorf, a New York real estate mogul, for $1,050,000. O'Malley always swore the offer was phony, but since he had no proof, he was forced to match Zeckendorf's offer.

Thus, explained Red Smith in the *New York Times*, "Zeckendorf received $50,000 for his trouble, Rickey got his million and O'Malley's enduring hostility." In fact, after Rickey went to Pittsburgh, O'Malley fined any Brooklyn employee $1 for mentioning Rickey's name in his presence (he later had the same rule for Marvin Miller, the powerful head of the baseball players union, but in Miller's case the fine was $5 per mention).

In the early 1950s, with O'Malley now in firm control of the franchise, one aspect of Brooklyn baseball stayed the same: The Dodgers dominated the National League, only to flop when they entered the postseason. Between 1947 and 1954 the team won four pennants for three different managers—Durocher, Charlie Dressen, and Walter Alston—but in 1947, 1949, 1952, and 1953, they dropped all four "Subway Series" to the Yankees.

Then came glorious 1955. After playing in seven World Series since 1916—and leaving their fans disheartened every time—the Dodgers finally triumphed over the Yankees for their first and only world championship in Brooklyn. Johnny Podres ended the drought on October 4 at Yankee Stadium with a 2–0 victory in Game 7. Afterward, Podres recalls, "There was champagne flowing all over Brooklyn."

In 1956 the Dodgers won their fourth pennant in five seasons, but lost in the Series again to the powerful Yankees. In 1957 the Dodgers came in third, then left Brooklyn for Los Angeles. The story of that famous move is where *True Blue* begins.

PART I

THE LATE FIFTIES

1

WALTER O'MALLEY'S RADICAL MOVE WEST

1 9 5 7

HARRY RUDOLPH TURNS 70 THIS SEPTEMBER. HARRY HAS NINE CHILDREN, plays golf about five times a week, and owns a cozy restaurant aptly named Harry's, located in La Jolla, California, the pretty coastal village just a few beaches north of San Diego.

And so as Harry puts it, "I don't have any complaints about California. I've been fortunate. But, yeah, there are still times I miss New York."

That's where he grew up. In fact, from 1945 to 1947, Harry had the greatest job in Brooklyn.

HARRY RUDOLPH: It was better than that. It was probably the greatest job a kid could have in the world at that time. I was the bat boy for the Brooklyn Dodgers.

In 1947 I got to see Jackie Robinson break the color line. I got to spend time around Pee Wee Reese. He was the captain of the team. He was a Southerner. And it's well documented that Reese befriended Jackie, and that helped Jackie break some barriers.

All those guys were magical to me. They were magical to everyone in Brooklyn. Ebbets Field was real small and the fans sat close to the field.

And most of the players lived in Brooklyn then. There was a love affair. There was a bond.

Then one morning they were gone. They announced they were leaving. Walter O'Malley was going to L.A. and Horace Stoneham was going to San Francisco. As it turned out, O'Malley got the much better deal. O'Malley was a very smart Irishman.

But nobody in Brooklyn ever forgave him. People were too broken-hearted. There was a void and a shock. Then I remember when they demolished Ebbets Field. They had the big balls ready, and they tore it down.

That was a big loss, a very sad time. Maybe there were some kids it didn't matter to. It mattered like hell to me.

Pete Hamill is a legendary New York newspaperman and the author of many books, including the bestselling novel *Snow in August* and the powerful memoir *A Drinking Life*. Hamill was born and raised in the borough of the Dodgers.

PETE HAMILL: The Dodgers were such a natural part of childhood. They were part of the dailiness of life, including the off-season, when the Brooklyn *Eagle* would carry a column they called the "Hot Stove League," which told you about what all the players were doing when there was no baseball season.

It was part of living, in a way. And I'm talking about the world before television, in which you experience something like baseball, and particularly the Dodgers, through newspapers and the radio. I mean, it wasn't until I was maybe 11 that I was able to actually go to games. So we imagined these games, and we imagined the players before we ever saw them.

The most important thing was Robinson. Here he comes in 1947, and what was so great to me was not that Robinson integrated baseball. He integrated those stands at Ebbets Field.

I was 12 in 1947. And Robinson quickly became as close to a role model as anybody that people my age had, black or white. Because we identified with him. I mean, Brooklyn itself was on the margin of New York. It was the butt of jokes in all those radio shows and war movies. There was always some dumb guy in the platoon who was from Brooklyn. And people would make fun of the way he talked.

When Robinson came along, everyone in the stands could identify with him. The blacks, the Jews, the children of immigrants could identify with him. He was on the edge of the goddamned thing. And into the bargain, he was a great baseball player. I mean, if he had been a .210 hitter, it wouldn't have been the same thing.

George Vecsey, the terrific sports columnist for the *New York Times,* was a die-hard Dodger fan who grew up in Queens.

GEORGE VECSEY: Have you ever been to the Brooklyn Museum? It's a wonderful museum on Eastern Parkway. You can stand in the botanical gardens, which is right behind the museum, and look out at where Ebbets Field used to be. Except now there is housing.

My wife and I went out to the museum the day after Thanksgiving a year ago. I'm in this beautiful garden on a beautiful November afternoon and there's a lump in my throat. That's my childhood over there I'm looking at.

So, yes, I hated O'Malley when they left Brooklyn. Then I hated him even more in '62—the first time I went to Dodger Stadium. Here was this gorgeous stadium up on a hill. You could drop a hamburger on the floor and pick it up and eat it.

And I hated and resented that this had happened. I felt: "They took my team. O'Malley took my team. Then he put it up on this hill."

Vecsey was hardly alone. For uprooting the Brooklyn Dodgers to Los Angeles, Walter O'Malley is despised by a number of New Yorkers to this day.

But did O'Malley truly abandon Brooklyn, or was he pushed into a corner by New York politics? Was he a devious traitor? Or was he a bold pioneer, which is how generations of Southern Californians see him?

From Brooklyn's point of view, the first glimpse of betrayal came in the glorious summer of 1955. With the Dodgers en route to their first World Series victory, O'Malley shocked the borough with this announcement: In 1956 his team would play seven "home games" at Roosevelt Stadium in Jersey City.

O'Malley had no interest in moving to New Jersey. In fact, he was sending a message to New York politicians. Ebbets Field, then in its 43rd season, all but reeked of history and tradition, but the stadium had grown old and badly outmoded. Now, after several years of agitating for a new stadium, O'Malley was running short on patience.

Robert Creamer believes he had a right to. Creamer, a former writer at *Sports Illustrated* and the author of books on Babe Ruth and Casey Stengel, says, "Ebbets Field by then was pretty much a slum of a ballpark."

ROBERT CREAMER: The Dodgers were still a terrific ball team, best in the National League. And the Dodgers were still making a profit in Brooklyn. But Ebbets Field was not an attractive place.

The grandstands were dirty and smelled of stale beer. The clubhouse was so small and cluttered, even the Dodger clubhouse, it was like somebody's attic. And the visiting clubhouse was worse. It was like the Black Hole of Calcutta.

This was a decrepit, antiquated old ballpark that just could not continue. That's all there was to it. They had to have a change.

Parking presented a major problem as well. Ebbets Field had opened in 1913, before the automobile was mass produced, and thus had 700 parking spaces. It seated only 32,111 fans, and even in those small confines attendance was sliding. In 1947, Jackie Robinson's exciting rookie year, Dodger attendance had peaked at 1.8 million. In 1955, when Brooklyn won its first and only World Series, barely one million customers showed up.

ROBERT CREAMER: I remember Duke Snider talking about it. The Dodgers had just come back from this terrific road trip and Ebbets Field was half empty. Snider was mad as hell. He was talking to one of the writers, and Snider just said, "Fuck 'em. They're the worst fans in the league."

So the glorious Brooklyn Dodgers and the glorious Ebbets Field is a myth. It's a nice myth, but it's a myth. And it wasn't just Walter O'Malley saying, "Screw Brooklyn. I'm gonna go to greener pastures." The pastures in Brooklyn were no longer green.

Meanwhile, in Milwaukee, the first major league franchise to change cities was setting attendance records. In 1952, their last year in Boston, the Braves had drawn only 281,000. But with a new 43,000-seat County Stadium, parking for 10,000 cars, and Hank Aaron and Eddie Mathews hitting home runs, Milwaukee drew two million fans in four straight seasons (1954–57), which was almost *twice* what Brooklyn drew those years. "If they take in twice as many dollars, they'll eventually be able to buy better talent," O'Malley muttered. "Then they'll be the winners, not us."

Of course, not everyone trusted his public statements. His detractors called the Braves a red herring. They said greed, pure greed, drove Walter O'Malley out to California.

Roger Kahn, Jerome Holtzman, and Neil Sullivan give their perspectives. Kahn is famous for writing *The Boys of Summer*, the poignant and funny account of the 1950s Brooklyn Dodgers, which the *New York Times Book Review* called "a classic." Holtzman has covered baseball for the *Chicago Sun-Times* or *Chicago Tribune* since 1957. Sullivan grew up in Los Angeles and is now a college professor in New York. His book, *The Dodgers Move West*, is the most significant study of why the team left Brooklyn.

ROGER KAHN: I wouldn't ever want to create the impression that Walter O'Malley was a nice fellow. But I will say this about him leaving Brooklyn. Walter O'Malley's wife had throat cancer, and she spoke in a whisper. She had built a circle of friends at Amityville, Long Island. Walter was born in the Bronx, but he lived in Brooklyn.

So Brooklyn was their home. And the idea that they wanted to uproot themselves at this point in their lives is just not so. Now, the question of greed? Yeah. George Steinbrenner is greedy. Capitalists are greedy. That goes with the franchise, doesn't it?

JEROME HOLTZMAN: Hadn't they made money the previous year? So what was the big deal? He just wanted to open up a bigger territory for himself.

Walter O'Malley abandoned the people of Brooklyn. It was a money move. That's all it was. You're gonna tell me he needed a new stadium?

That's the old excuse. Everybody says that. Whenever they want to move, they need a new stadium.

NEIL SULLIVAN: Was he interested in making money? Yeah, he sure was. But he gambled *his* own money when he moved.

There's a mythology that he planned all along to go to L.A., because he knew they'd be drawing three million a year in attendance. But if Los Angeles was such an obvious gold mine, why didn't the Boston Braves move to L.A.? Why didn't the St. Louis Browns or the Athletics? They all went someplace else.

Walter O'Malley knew New York. He did not know Los Angeles. So it was a very bold, even reckless, move on O'Malley's part. It was an extraordinary move.

Mark Reese agrees with Sullivan. The son of the late Pee Wee Reese, he is also a film producer whose documentary series for ESPN (*The Original America's Team: The Brooklyn Dodgers*) was described by the *New York Times* as an "elegant, intelligent, evocative film."

MARK REESE: I think Walter O'Malley, and the entire country, were becoming more aware of what Los Angeles was. The postwar years were highly prosperous. The population was booming. Then Disneyland opened in 1955. It was hugely successful. It was family-run entertainment. And I believe that pushed O'Malley over. He started thinking, man, this thing could work!

But Disneyland started out here. So in 1957, it was still a radical thing to move the Dodgers out west. It took a lot of balls for him to do that.

PETE HAMILL: I think greed was a factor. But I think he was also a visionary. O'Malley understood—in the same way that Bugsy Siegel was a visionary—that airplanes and air-conditioning were changing the perception of the West.

So there had to be a ballpark out there. There had to be major league baseball. To think that major league baseball would end at the Mississippi was just nuts.

So I think he was right about that. But what the people in Brooklyn resented was, yeah, there ought to be baseball there. But do you have to take *our* team? I mean, that was bound to infuriate them.

And what about the issues of race and class? During the late 1950s, as a majority of white Brooklyn moved to the suburbs, did the neighborhood surrounding Ebbets Field become too black, too Puerto Rican, too poor for Walter O'Malley's patrician tastes?

ROGER KAHN: Brooklyn was changing ethnically and economically. The upper-middle-class people were moving out to Long Island. And you were getting a different group of people, a lot of Latins and blacks.

That was a concern in the Dodgers' front office. It was never expressed publicly, because it was so politically incorrect, but more or less you heard that a black tide was gonna sweep down from Eastern Parkway over to Ebbets Field. And then who could afford to buy tickets to a game?

NEIL SULLIVAN: In Peter Golenbock's book, *Bums,* he talks about tension at Ebbets Field between blacks and whites. I imagine there's something to that. Hell, there's something to that today from time to time. But would you make this kind of business decision based on that?

You know, Tom Yawkey might have. The guy had about as appalling a record on race as any owner in the major leagues. The Red Sox were the last team to integrate. They waited until 1959, which was after Jackie Robinson had retired. Yawkey's record was deplorable. So if Yawkey had owned the Dodgers and they moved and somebody said, "Well, it was because of the racial climate," that would be a fairly credible theory.

But it just doesn't seem to fit Walter O'Malley. If he were motivated by racial considerations, I think he would have gotten out of Brooklyn entirely. But he didn't want to. The evidence is that if he could build a new stadium, privately, Walter O'Malley wanted to stay in Brooklyn.

Carl Erskine feels the same way. Erskine, the courageous and classy pitcher whom Brooklyn fans called "Oisk," injured his right shoulder as a rookie and pitched in pain throughout his 12-year Dodger career. Yet he still threw two no-hitters, went 122–78, and struck out a then-record 14 batters in Game 3 of the 1953 World Series.

CARL ERSKINE: When this whole problem got started, I don't think he wanted to leave Brooklyn. You have to understand the political climate up there. Brooklyn didn't have big entertainment, big hotels, big restaurants. Brooklyn didn't have the political clout. It was kind of an orphan borough.

So when Walter O'Malley tried moving—but only to another part of Brooklyn—the city fathers wouldn't go for that.

O'Malley had dreamed of building baseball's first domed stadium at the intersection of Flatbush and Atlantic avenues in downtown Brooklyn. So he could finance this stadium himself, he asked government officials to condemn the property for him. But in 1955 O'Malley's ambitious plan was blocked by Robert Moses, the single most powerful man in New York City.

The autocratic head of New York's highways, parks, and urban renewal, Moses didn't mind if the Dodgers left Ebbets Field. In fact, he planned to build a housing project there. But Moses instructed O'Malley to relocate to Queens, to which O'Malley famously replied, "If my team is forced to play in the borough of Queens, they will no longer be the Brooklyn Dodgers."

Thus began a monstrous clash of ego: Walter O'Malley versus Robert Moses, a man so formidable he sparred for years with Franklin D. Roosevelt, and a man described by his brilliant biographer Robert Caro as "blind and deaf to reason, to argument, to new ideas, to any ideas except his own."

MARK REESE: Robert Moses was absolutely ferocious. He ran right over anyone in his way. Well, he and O'Malley had a power struggle. And Robert Moses won. There was no way O'Malley was getting that land.

In August 1955, immediately after Moses spurned him, O'Malley made his announcement about playing seven home games in Jersey City. Then he quickly sold Ebbets Field to a real estate developer who leased it back to O'Malley for only three years. In January 1957, after New York mayor

Robert Wagner had formed a do-nothing committee to study the stadium issue, O'Malley issued a terse ultimatum: "Unless something is done within six months, I will have to make other arrangements."

PETE HAMILL: Clearly the combination of Moses' autocratic methods and Wagner's indecision made it easier for Walter O'Malley. I mean, I think he had his heart set on the West. But they sure didn't do much to keep the move from happening.

Meanwhile, in 1957, Los Angeles was a sprawling metropolis with 5.5 million people, and a city getting fat on defense contracts and a nonstop housing boom. Now its powerbrokers coveted major league baseball.

Two famous ex–Los Angeles newspapermen, Mel Durslag and Bud Furillo, recall the local desire for a big league club. Durslag wrote graceful sports columns for more than 30 years, most of that time for the *Herald Examiner*. The blunt-spoken Furillo has worked in print or radio since 1946. From 1964 to 1974, he served as the *Herald Examiner*'s sports editor.

BUD FURILLO: Red Smith once said to me, "Bud, I have nothing against Los Angeles. I like Los Angeles. Tell me one thing. Where is it?"

So the city needed more identity. Especially downtown Los Angeles. City Hall knew that major league baseball could do that.

MEL DURSLAG: L.A. had been fighting for years for major league baseball. And Walter O'Malley came close to missing out. In 1957 it was all offered to the Washington Senators.

BUD FURILLO: The Senators were coming to Los Angeles. Their owner, Calvin Griffith, was tired of losing money in the nation's capital. But then at the 1956 World Series, O'Malley sent a note to Kenneth Hahn. Hahn was the county supervisor from L.A. He came to the World Series to meet Calvin Griffith. But O'Malley found out and sent this note to Hahn. It said *he* was interested in Los Angeles. So now, all of a sudden, do you want the Washington Senators or Brooklyn Dodgers?

MEL DURSLAG: It was a very easy decision for Los Angeles. So it was full speed ahead with Walter O'Malley. And Cal Griffith had to settle for moving to Minnesota.

In February 1957, O'Malley's next slick move came at Phil Wrigley's expense. The chewing gum tycoon owned the Chicago Cubs as well as the minor league Los Angeles Angels. When O'Malley learned Wrigley was feuding with L.A. politicians, he secretly offered a trade: Wrigley's minor league franchise and its ballpark, Wrigley Field, for O'Malley's minor league franchise in Dallas–Fort Worth.

O'Malley didn't care about the Angels, and he had no long-term plans for Wrigley Field, which had been built in 1925 and now sat next to a brothel. O'Malley urgently wanted, and received, only one thing from Wrigley: the territorial rights to major league baseball in Los Angeles.

JEROME HOLTZMAN: They made an even swap: Fort Worth for Los Angeles. What a deal that was, huh? Phil Wrigley let Walter O'Malley come into L.A. scot-free.

O'Malley next turned his lethal charm on Horace Stoneham, the New York Giants owner who had already decided to leave East Harlem. The Polo Grounds had decayed, and by 1957, even with Willie Mays in center field, attendance had plunged to 9,000 fans a game.

MARK REESE: The myth is that Walter O'Malley talked Horace Stoneham into leaving New York. He actually talked Stoneham into moving to California. Until then, Stoneham was headed for Minnesota.

Reese's point is confirmed by Buzzie Bavasi, the colorful and shrewd negotiator who spent almost two decades (1951–68) in the powerful role of Dodger general manager. In 1967, after his teams had won eight pennants and four World Series, *Sports Illustrated* called him "baseball's most successful executive."

BUZZIE BAVASI: Stoneham had the major league rights to Minneapolis. But O'Malley needed Stoneham in California, because the other National League owners said Walter couldn't move out there alone. They needed another team for the purposes of scheduling and transportation.

So that's when Walter called Stoneham. Walter said, "Why don't you go to San Francisco? We'll go out west together."

NEIL SULLIVAN: Even to this day, nobody talks about Stoneham being a villain. Probably because the Giants didn't have the borough identity the Dodgers did.

Stoneham was also known to take a drink. If you caught him at the right time of day, you could probably get Willie Mays for a second baseman. So I think people understood that Stoneham just wasn't a force. And Walter O'Malley was.

MARK REESE: Walter persuaded Horace to take a look at this place called the Candlestick area. Walter took Horace out there during the winter. It was 70 degrees at Candlestick, the sun was shining, and after a five-martini lunch, Horace was sold.

Little did he know that in June and July, the fog would roll in off the bay, Giant pitchers would get blown off the mound, infield fly balls would turn into home runs, and Giant fans would be wearing turtlenecks.

But that was Walter O'Malley. As a friend of mine once said, he could sell you a dead horse—twice.

By this time, O'Malley and Kenneth Hahn had taken their fabled ride over Los Angeles in a borrowed Sheriff's Department helicopter. Scanning potential sites for a new stadium, O'Malley saw 300 acres of sparsely developed land in the downtown area known as Chavez Ravine.

Hahn instantly promised O'Malley the rugged tract, but nearly couldn't deliver it in the end. Political resistance kept the Dodgers out of a new stadium until 1962. They would actually play in a football stadium, the Los Angeles Coliseum, in the meantime.

In August 1957, Horace Stoneham made the first hurtful announcement. "We're sorry to disappoint the kids of New York," he said, "but we didn't see many of their parents out there at the Polo Grounds in recent years."

On September 24, 1957, the Dodgers played their last game at Ebbets Field. Brooklyn won 2–0 while organist Gladys Gooding played *Auld Lang Syne* and fans hoping for a last-second miracle unfurled signs saying, "KEEP THE DODGERS IN BROOKLYN."

It became official on October 8. New York had lost another baseball team.

The Brooklyn faithful wept. They cursed O'Malley in bars and hung him in effigy on city streets. Dick Young wrote in his hard-bitten *Daily News* column, "O'Malley leaves town a rich man and a despised man." Then Young went over the top in a story for *Sport* magazine. "To hell with the Los Angeles Dodgers!" he seethed.

CARL ERSKINE: It was kind of a shattering thing for the borough of Brooklyn. This was a pretty deep hurt in a love affair.

GEORGE VECSEY: You can't underestimate the pain that was left behind. My God, the Dodgers moved?

HARRY RUDOLPH: If it was another team, there wouldn't be that much sadness. Brooklyn was always different. The Dodgers were always different. They were the bums.

PETE HAMILL: After the Dodgers left, I never went to another baseball game for 12 years. Then one night I was having dinner with Jack Newfield. Jack used to write these pieces for the *Voice*. Very good pieces on the ten worst landlords and the ten worst judges and so on.

And I said at dinner, "Geez, Jack, you ought to expand this and do the ten worst people of the twentieth century." He said, "You make your list and I'll make mine." We both only got to three, and they turned out exactly the same: Hitler, Stalin, and Walter O'Malley.

2

STRUGGLE IN PARADISE

1958

IN 1958, WHILE NEW YORKERS VENTED AND MOURNED, SOUTHERN CALIFORNIANS cheered the arrival of major league baseball. One of their staunchest fans was Bill Caplan, a 66-year-old boxing publicist who has attended Dodger games since the season they were reborn in Los Angeles.

BILL CAPLAN: When I was seven years old, the team that I picked as my favorite was the Brooklyn Dodgers. They were my childhood team, even though I grew up in Iowa.

I moved to L.A. in 1957. And when I found out my Dodgers were coming here? To Los Angeles? It was the greatest present anyone could give me.

Then I never missed a pitch the first 15 or 20 years they were here. I probably went to 80 percent of the games, and if I couldn't get to the game, I had a transistor radio to my ear, listening to Vin Scully and Jerry Doggett. If I went to a movie, dinner, *anything*, I knew if the Dodgers were winning.

There were a lot of fans like that in the early days. The Dodgers took over this town and never let go.

For the original Los Angeles Dodgers, however, their first year out West brought difficulties. In fact, Don Drysdale called it "one totally screwed-up season. . . . If you'd have asked the players on the Dodgers to take a vote, it might have been 25–0 to stay in Brooklyn."

Drysdale grew up in Los Angeles, no less. So did the great Duke Snider, the 1958 team's only other native.

DUKE SNIDER: My wife and I had tears in our eyes the day we packed up and moved. I was born in Los Angeles. But I was born in Brooklyn, baseball-wise.

ROGER KAHN: I think the players were sort of disoriented. Clem Labine said you're on the mound, you got a man on second and third, you go into your stretch, you take a look around, and where is Ebbets Field? Where the hell is Brooklyn?

The sinkerball-throwing Labine was one of baseball's top relievers in the 1950s. He went 13–5 for the sainted 1955 World Champions and his 83 saves in Brooklyn set a club record.

CLEM LABINE: You establish certain roots, especially in a close-knit town such as Brooklyn. Now, suddenly, we live in Los Angeles. We don't know the fans, we don't know the city. Where are we gonna live? What schools should we put our kids in? So, yes, that first year we struggled.

ROGER KAHN: Remember, Walter O'Malley had also dumped Jackie Robinson, cynically, before they left Brooklyn. I don't know how much Jackie could have played if he had continued, probably not more than 100 games a year, but it was still a symbolic, disturbing sort of thing.

Then Roy Campanella goes down in a car accident. Then the team comes to L.A. and right off they stumble.

MARK REESE: My father didn't want to go to Los Angeles. His playing days were numbered and he wanted to retire with his whole career in Brooklyn. Then Walter O'Malley said, "I need you to come. I need you and Gil

Hodges and the old-timers. I want to bring the legacy to L.A., and then gently make the transformation."

So Pee Wee did it for Walter. But he was past his prime and so were most of the other Brooklyn stars.

In 1958 the team that had won four pennants in six years finished a stunning 21 games out of first place. In fact, only the eighth-place Phillies kept the new western Dodgers (73–81) out of the cellar.

Then again, maybe they had stadium shock. After a decade of hard-hitting teams in that bandbox, Ebbets Field, the 1958 Dodgers still had Duke Snider, Gil Hodges, and Carl Furillo in their starting lineup, but with Dodger Stadium not yet constructed, the team now played in the enormous Los Angeles Coliseum.

The Dodgers only expected to be there two seasons. They remained there twice that long—in a ballpark that quickly became the talk of baseball.

CLEM LABINE: That's because it *wasn't* a ballpark. It was a football stadium. The Los Angeles Coliseum held 100,000 people. That was a bit of a jolt after Ebbets Field.

So was the Coliseum's left field line. It was the shortest in the majors at only 250 feet from home plate. So to prevent a ridiculous number of home runs, the Dodgers put up their infamous left field screen: 40 feet high and 140 feet long, suspended in the air by two steel poles. As *Sports Illustrated* wryly pointed out, it looked remarkably like the Brooklyn Bridge.

Nearly as strange as the screen were the lopsided dimensions in the outfield. The center field wall was a normal 410 feet. But the right field wall was 300 feet down the foul line, quickly curved out to a radical 400, and then finally reached a mind-boggling 440 in right-center.

Thus in 1958, even with the towering left field screen, 182 homers went out that way. Only 11 homers were hit to center and right.

NEIL SULLIVAN: They tried to palm it off. But the Coliseum was a very weird place. The one guy who made his bones there was Wally Moon. He batted left-handed, but he learned how to slice home runs to left. The head-line writers loved it. They called them Moon Shots.

BUD FURILLO: Moon developed that opposite field swing. But Duke Snider wasn't an opposite field hitter. In those days they called guys who did that "piss hitters."

Well, Duke Snider was not a piss hitter. Snider pulled the ball, just like Ted Williams.

The comparison to Ted Williams isn't a stretch. In the mid-1950s, during the golden age of New York baseball, some considered Duke Snider the best all-around center fielder in Gotham (ahead of Willie Mays and Mickey Mantle). From 1953 to 1957, Snider hit more than 40 home runs every season. Even today the Duke of Flatbush still holds the home run record (389) for both the Brooklyn and Los Angeles Dodgers.

Yet in 1958, his first season playing in his hometown, Snider batted what he calls a "weak" .312. And coming off knee surgery, in a stadium that devoured left-handed power hitters, he hit just 15 homers after those five straight years of 40-plus.

DUKE SNIDER: A lot of it was my knee. But, sure, I lost some home runs in the Coliseum. The first time Willie Mays played there, he said, "Duke, they killed you. Man, they took the bat right out of your hands."

Then he walked away laughing. Of course, Willie batted right-handed. So he had that nice short distance to left field.

Snider says he and Mays talked on April 18, 1958, the blazingly hot and historic afternoon when the Dodgers defeated the Giants 6–5 in the first major league game played in Los Angeles. The sweaty but grateful crowd of 78,672 (a National League record the first time out!) included such luminaries as Nat King Cole, Dinah Shore, Danny Kaye, and Edward G. Robinson. Not that the Dodgers noticed their glitzy new fans.

CARL ERSKINE: Are you kidding me? One time I was pitching in the Coliseum. I glanced over at our dugout and five or six of our guys all had their necks craned. They were gawking into the stands at Lana Turner.

Hollywood producer Joseph Siegman has co-organized the Hollywood Stars Game for more than 35 years. This is the annual exhibition at Dodger Stadium, where the celebrities take the field to actually play semidecent baseball.

Siegman recalls Hollywood's instant embrace of the city's first major league franchise.

JOSEPH SIEGMAN: Cary Grant. Bing Crosby. Bob Hope. Jack Benny. George Burns. Milton Berle. Nat King Cole. Danny Kaye. Dean Martin and Jerry Lewis. Now, they were split up by then. So they came separately. But all of these stars came out to see the Dodgers.

BUD FURILLO: A lot of Hollywood people come from New York. So as soon as they left Brooklyn, the Dodgers became Hollywood's domain. Good grief, I can still see Milton Berle in their clubhouse. He looked like he shared a locker with Sandy Koufax.

The 93-year-old Berle grew up playing stickball in Harlem. During the 1940s, as the incredibly hammy host of *Texaco Star Theater*, he was the first superstar of the new American medium called TV.

MILTON BERLE: I rooted for them when they played in Ebbets Field. Then Danny Thomas and I tried investing in them when they came here. We wanted a piece of the Dodgers, but O'Malley turned us down. He wanted to own them himself without any partners. Which I totally understood.

So I became one of the Dodgers' biggest boosters. My wife and I had season tickets. We had eight box seats between home plate and first. And we would take other performers. Walter Matthau, Jack Lemmon, Neil Simon. Everyone wanted to go and see the Dodgers. That was the great place to be in Los Angeles.

But if the show business crowd brought glamour, it was the ordinary fan who proved that this movie and beach town could also rally around major league baseball. In 1958, in spite of a seventh-place team and a freakish stadium, the Dodgers drew 1.85 million fans. This total squeaked past their all-time high in Brooklyn (1.81 million) and marked an enormous increase over their last season there (1 million).

Meanwhile, however, in Walter O'Malley's bid for a new stadium, he found himself engaged in a serious land war. Back in October 1957, the Los Angeles City Council had made O'Malley an offer he couldn't refuse: the 300-acre site at Chavez Ravine in exchange for his minor league ballpark, Wrigley Field. To further gift wrap the package, the city and the county also agreed to spend $4.7 million for grading, street construction, and access roads.

But in 1958, as O'Malley's opponents closed ranks, the land deal was challenged. This led to a public referendum, which very nearly derailed O'Malley's dream.

BUZZIE BAVASI: Chavez Ravine was a dump. I mean, literally a dumping ground. Nobody wanted it. But the opposition felt that we were getting too much land for nothing. I mean, all the city got was Wrigley Field.

But we still thought the vote would be a cinch. Then it started getting tighter and tighter. So Walter O'Malley went out and got people like Cary Grant and Ronald Reagan to go on TV and say how good it would be for the city of Los Angeles. We won by *that* much. If not for Hollywood, we might have lost.

In June 1958 the referendum passed by just 24,000 votes out of 668,000. This narrow result reflected a common belief: Walter O'Malley made a sweetheart deal. He "stole" Chavez Ravine from Los Angeles.

BILL CAPLAN: O'Malley made a great deal for himself. But it was also a great deal for L.A., because Dodger Stadium wasn't built with public funds. O'Malley financed it himself for $12 million, which is what it would probably cost to paint it now. And even though he ended up making a killing, he always kept the ticket prices low.

JEROME HOLTZMAN: It was a deal that was good for both parties. Who got the best of it I don't think is of any real concern. I know L.A. sure as hell didn't get the worst of it.

BUD FURILLO: Considering how many property taxes he paid, how he gave an identity to downtown Los Angeles, and how much money came in from every World Series played out here, I would say L.A. got the sweetheart deal.

MEL DURSLAG: A big American city finally got major league baseball. But it was more important than that. It opened up the entire West to major league baseball.

CARL ERSKINE: People always loved baseball in Kansas City, Denver, Los Angeles, but they had to take minor league teams. Then the jet plane and Walter O'Malley came along.

Before O'Malley journeyed 3,000 miles (and took along Horace Stoneham), the 16 major league teams were found in only ten cities, with most of them confined to the Northeast. To both the west and south, the major league map stretched only to St. Louis.

ROGER KAHN: Frank Graham was Walter O'Malley's publicity man. So Frank knew that the rivalry between O'Malley and Branch Rickey was ferocious. And Frank said that on one level or another, Walter wanted to do something great in baseball. Just as his hated adversary, Branch Rickey, had been a pioneer with Jackie Robinson.

The way the cards fell, this was it. Walter O'Malley nationalized the big leagues.

3

"THE WEAKEST WORLD CHAMPIONS OF ALL TIME"

1959

THE 1959 DODGERS HAD THREE YOUNG POWER PITCHERS ON THEIR STAFF. Sandy Koufax and Don Drysdale became Hall of Famers. Stan Williams threw just as hard—between 95 and 100 miles per hour—but his fastball never took him to Cooperstown. It wasn't even his trademark. He was what baseball calls a "headhunter."

STAN WILLIAMS: When I was a teenager, I had a coach who told me, "Knock your grandmother on her ass if she has a bat in her hands." That was pretty much my attitude.

Reliever Larry Sherry, a rookie sensation in 1959, calls Williams "the most ferocious" on a young Dodger pitching staff known for throwing beanballs.

LARRY SHERRY: People said me and Drysdale were mean, but Stan had it down to a science. He actually kept a book inside his locker. It listed the guys that he was gonna hit, and *where* he was gonna hit them.

Stan was also big. So none of the batters really wanted to fight him. Plus they knew if there was a fight, he'd hit the next six batters in a row.

STAN WILLIAMS: Well, the game was played differently then. It was a knockdown era. You tried every possible way to get a hitter out. If nothing you tried worked, you drilled him in the ribs and started all over again.

After the six-foot five-inch, 240-pound Williams retired, the *Los Angeles Times* dubbed him "the meanest pitcher of his time." But ask Williams today about the famous night of May 7, 1959, and the strapping ex-pitcher sounds anything but nasty.

STAN WILLIAMS: There were 93,104 fans at the Coliseum. It was the biggest crowd in baseball history. They all came out to honor Roy Campanella.

In the middle of the game they called time-out. Then they turned out all the lights and everyone in the stands lit a match for Campy. That was quite a beautiful sight. Very emotional.

MARK REESE: My father rolled Roy Campanella out to the mound. Roy was in a wheelchair from his automobile accident. And when 93,000 people started cheering, they were saying goodbye to Campy and Pee Wee and all the old Brooklyn Dodgers.

But I've always felt those fans were also saying: "There are 93,000 of us here tonight. This team is in Los Angeles to stay." And that year the Dodgers won the World Series.

Still, 1959 was a difficult ride, especially for Walter Alston, the team's embattled manager that season. In 1958 his critics had howled at the Dodgers' seventh-place finish. Then the grumbling grew louder when Los Angeles plunged to fifth in June 1959.

MEL DURSLAG: He was suddenly fighting for his job. But that's how it was for Alston. This guy lived in crisis all the time.

LARRY SHERRY: Alston managed the Dodgers for 23 straight years! But when he didn't win, you'd start hearing the rumors every winter. Is Walter O'Malley going to fire Walt Alston?

BUD FURILLO: Walter O'Malley only gave one-year contracts. In fact, that's how Alston got the job. Charlie Dressen, his predecessor, won three straight pennants. So right after the third one in '53, Dressen's wife Ruth said, "Honey, go in and tell Walter O'Malley you want a two-year contract."

He did, and O'Malley fired him. That's when they signed Alston. But he had only managed in the minors. Nobody knew a goddamn thing about him.

When his hiring was announced on November 24, 1953, even the jaded New York press was flabbergasted. One *Daily News* headline read, WALTER WHO? And a New York writer charged, "The Dodgers do not need a manager and that is why they got Alston."

DUKE SNIDER: Alston had actually played in the major leagues. But he only batted once, and he struck out. So he seemed insecure to us at first. Sometimes he'd ask a player on the bench, "Hey, you think I should bunt? Should I hit and run?"

One time he made a mistake and asked Jackie Robinson. Jackie told him, "You're the manager. You want to bunt, bunt. What are you asking me for? That's why they hired you."

Jackie had a penetrating voice, and our whole dugout heard him. Alston never asked anyone again. But he and Jackie never really connected.

This incident took place in 1954, Alston's rookie year, and it wasn't the only time that Robinson and Alston had hard words. Moreover, in 1954, the Dodgers finished second after winning those three straight pennants under Dressen.

In spring training 1955, Alston reportedly challenged Robinson to a fight. Other players intervened, and the 1955 Dodgers won the pennant. Then they finally vanquished the Yankees in the 1955 World Series, making

Alston the first manager to win a championship in the long and gut-wrenching history of the franchise. But it never seemed to earn him much respect. In both Brooklyn and Los Angeles, Alston was always too dour for his detractors, who considered him little more than a caretaker for teams bulging with talent.

STAN WILLIAMS: We weren't all Alston fans, let's put it that way. He never said much to his players. And when he did have something to say, frequently you read it in the paper, rather than have him tell you face-to-face.

Not that he was a coward. Not by any means. Walter Alston was a strong old farm boy.

MEL DURSLAG: Alston had arms like a blacksmith. And he was bigger than most of his players. Probably six foot three, 220 pounds.

But he wasn't a ferocious person. Alston was a quiet, repressed person, who, when he lost his temper, got pretty angry.

MARK REESE: When my father became a coach, some of the Dodger players stayed out late. Then they stopped by Pee Wee's hotel room just to BS. Then there was a knock on the door. Walter Alston was doing a late bed check.

He said, "Hey, it's Walter. What's going on in there?"

Well, everybody would always impersonate Alston. So somebody said, "Hey, Walter, kiss my ass. If it's really Walter Alston, prove it."

So Alston kicked down the door. He said, "Is that proof enough?"

BUD FURILLO: Alston didn't take shit from anybody. He challenged Jackie Robinson to a fight! All that "silent Walter Alston" stuff is bullshit.

And yet, according to Bavasi, O'Malley wanted more than a manager who was physically imposing. He wanted someone to charm the Dodgers' new constituents out west.

BUZZIE BAVASI: In 1958 Walter O'Malley wanted to fire Alston. We had just finished seventh our first year in L.A. And Walter O'Malley's friends in Hollywood were saying, "Why don't you bring in someone more vivacious?"

Alston avoided the ax when Pee Wee Reese and Bavasi threatened to quit. But when the Dodgers slumped again in June 1959, Alston was rumored to be on his way out.

Dodger historian Tot Holmes, who has also been a fan since 1946, despite living in Gothenburg, Nebraska, recalls what happened next.

TOT HOLMES: The Dodgers had brought out most of the great old stars from Brooklyn. Hodges and Snider and Reese and all of them. But in 1958 they found out these guys were past due.

So in 1959, almost midstream, they switched to a younger team of speed and pitching. They brought up Maury Wills and Larry Sherry in midseason. And they won a pennant. Which was kind of a miracle, to rebuild the team that quickly. They went from seventh place one year to first the next.

In fact, it was the biggest jump in the 84-year history of the National League. But the 1959 Dodgers were hardly a powerhouse. They won 86 games in the regular season, leaving them in a first-place tie with Milwaukee. Then, after beating the Braves in a best-of-three playoff, they still had a measly 88 victories.

Thus, in the 1959 World Series they were expected to lose to the Chicago ("Go-Go") White Sox. In fact, after getting thrashed 11–0 in Game I, there was even talk of a four-game White Sox sweep.

These gritty Dodgers didn't panic, though. Sherry, only a rookie, but suddenly the best reliever in baseball, won two World Series games himself, saved two others, and earned Most Valuable Player. An unknown outfielder named Chuck Essegian blasted two pinch-hit home runs. Snider, Hodges, and Furillo, three of the immortal Boys of Summer, each helped win games with key hits in their final World Series.

Back on May 9, the largest crowd in baseball history (93,103) had jammed the Coliseum to light candles for a paralyzed Roy Campanella. Five months later, in the three Series games played in Los Angeles, each crowd set a new postseason record. The three remarkable figures: 92,394, 92,650, and 92,706.

LARRY SHERRY: The Coliseum was 92,000 for three days in a row! And it was deafening. You couldn't hear a thing, and this was for *baseball* games.

The Dodgers won the Series in Chicago with an easy 9–3 victory in Game 6. And then it was bedlam back in California. The Dodgers were World Champions, the Western Dodgers, mind you, this Los Angeles crew achieving in year number two what it took the Brooklyn Dodgers 73 years.

Still, how would they be judged by history?

Wrote baseball author Bill James in 1997: "They were, in my opinion, the weakest World Championship team of all time."

BUZZIE BAVASI: I agree. It was the worst club ever to win a World Series. But it's also my favorite club. Those kids won on sheer courage and fortitude. That's really all it was.

MAURY WILLS: That was my rookie year after eight and a half years in the minors. And the winner's share was $11,000! That was more than twice what I was making. Man, I was gonna retire, get that place in the country I always wanted. Wow, an $11,000 check!

LARRY SHERRY: Of course, you saw what the Yankees just got for winning the Series. $320,000 a man. While we got about $12,000. But what the hell, that team made history. We won the first World Series for L.A.

PART II

——

THE SIXTIES

4

THE TRANSFORMATION
OF KOUFAX

1960–61

IT WAS THE YEAR THE "PILL" WAS APPROVED AS A SAFE CONTRACEPTIVE. Movie-goers shrieked at Alfred Hitchcock's *Psycho*. John Kennedy edged Richard Nixon in the closest presidential race in American history.

In baseball in 1960, the demolition of Ebbets Field began. The Yankees lost the World Series and promptly fired their 70-year-old manager, Casey Stengel. Ted Williams ended his storied career by hitting a home run in his final at bat.

As the 1960s proceeded, 12 new major league stadiums were erected, as cities either tried to keep their existing teams or attract new ones. Most of these stadiums were pitchers' parks, which along with an expanded strike zone led to a pitching dominated era. In fact, batting averages sunk so low—and fans became so turned off by the lack of scoring—that in 1969 the strike zone was reduced, and the pitching mound was lowered by six inches. These changes shifted the advantage back to the hitters, and attendance began to climb accordingly.

Influenced by the flight west of the Dodgers and Giants, baseball also expanded during the sixties (for the first time since 1901) by adding eight new franchises in Houston, Washington, D.C., New York City (the Mets),

Los Angeles (the Angels), Kansas City, San Diego, Seattle, and Montreal. Thus, with 24 teams by 1969, each league was split into Eastern and Western Divisions, and a playoff series was created to determine which clubs would advance to the World Series.

And yet, amid all this change, the owners still paid their players pitifully. In 1965, according to Marvin Miller, the razor-sharp new head of the players union who was just beginning the fight for free agency, "The average salary was a paltry $19,000, and since World War II, only superstars like Ted Williams, Stan Musial, Joe DiMaggio, Willie Mays, and Mickey Mantle had reached the unoffical maximum of $100,000."

In Los Angeles as the decade started, the 1960 Dodgers could not defend their World Series title, fading in August and finishing in fourth place. Maury Wills emerged as a star in his first full season, batting .295 and leading the league with 50 stolen bases. Rookie outfielder Frank Howard led the Dodgers with 23 home runs, while Drysdale's 15 victories topped the pitchers.

Oh, yes. Something else. It was the year Sandy Koufax almost quit baseball.

By this time, after six years of struggling with his control, he had won only 36 games while losing 40. Now, at the end of the 1960 season, a frustrated Koufax wondered if he was merely a baseball cliché: the flame throwing left-hander who can't throw strikes.

While growing up in Brooklyn, as he later wrote in his 1966 autobiography, Koufax didn't even consider baseball to be his best sport. He could "jump through the roof" at Lafayette High School, and he accepted a scholarship to play college basketball at Cincinnati. But when he also played baseball as a freshman, Koufax struck out 17 batters in his first start. Then he fanned 18 his next time out, which brought the big league scouts hustling to campus.

In December 1954, two weeks before his 19th birthday, he signed with his hometown Brooklyn Dodgers for a $14,000 bonus and $6,000 salary. The size of his bonus made Koufax a "bonus baby," meaning the Dodgers were now required to keep him on the parent team for at least two years.

Former pitching mate Ed Roebuck explains how this fact shaped Koufax's early years in professional baseball.

ED ROEBUCK: It's the same old story, and it's a shame. I'm a scout today and we still do it. We sign a young kid and hurry him into the majors.

That's what happened to Sandy. He just sat around in Brooklyn. Then every once in a while, he would mop up. Well, he really should have been in A ball, learning how to throw strikes. But Sandy never pitched a day in the minors.

Roger Craig pitched with Koufax in Brooklyn and Los Angeles. In 1959 his five clutch wins in September helped send the Dodgers to the World Series.

ROGER CRAIG: Before he was a star? They didn't even like taking batting practice off Sandy. That's how wild he was. Sometimes he'd throw the ball outside the batting cage. He was just another kid with a great arm, but a kid with no idea how to pitch. A lot of guys thought Sandy would never make it.

In 1955 and 1956, his first two big league seasons, Koufax went 2–2 and 2–4. In 1957, when he was 5–4, *Sports Illustrated* called him "a young lefty with a wicked fastball and a minimum of control."

Still, his 9–10 record in Brooklyn was built in only 68 innings per season. Thus, two schools of thought arose regarding his early relationship with Alston: (1) Alston was patient while the young Koufax struggled, (2) Alston never gave Koufax a real chance.

Buzzie Bavasi supports the former theory. So, too, does baseball maven Bill James, who once described Alston as an optimist. "Alston waited for six and a half years for Sandy Koufax to find home plate. I doubt that any other manager in baseball history would have, except perhaps for Connie Mack."

The opposing view is presented by Tot Holmes and Roger Kahn.

TOT HOLMES: In 1958 the Dodgers finished in seventh. I mean, what are we waiting for? Why not stick a kid like Koufax in there?

Koufax is hard to read. You can never get anything out of him. But from what I understand, he was very put out with Alston over that. He thought if Alston gave him a shot, he would have learned his craft a lot earlier.

ROGER KAHN: Walter Alston handled Koufax poorly. You did not have to be a genius to see that the arm was there. So let him work. Let him pitch. Put him in games.

I used to play a little basketball with the Dodgers during spring training. It would be Joe Black and myself against Koufax and their PR man, Frank Graham Jr. We'd get ahead and then Koufax would turn it on. He'd start making these beautiful left-handed hook shots.

I said to Joe Black one day, "Geez, how do you figure? The guy goes on the basketball court, he throws in a hook from the corner. Put him on the batting practice mound, and he's bouncing his pitches in the dirt."

Joe Black said, "Up here," and pointed to his head. Well, nobody really seemed to work with Sandy on that. Here you had this sensitive young pitcher, and Alston just ignored him.

The intensely private Koufax declined to be interviewed, but his close friend, Kevin Kennedy, says Holmes and Kahn may have a point. Kennedy, who used to manage the Texas Rangers and is now a baseball analyst for Fox, befriended Koufax in the 1980s when both worked as instructors in the Dodgers' minor league system.

KEVIN KENNEDY: Sandy's not the type to bash guys, but we did talk about Alston. We talked about him a lot. Sandy told me, "People thought I was wild. But I would pitch every 25 days or so. I would pitch six innings, strike out nine, and walk four. Then I wouldn't get called on again for a month."

Sandy really disagreed with that. He didn't feel Walt Alston pitched him enough.

TOT HOLMES: Even after Koufax became a huge star, he only pitched on one opening day. Nobody knows why that is. In fact, someone asked Koufax once and he muttered that it was a puzzlement to him, too. So there must have been something between him and Alston. When you have a great pitcher like that, wouldn't you let him start the season for you?

MAURY WILLS: Opening day is an honor. It goes to the star of the staff. And they kept giving it to Drysdale. Well, Drysdale was very good, but he was no Koufax. There was no comparison.

After a while, Koufax got tired of it. Then one day we had a double-header and both of them were scheduled to pitch. Drysdale followed Koufax in the rotation, which means Sandy should pitch the first game and Don the second.

Well, somehow Don got himself picked to pitch the first game. And for the first and only time, I saw Koufax go through the clubhouse, throwing things and swearing. Then he went into the manager's office and raised hell. Then Alston switched it back and Koufax pitched the first game.

In 1958, the first year out west, Koufax won more than five games in a season for the first time. But along with going 11–11, he threw 17 wild pitches, a dubious Dodger record he still holds today.

In 1959 Koufax once again blew hot and cold. He struck out 18 Giants in one riveting performance at the Coliseum. Then, in his first World Series start, Koufax threw a five-hitter while losing 1–0 to Chicago. For the entire season, however, he was just 8–6 with a 4.09 ERA.

In 1960 the *Herald Examiner*'s Mel Durslag was standing behind the backstop at the Coliseum before a night game when he eavesdropped on an argument between Koufax and general manager Buzzie Bavasi. Durslag printed this account in a freelance piece for the *Saturday Evening Post*:

"I want to pitch," Koufax screamed at Bavasi, "and you guys aren't giving me a chance!"

"How can you pitch," Bavasi answered, "when you can't get the side out?"

"Who the hell can get the side out sitting in the dugout?" Sandy snapped.

At the low point of that 1960 season, Koufax's record plunged to 1–8. He ended up 8–13, which made him 36–40 after six years. That's when he thought about finding a new line of work.

KEVIN KENNEDY: Sandy sold electronics after that season. He was seriously thinking about leaving baseball.

ED ROEBUCK: Sandy and I were roommates. One day he said to me, "Maybe I'll quit." I said, "Sandy, if you do, give me your arm."

BUZZIE BAVASI: Koufax came to me during the '60 season. He said, "Alston's not pitching me. I'm going home." I said, "When do you want to go?" Koufax said, "Tomorrow." I said, "Fine, I'll get you a ticket."

Thank goodness he stayed. He suddenly became the best in the business.

As Johnny Podres explains, the turning point came in spring training 1961. Podres himself would go 18–5 that season, but he is most revered for his money performance in the glorious 1955 World Series when he shut out the Yankees 2–0 in Game 7.

JOHNNY PODRES: Sandy Koufax always had the talent. Hell, I remember in '58 when he struck out 18 guys. Nat King Cole was dancing on top of our dugout. But Koufax was erratic. He would pitch a couple good games. Then one day he'd throw one all the way to the backstop.

Then all of a sudden, during spring training, Sandy Koufax finally discovered control. And the man he really credits is Norm Sherry. Norm was one of our catchers and Sandy's roommate.

NORM SHERRY: We had an A game in Vero Beach and a B game in Orlando. Koufax was going to pitch five innings in Orlando, but one of the other pitchers missed the flight. So Koufax was probably going to have to go seven.

Koufax was telling me on the plane ride over there that he wanted to work on his change-up and his curve. I said, "Sure, that's great."

So then the game starts. I called a few change-ups and curves for the first hitter. Sandy walked the guy, and he didn't throw a strike with anything. Next batter comes up. Another change-up and curve, and two more balls. Sandy's getting madder and madder out there. Now suddenly he wants to throw all fastballs. And pretty soon he's walked the bases loaded.

So I went out to the mound. I said, "Sandy, we only got one other pitcher here. And at this rate, you're gonna be out here all day. Why don't you take something off the ball? Don't even try and strike these next guys out. Just throw it over the plate and let them hit it."

So I go back behind the plate. And lo and behold, he did it. He wound up nice and easy, like he was saying, "Here, hit it." Well, he struck out the side. Then he pitched a no-hitter for seven innings. And I guess the light bulb just went off in his head.

KEVIN KENNEDY: Seven innings, no hits. Still throwing hard, but not trying to blow away every hitter. That was Sandy's defining moment.

JOHNNY PODRES: After he started throwing strikes, it was all over. For the next six years, he was the best pitcher who ever lived.

Tim McCarver was a two-time All-Star who won World Championships with the 1964 and 1967 St. Louis Cardinals. Now a brilliant TV analyst for Fox, he is asked what made Koufax so remarkable.

TIM MCCARVER: His curveball. People that talk about his fastball really don't know what they're talking about. I mean, it was a good fastball. It was a very good fastball. And Sandy felt like nobody could hit his fastball. And very few people did.

But I never saw a curveball like Sandy Koufax had. It's the best curveball I've ever seen, either as a player or as a broadcaster. It was a very hard curve, and it had *tremendous* downward movement. There was nothing even close.

JEROME HOLTZMAN: He was the best pitcher I ever saw and I'll tell you why. He had a curveball that started at your head and broke straight down to your ankles.

I would say to myself, "The hitters don't have a chance. They're lucky if they just make contact." That's how good Koufax was.

In 1961, as he began his extraordinary rise, Koufax pitched in his first All-Star Game. He finished 18–13 with 269 strikeouts, breaking Christy Mathewson's National League record of 267.

Then came the really hard part. Dealing with fame. The kind of extravagant fame which the fiercely private Koufax never wanted. In fact, even his own ex-teammates repeatedly describe him as a "loner."

But what is Sandy Koufax if not enigmatic? For his teammates also call him warm and humble, funny and sincere. Above all, says Ron Fairly, a former roommate, "He was a great team player who also happened to be a superstar."

Fairly, a sweet-swinging outfielder–first baseman, had his best year in 1961 when he batted .322. Here he recalls a favorite Koufax story.

RON FAIRLY: We were fighting for a pennant and we brought up a guy from the minors named Jimmy Barbieri. One day in St. Louis, we caught Jimmy talking to himself in the shower. That's how nervous he was.

Jimmy was making the major league minimum. And Koufax said to me, "Ron, do you realize that if I pitch well between now and the end of the season, I can double that man's income?"

Sandy meant the World Series money. Then Sandy went out and he pitched brilliantly. And sure enough, he doubled the guy's income.

Dick Tracewski also roomed with Koufax, and they remain close friends. The sure-handed Tracewski played infield for four World Series winners, including the 1963 and 1965 Dodgers.

DICK TRACEWSKI: As he became a big star, we would go on these long road trips, and Sandy would pitch in Chicago, Cincinnati, Philadelphia, New York. And people in every city started asking, "When is Koufax pitching? I'm going to that game." Then they sold out every ballpark where he pitched.

Well, it was a burden for him. Not only did he not care about the full house, he didn't need all that coverage from the press. He was a private person. In fact, most nights we ate dinner in our hotel room. Sandy just didn't crave all the attention.

Catcher John Roseboro played with Koufax for 10 years. Although he is most famous for his bloody fight in 1965 with San Francisco pitcher Juan Marichal, he also made the All-Star team four times and won three World Championships in Los Angeles (1959, 1963, and 1965).

JOHN ROSEBORO: With us, Sandy Koufax was happy-go-lucky. He was a jokester. He had every stewardess trying to get to him on every airplane.

But if you look at Sandy then and you look at Sandy now, one thing hasn't changed. It doesn't take very much to get him pissed off at the "establishment."

To show you his personality, one year he volunteered to come to Vero Beach. He was retired by then. And one day he got pissed off because the Dodgers printed some publicity pictures that he was supposed to get first right of refusal on. But they never gave him first right and he got angry. So he packed up and left.

That was Sandy Koufax. If it don't go the way you said it would go, fuck it, I'll go someplace else.

BUD FURILLO: I'll tell you how private he was. Walter O'Malley didn't even have his phone number. If he wanted to get in touch with Koufax, he had to send a Western Union wire.

MEL DURSLAG: After he stopped playing baseball, he moved somewhere in the woods of Maine. Then he lived in the woods in Idaho. Then he lived, of all places, in the hills of Paso Robles, California. Then he moved to Carpinteria, the little coastal town near Santa Barbara. Away from everything.

And now the last I heard, unless he's moved again, he lives in Vero Beach. So Koufax is kind of a mystery, you see.

And how do you penetrate a mystery? With the very best of them, you don't.

But maybe Dave Wallace comes closest to summing up how his best friends view Sandy Koufax. Wallace, the New York Mets' pitching coach, became tight with Koufax when Wallace coached in the Dodgers' minor league system.

DAVE WALLACE: I'll tell you how much I trust him. If I knew I was dying, and I had to split up what property I had, what money I had, I would want it in Sandy's hands. Then I could die peacefully.

In 1961, even as Koufax began his six years of glory, the Dodgers swooned in late August and finished four games back in second place. This also marked the end of their four years in the bizarre Los Angeles Coliseum. Now, beginning in 1962, the Dodgers would occupy a genuine big league ballpark. Maybe the prettiest ballpark in the world.

5

THE FAMOUS COLLAPSE

1962

How remarkable a season was 1962?

Dodger Stadium opened to critical raves. Maury Wills stole 104 bases, breaking Ty Cobb's supposedly bulletproof record. Don Drysdale won 25 games and the Cy Young Award. Third-base coach Leo Durocher tried sabotaging Walt Alston. And the 1962 Dodgers, who had a four-game lead with only seven to play, suffered one of the epic collapses of all time.

Roger Owens says he remembers it clearly. In 1958, at age 15, he had started working as a soft drink vendor at the Coliseum. By 1962, when Owens moved to Dodger Stadium, he had graduated to selling peanuts.

He is now 58 and still pushing peanuts at Dodger Stadium. But even more than his longevity are his unique tosses—between his legs, behind his back, two bags at once to customers in different rows—that make him the most famous vendor in the majors. Billed as "the Peanut Man at Dodger Stadium," Owens has appeared on the *Today* show, *Entertainment Tonight, Good Morning America,* and *The Tonight Show* when it was ruled by Johnny Carson.

But mostly Owens belongs to Dodger Stadium, where in his good-natured way, he is as much of a landmark as the infield's crushed red brick and the purple San Gabriel Mountains behind right field.

ROGER OWENS: I'm the oldest of nine children and I come from a really poor family. We barely had any clothes. So my father asked me to start vending just to help bring in some family income.

It was also a great way to see the games. I was a baseball pitcher at Manual Arts High School, which is just three blocks away from the Coliseum. And so even though I couldn't afford the tickets, being a vendor gave me a chance to watch my favorite team.

I still remember when Dodger Stadium opened. The vendors were just in awe. I mean, look at it! They just keep this place immaculate. And the setting, with all the trees and the mountains in the background. Most ballparks in other cities, all you see is cement and smoggy skies. But this place is so therapeutic. It's almost like you're going to the country. Except you know downtown is right over there.

Over the years, I've missed very few games. And I try making it fun for people who watch me. I'm the only peanut vendor at Dodger Stadium who throws behind his back. But it's not in the arm, you know. It's the power in the wrist that really flicks that bag of peanuts. And I'm right on the money up to 30, 40 rows behind my back. Of course, I've also got the basic tosses. The fast nut, the curve nut, and knuckle bag. I've got those down pat.

Honestly, as you get older, it gets harder to run up and down these stairs. But I still love this job, and I can't visualize when I'll ever stop. I wouldn't quit if I won Lotto tomorrow. Not even if I won the $50 million.

O wens was present, of course, on April 10, 1962, the delightful day when Dodger Stadium opened and 52,564 fans passed through its gleaming new turnstiles. So what if the Dodgers lost 6–3 to the Reds? Koufax pitched a four-hitter the next evening, Los Angeles won four straight, and the crowds kept streaming into Chavez Ravine. In fact, the 1962 Dodgers drew more fans (2.7 million) than any team in baseball history to that time.

With its 56,000 seats and parking for 16,000 automobiles, Dodger Stadium was just one of 12 new stadiums built in the 1960s, but it was the only one financed privately, which was a nice thing both for the fans and Walter O'Malley. Dodger Stadium had awesome hot dogs, pristine floors and restrooms, and a full-time staff of gardeners to nurture the roses, begonias, and marigolds dotting the grounds.

And in return for building what Jim Murray dubbed "the Taj Mahal" of baseball? O'Malley cleared a then whopping $4 million a year in the 1960s.

BUZZIE BAVASI: The only thing we forgot was water fountains. There wasn't a water fountain anyplace. Some people thought Walter O'Malley did it on purpose, so people would have to buy beer. This one writer, Sid Ziff, carried on for months about what cheap bastards we were.

But while the cynics poked fun at the stadium's plumbing, the pitchers fell in love with its dimensions. About 400 feet to center, 370 to the power alleys, and 330 down the lines, its spaciousness made it tough to hit home runs. So, too, did the night air that flowed cool and moist through Chavez Ravine.

"No question about it. Dodger Stadium was a pitcher's park," says outfielder Frank Howard, who still hit 32 homers in 1962. Then again, the six-foot-seven, 258-pound Howard could have hit with power anywhere.

FRANK HOWARD: That ballpark was designed to fit the Dodgers' new style. They no longer played in the confines of Ebbets Field, where the emphasis was on a power-hitting ballclub.

In Los Angeles the Dodgers had all this great pitching and speed. So they built a big ballpark to exploit that.

The three biggest stars in this roomy new stadium? Koufax, Drysdale, and Wills, the determined little man who had bounced around the minors for eight years before helping the Dodgers win the 1959 World Series. In 1962, when he won Most Valuable Player, Wills batted .299, scored 130 runs, and electrified the sports world by stealing a record 104 bases.

BUD FURILLO: He revolutionized baseball when he did that. Ever since Babe Ruth, baseball had been all about hitting home runs. Then Maury Wills brought back the stolen base. He brought back speed and daring. He was the most exciting player I've ever seen in my life.

BUZZIE BAVASI: Every time he got on, the Dodger fans would start chanting, "GO, GO, GO!"

JOHN ROSEBORO: Maury was the gasoline in our engine. If he didn't get on base, the Dodgers were in deep shit.

TIM McCARVER: We used to kid around that a Dodger rally consisted of a Maury Wills bunt for a single, Wills stealing second base, Wills moving to third on a sacrifice, and then Wills scoring on a wild pitch. That was a Dodger rally.

Now, obviously, it was exaggerated. The Dodgers had more hitting than they got credit for. But they had such strong pitching that you knew you had to stop Wills, because if he scored just a few runs, that could be enough for the Dodgers to thwart you.

JOHN ROSEBORO: His life changed drastically when he broke Ty Cobb's record. Maury got very popular, and he liked it. Anybody would like it. He was "the man."

MAURY WILLS: Yeah, the fame changed my life tremendously. I would be in Las Vegas, hanging around with stars like Frank Sinatra, Sammy Davis, Dean Martin, Jerry Lewis. Man, that's a long way for a guy who rode minor league buses for eight years.

Though he won't give out details, Wills also confirms his hotly rumored affair with Doris Day, the enormously popular actress and loyal Dodger fan who took a particular liking to the team's dashing shortstop. Wills says the romance ended around 1963, shortly after the press began sniffing around.

In 1962 Wills wasn't the only Dodger with Hollywood connections. Leo Durocher, the flashy third-base coach, partied with Frank Sinatra and George Raft, and bedded a string of starlets after his divorce from film star Laraine Day.

But if Durocher was a flat-out rogue, he was also a respected baseball man. In 1941 he managed the Brooklyn Dodgers to their first pennant in 21 years. Then in 1948 Durocher shocked everyone when he skipped

Brooklyn to manage the hated Giants. In 1954 he won his only World Championship when the Giants swept the Indians in four games. Still, Durocher was fired the very next season for publicly ridiculing Horace Stoneham.

Durocher, who insisted he'd been blackballed, spent his next five years outside of baseball. Then in November 1960 it was Walter O'Malley's turn to shock the industry when he hired the brash Durocher to coach third base for taciturn Walt Alston.

Of course, the newspapers were filled with pointed questions. Was Durocher coming in to ease out Alston? Otherwise, why hire Leo the Lip?

BUZZIE BAVASI: O'Malley hired Durocher because he needed a dollar. He was going through a tough time. And Durocher was good for baseball anyway. He was controversial.

TOT HOLMES: I think Walter O'Malley enjoyed a good conflict. So this was his reminder to Walt Alston: If things don't work out with you, I got this other guy.

Carroll Beringer, the Dodgers' bullpen coach from 1961 to 1972, cites what he believes is another key factor.

CARROLL BERINGER: The Dodgers were always very publicity-minded, and there was no question his presence would boost attendance. But Leo also had a great baseball mind. Even Leo's enemies would admit that.

Tommy Davis calls Durocher a "politician," but a fiery politician "who we needed." In his sparkling 1962 season, the Brooklyn-born outfielder hit 27 home runs, won the batting crown at .346, and drove in more runs, 153, than any major league player since 1950.

TOMMY DAVIS: Durocher was good for the players because he *talked* to the players. Alston would hardly say anything to the players.

And Leo had been around. He knew some nice people and some shady people. He could talk about baseball, he could talk about gangsters. He was interesting, and the guys liked hanging around him. I think Alston was a little uncomfortable with that.

BUZZIE BAVASI: The older players liked Durocher because he was a party man. He'd go out and have drinks with then, have broads with them.

This wasn't the case, however, with rookie pitcher Joe Moeller. An $80,000 bonus baby, Moeller was ostracized by the old school Durocher.

JOE MOELLER: I didn't drink and carouse, I was 19 years old, and I signed for a large bonus. Leo was very outspoken about that. He said I didn't pay my dues.

You know, to be honest, my rookie year with the Dodgers was disappointing. Because that '62 team was really divided. Mostly you had Durocher against Alston. But then you also had players taking sides. When it got to the pennant race and we began struggling, Leo did a lot of second-guessing. Every move Alston made, Leo said, "How can he do that?"

STAN WILLIAMS: Like I said, we weren't all Alston fans. But Durocher was bad because he had a knife in Alston's back all the time. Leo would stand behind him and make gestures while Alston was talking.

ROGER KAHN: Leo thought Alston was dumb because he was a farmer. Look, the Dodgers were the first team Leo managed. Leo with his silk shirts and his wing-tip shoes and his Broadway pals. Now you got this guy from Ohio who doesn't talk so quick running the team and making mistakes. It drove Durocher nuts.

LARRY SHERRY: Durocher was after his job. One time in San Francisco, he took us out to see Buddy Greco. Good piano player, good entertainer. Durocher picked up the tab for several players, and we stayed out for the late show, which was after one o'clock.

We found out afterwards that somebody ratted on us. Then we did some detective work and found out it was Durocher. He went in and told Alston, "Your players are out drinking and chasing women at night."

Leo was the one who invited us out. But he wanted to make Walt look bad. Why else do you think he did it? Durocher wasn't born in an incubator. He knows what the hell he's doing. He wanted it make it look like Alston didn't have control of his players.

By July 1962, with the Alston-Durocher conflict still mostly covered up, the first-place Dodgers had swept five straight doubleheaders. Wills, Davis, Drysdale, and Howard were all en route to having their best seasons.

Meanwhile, Koufax had been spectacular. In April he had struck out 18 batters, tying a record he already held with Bob Feller. In June he'd thrown the first of his four no-hitters.

Now, with Koufax's 14–4 record, his 209 strikeouts, and the season barely half over, he had done even more than establish himself as baseball's most dominant pitcher. He was putting together a season for the ages.

Then on July 17 Koufax left the mound after one inning. His ravaged left index finger, which had turned purple and swelled up grotesquely in his last few starts, finally split wide open. The root of the problem, called Reynaud's Phenomenon, was later found to be caused by a circulatory disorder that had resulted from a blood clot in his left palm.

FRANK HOWARD: Koufax was doing things that very few pitchers in the history of this game have ever done. Then we lost him for two months.

So with all due respect to the Giants, I don't see them catching us if we had Koufax. With Koufax for a full year, you're not gonna have a slide like we had at the end of '62.

Although Koufax would return in late September, he could not regain his command after such a long layoff. Still, the Dodgers seemed to have won the pennant without him, since they had a four-game lead over the Giants with only seven games left.

But as Los Angeles went a horrendous 1–6, San Francisco finished 5–2, leaving the two transplanted rivals tied for first. This brought a best-of-three playoff, in which the first two games were split. In the third and decid-ing game in Los Angeles, the Dodgers went into the ninth with a 4–2 lead. They were three outs away—awful collapse and all—from playing the Yan-kees in the World Series.

But Alston had a tough decision to make. Should he stay with his reliever, Ed Roebuck, who might be tiring after two strong innings? Should he call on hard-throwing Stan Williams, who was normally a starter? Or should he turn to Drysdale, also a starter, but who'd already won a league-high 25 games?

Snider, whom Alston had just removed for defense, recalls what hap-pened next at a tense Chavez Ravine.

DUKE SNIDER: First you gotta remember something: I was there in 1951 when we had a 4–1 lead in the ninth inning and the Giants beat us 5–4 on Bobby Thompson's home run. So now I'm sitting next to Drysdale on our bench. I said, "What are you doing sitting here? Go tell Walt you'll warm up and pitch the ninth inning."

Drysdale talked to Alston and came back. I asked him what Alston said. He said, "Walt said I'm pitching against the Yankees tomorrow in the World Series."

I said, "If we don't win, there *is* no World Series." But Drysdale never went in. Alston stayed with Ed Roebuck for the last inning.

MAURY WILLS: You want to know why he didn't put Drysdale in? Durocher got real vocal in our dugout. He kept saying that Drysdale should go in. Well, Alston didn't like that it was Durocher's idea and not his. So he kind of cut off his nose to spite his face.

In one of the most nightmarish half-innings in Dodger history, Matty Alou led off the ninth with a single. Harvey Keunn hit a one-hopper to Maury Wills. A perfect doubleplay ball. But second baseman Larry Bur-right was shaded too far toward first base. Wills had to wait for Burright to rush back to second, and by then it was too late to turn the double play.

LARRY SHERRY: Everybody was screaming, "Who moved Burright?" Because we knew it was either Alston or Durocher. But nobody ever took the blame for it.

With Keunn on first and one out, Roebuck walked two straight batters to load the bases. Willie Mays lined a single that tore off Roebuck's glove. The Giants trailed 4–3, still had only one out, and the bases still were loaded. Then, passing over Drysdale a second time, Alston replaced Roebuck with Stan Williams.

By the time the ninth inning ended, Williams had walked in the winning run, the Giants had won 6–4, Chavez Ravine had fallen deathly silent, and the shell-shocked Dodgers had staggered back to their clubhouse, where they locked the door to reporters and got drunk.

JOHN ROSEBORO: Holy shit. It got ugly. Drysdale had volunteered to come in, and Alston wanted to save him for the World Series.

So we were very pissed off. And there was Champagne in our clubhouse, there was whiskey, all the celebration stuff they couldn't get out. So you had a lot of players drinking and cussing. Then Alston went into his office and wouldn't come out. Guys were yelling, "Come out, you gutless son of a bitch."

CARROLL BERINGER: Well, you're talking to one of his coaches. So maybe I didn't see things the way some players did. But I thought Alston handled it just right. I mean, Alston had a temper. He would charge a bulldozer. But he just stayed in his office and let some players vent.

JOHNNY PODRES: The clubhouse guy passed out some bottles of booze. There were guys drunk in the shower. Nobody really left. I can still remember Tommy Davis. He told Walter Alston that he stole his money.

TOMMY DAVIS: I was very peeved when he went with Stan Williams. I love Stan and I thought he was a great pitcher. But if you had Stan Williams or Don Drysdale, who would you bring in?

So I started yelling at Alston, "You stole my money!" I said it loud enough for anyone to hear. But there weren't any reporters in there yet, because they didn't open the clubhouse right away. Hell no, they didn't open the clubhouse. It would have been an *Enquirer* situation.

BUD FURILLO: Fifty-eight minutes. The clubhouse was closed to us for fifty-eight minutes. They were still crying when we got in. Man, I felt so sorry for them. No way in hell the Giants should have caught them.

DUKE SNIDER: I don't remember Durocher being in there. I think he took his shower and got right out. Then Durocher talked that night from what I hear.

TOT HOLMES: Leo was quoted as saying in the papers, "We would have won the pennant had I been the manager."

Now did Leo really say exactly that? There seemed to be some question. But he did talk about that season when he wrote his book. He said Alston froze that year. He said Alston had the guys so tight, you couldn't drive a needle up their butts.

BUZZIE BAVASI: The night after I heard about Leo's comments, there was a dinner for the Dodgers. I was furious. And I told Leo, "You're through, you're fired, you're finished."

The next day I called Alston. I told him I fired Leo. And Alston said, "Buzzie, don't do it. Let him keep his job." That's why Leo Durocher stayed with us. Walter Alston wouldn't let me fire him.

Bavasi doesn't say so, but neither, perhaps, would Walter O'Malley, who (as we will see shortly) was itching to fire Alston and replace him with Durocher. And so to the surprise of the baseball world, Durocher kept his job in spite of his glaring insubordination.

On the other hand, Snider was through after 16 glorious years with the Dodgers, who sold him for $40,000 to the Mets, whose 102 losses had just established them as the lousiest team of all time.

History books have told us it was straightforward. The Duke of Flatbush, 36, was slowing down. But Snider, a Hall of Famer whose uniform was retired by the Dodgers, says there may be more to the story of his departure.

DUKE SNIDER: I've never told this to anyone before. But it could have been how the postgame thing was handled. After we lost to the Giants, I was the one who kept the reporters out. I didn't want them to see our players that way.

Well, it appeared that I was running the team. It appeared I took the reins away from Alston. I assume Alston was very upset about that. That may have been the reason I lost my job.

Stan Williams got shipped out as well. Williams, who had walked in the winning run, got traded to the Yankees after averaging 14 wins the past three seasons. Williams says he believes that he was a scapegoat for the famous collapse of 1962.

Still, nobody got treated more harshly than Alston. In fact, according to Bill James, "It may be that no manager in baseball history was ever more second-guessed for losing a pennant race than was Walter Alston in 1962."

BUZZIE BAVASI: We had the thing won, and we lost it. And right after we lost, O'Malley said he wanted Alston fired. And O'Malley wanted Durocher to replace him. He was in love with Durocher.

I said, "If you fire Alston, I'm gone too. He didn't make those errors, he didn't give up those base hits. How the hell can you say it was Alston's fault?"

O'Malley, the businessman, knew he would have netted millions had the Dodgers and Yankees played in the 1962 World Series. And yet, he trusted Bavasi on baseball matters, and Alston was allowed to keep his job.

Then in 1963, with Alston under fire yet again, he was rescued by a dignified man named Koufax.

6

KOUFAX KILLS THE YANKEES

1963

IN ITS MARCH 1963 ISSUE, *SPORT* MAGAZINE ANXIOUSLY ASKED IN A BIG BLACK headline: WILL DISSENSION DESTROY THE DODGERS? The bulk of the article dealt with the Alston-Durocher conflict, which had gone public the previous October when Durocher criticized Alston in the papers. The story also printed this blunt quote from Drysdale on the 1962 season's disastrous last inning: "You're damn right I would have liked to pitch. Only they didn't ask me."

By May 5, 1963, Los Angeles had plunged to seventh place and the columnists all but wanted Alston's head. Then on Sunday, May 6, at the end of a long, grim road trip, the Dodgers lost a doubleheader at Pittsburgh.

This set the stage for the fabled "bus incident."

DICK TRACEWSKI: We just stunk up the joint, and everyone was tense. Then we took this old bus from the stadium to the airport. It was hot and it was humid and some of our guys started yelling at Lee Scott.

MAURY WILLS: He was our traveling secretary. And while we're bitching at him, suddenly here come the Pirates. They're also leaving town to go on the road. But they're in this new air-conditioned Greyhound, and they go flying right by us.

TOMMY DAVIS: So now we're *really* on Lee Scott. "Goddamn it, next time get a better bus!" Well, Alston got tired of that. He got *very* upset.

CARROLL BERINGER: I was sitting right across from him and I saw the veins in his neck were popping out. He told the bus driver, "Pull this damn thing over!"

RON FAIRLY: Alston challenged our whole team. He said, "Anybody who doesn't like this bus? Get off it and come outside. We'll settle it right there."

That's when everyone realized, well, maybe we should shut up. Then Alston went outside. And I don't mean he stood out there for a few seconds.

MAURY WILLS: Alston took his time. He lit a cigarette up, just walking back and forth, looking into the windows. Nobody got off the bus.

Then he came back inside. Alston looked right at Frank Howard, who was huge, and a couple other big guys. He said, "Anybody got anything to say?"

Nobody said a word.

MEL DURSLAG: I said to him after everyone calmed down, "Walter, what would you have done if Frank Howard had accepted your challenge?" He said, "I'd have crapped in my pants."

FRANK HOWARD: That's the first I've ever heard that. But let me tell you something about Walter Alston. He's the only guy I know who managed 23 straight years in one place. So Alston must have been doing something right.

MAURY WILLS: I thought the bus incident was our turning point. We got real hot after that.

DICK TRACEWSKI: Well, our discipline improved. But we had a pretty strong team in '63. We were probably just too good to stay down for long.

For whatever reasons, the Dodgers won 15 of their next 19, soaring from seventh place to one game out of first. Then, when Los Angeles faltered again in June, there were published reports that had several players ripping Alston to the front office. "If the Dodgers lose today," said Cub head coach Bob Kennedy before a game in Chicago, "Durocher will be manager tomorrow."

LARRY SHERRY: I really think that saved Walt Alston's job. Walter O'Malley, if you understand the inside stuff, wanted to fire Alston and give Durocher the job. But then Bob Kennedy came out with that statement. That pissed off O'Malley. He was not gonna make a change right after Bob Kennedy said that.

With the Alston-Durocher rumors unabated, the Dodgers warmed up again during July, built a six-game lead by August, and then saw that lead shaved to one game in September. Then, amid charges they were choking again, the Dodgers pulled away to win the pennant by a solid six games.

Maury Wills, Tommy Davis, and Frank Howard all had strong years, but the mightiest Dodger by far was Sandy Koufax, who went 25–5 with a 1.88 ERA and a league record 306 strikeouts. For this stunning performance, he later became the first pitcher in baseball history to win both the Cy Young and Most Valuable Player awards.

RON FAIRLY: There were actually times that year when I felt sorry for the other team's hitter. I would think, "He's not even gonna foul tip one." And then he wouldn't.

In the 1963 World Series, the Dodgers were matched against the formidable Yankees, who had won the previous two World Series and six of their seven World Series against the Brooklyn Dodgers. Now, in the teams' first transcontinental Series, the Yankees were solidly favored (8–5) to triumph again.

DICK TRACEWSKI: When we went over them in our meetings, it was kind of scary. Their catcher, Elston Howard, won MVP. They had Joe

Pepitone, Bobby Richardson, Tony Kubek, and Clete Boyer in their infield. Their outfield was Roger Maris, Mickey Mantle, and Tommy Tresh. And they had good starting pitching: Whitey Ford, Al Downing, and Jim Bouton.

So there wasn't too much said after these meetings. We walked out with a big lump in our throats. These were the Yankees. And we were opening in New York.

MEL DURSLAG: God, there was tension before that opening game. It was the Yankees against the Dodgers, who had left Brooklyn. It was Sandy Koufax against Whitey Ford. It was the perfect matchup. That's what it was.

Roseboro felt so nervous before Game I, he snuck a few sips of peach brandy at his locker. Then, properly relaxed in the second inning, he blasted a three-run homer off Whitey Ford.

Meanwhile, Koufax struck out the first five Yankees he faced. Then he fanned I5 in all, a single-game Series record, and the Dodgers won 5–2 in front of 69,000 people in the Bronx.

ROGER KAHN: I remember Koufax taking the mound that game. The second hitter for the Yankees was Bobby Richardson. The scouting report on him was, don't throw him a high fastball.

So Koufax threw Richardson three high fastballs. Three pitches, three strikes, sit down. Then Koufax looked straight into the Yankee dugout. I could see Sandy saying in that look, "I can pitch it to your power and I'll still strike you out."

FRANK HOWARD: Scouting reports will give you tendencies, but you gotta look at who's out there. You got a Hall of Famer that throws 95-plus, and a curve ball that crosses your eyes. He's gonna do what he wants to. He's gonna pitch his ballgame.

From I960 to I964 Bobby Richardson played in a record 30 straight World Series games. He won Series MVP in I960, batting .367 with a record 12 RBIs. In the 1962 Series he batted .391 with nine hits in only five games.

Richardson recalls his first encounter with Koufax in the 1963 World Series opener.

BOBBY RICHARDSON: Our scouting report said Koufax had a good fastball, a good change-up, and a good curveball. And by that time, we knew he had good control.

But after I faced him the first two times up, I realized that didn't say it all. He had tremendous stuff. I base that on the fact that I didn't strike out much, and he struck me out three times.

After I struck out the third time, I walked by Mantle in the on-deck circle, and Mantle just said, "There's no use for me to go up there."

He got Mantle three times, too. That night, on the TV highlights, all you saw was all the Yankees whiffing.

Podres won the second game 4–1 in New York. Then, in the first World Series game played at Dodger Stadium, Drysdale three-hit the Yankees and won 1–0. Koufax in Game 4 was not quite as masterful as in Game 1, but he still closed out the Yankees 2–1.

Now, who would have figured that? Los Angeles beat New York in a shocking four games. The Yankees scored only four runs the entire Series. The Yankees never led in any game. Mantle actually tried to bunt his way on.

TOT HOLMES: It was remarkable. *Nobody* swept the Yankees in the World Series. But it just confirmed the old saying: Great pitching can stop even great hitting.

MEL DURSLAG: The impact of that hit hard. What were the odds against a Dodger sweep?

TOMMY DAVIS: A hundred to one. That's what we heard. They said some guy bet a thousand dollars in Vegas on us winning four in a row. He won $100,000.

BUD FURILLO: That was the pinnacle of Walter O'Malley's career. The L.A. Dodgers sweeping the New York Yankees.

JOHN ROSEBORO: Hell yeah, O'Malley liked it. After the Yankees kicked the Dodgers' ass all those times? I can see where beating them four straight might ease the pain.

And, man, we didn't just beat them. We gave them a pitching lesson. One time Koufax struck out Mantle on three pitches. Mantle never took his bat off his shoulder. Then he turned around and said to me, "How the hell are you supposed to hit that shit?"

7

THE ROSEBORO-MARICHAL BRAWL

1964–65

One year after humbling the powerful Yankees, the Dodgers felt some embarrassment of their own. In 1964 they never contended, sliding from first place to sixth, winning 80 games and losing 82.

Hobbled by a spate of injuries, the Dodgers suffered their biggest single blow on August 8 when Koufax (19–5) slid into second base and jammed his pitching elbow. He would not only start just twice the rest of the season, but his doctors would also announce that his left elbow now had "traumatic arthritis," a condition which could be treated but not cured.

Then more bad news arrived when Tommy Davis broke his ankle sliding on May 1, 1965. He had the biggest bat in a rather weak offense, he was now done for the season, and everyone figured the Dodgers had no chance. Everyone but the 1965 Dodgers, one of the more relentless teams in franchise history. With left fielder Lou Johnson stepping in smoothly for Tommy Davis, second baseman Jim Lefebvre winning Rookie of the Year, Koufax racking up wins through elbow pain, and Wills and Drysdale their usual stellar selves, Los Angeles held first place for all but 16 days of the regular season.

However, the Dodgers were just a half-game in front of the Giants when the two teams began a key four-game series on Thursday, August 19, 1965.

Then, on that shocking Sunday at Candlestick Park, the tight pennant race was briefly forgotten when Juan Marichal struck John Roseboro with a bat.

The *Los Angeles Times* called it, correctly, "The ugliest incident in the history of West Coast major league baseball." But while this marked the bloody climax of the San Francisco–Los Angeles rivalry, the Giant-Dodger feud had not originated in California. It had its violent roots back in New York, where Leo Durocher's Giants and Jackie Robinson's Dodgers engaged in a nasty string of beanball wars.

After the teams moved west in 1958, it was probably Don Drysdale who was most responsible for keeping the torrid rivalry alive. "Don was one of the nicest guys in baseball," says Dodger catcher Jeff Torborg. "Until he got out on the mound."

JEFF TORBORG: You know how every hockey team has a policeman? Don was our policeman. And he always talked about that two-for-one thing. You knock down one of our hitters, and I'll knock down two of yours.

TIM MCCARVER: There were pitchers in those days who would throw at you for trying to bunt on them. But Drysdale would throw at you whether you bunted on him or not.

And Don was pretty intimidating out there. He was a big guy, six foot six, and he always gave you the impression that he really didn't care. If he hit you, it didn't matter. Big deal, it's part of your job.

ROGER CRAIG: If you were a rookie, you could expect it. First time you faced Drysdale, you went down.

This is confirmed with a smile by Giant Hall of Famer Orlando Cepeda, who recalls his first encounter against the snarling Drysdale.

ORLANDO CEPEDA: When I came up in 1958, people wondered if Dodgers-Giants would be the same as New York. Then my first big league game was against the Los Angeles Dodgers and Don Drysdale. His first pitch came right at my head. Drysdale knocked me down. And I knew, from the beginning, Dodgers-Giants is the same as in New York.

JOHN ROSEBORO: He was the meanest white boy in baseball. In fact, had Don been pitching in 1965, we wouldn't have had the incident at all. Because when Marichal started throwing at Wills and Fairly, Drysdale would have knocked down Mays and McCovey.

That shit would have ended right there. No need for me to even get involved.

B<small>UT</small> on that notorious day at Candlestick Park, it was Koufax and not Drysdale on the mound. And just how differently did they view throwing at batters?

Koufax hit only 18 throughout his entire career. Drysdale drilled 154, second only to Walter Johnson in baseball history.

CARROLL BERINGER: Koufax didn't believe in throwing at people. But he also didn't have to. He just said, "Here's my best stuff. Now try and hit it."

TOMMY DAVIS: Sandy said he did. He said he threw at guys. But Sandy threw so hard, I think he was afraid he'd kill someone.

TIM MCCARVER: Koufax just didn't do it. The only time I remember him intentionally throwing at somebody is when he threw at my teammate Lou Brock.

JEFF TORBORG: That's exactly right. Lou Brock. And I don't know if Sandy ever admitted it, but he really nailed him. Brock had stolen five bases against us that game. Finally, Sandy drilled him in the rib cage. He *buried* it in there. You could see the ball spinning in Brock's rib cage.

O<small>N</small> Thursday, August 19, 1965, three days before the Roseboro-Marichal brawl, Los Angeles won a tight game to open the big four-game series. Then on Friday the atmosphere turned from tense to hostile.

DICK TRACEWSKI: I remember the whole thing. And what I remember is Maury Wills started it all.

MAURY WILLS: I was frustrated because I couldn't get on base that game. And if I don't get on base, we have a problem winning. So I pulled back my bat like I was bunting. Except I didn't bunt. I hit Tom Haller, their catcher, in his mask. The umpire yelled, "Interference!" Haller said, "No! He came back with the bat!"

Man, the Giants went crazy. But the umpire gave me first base.

JOHN ROSEBORO: Matty Alou came up for them later that game. And damn if he didn't try doing the same thing to me. I said, "You little rat-faced SOB, I'll drive you into the ground if you try that crap again."

TOM HALLER: Matty Alou and Juan Marichal were like brothers. And Marichal, who was standing in our dugout, started jawing back and forth with Roseboro.

JOHN ROSEBORO: Marichal was standing behind their manager, running his goddamn mouth. So I yelled, "Shut the fuck up. If you want to run your mouth, you chicken shit, come out here on the field."

Then I saw Cepeda after the game. I said, "You tell that son of a bitch if he wants any part of me, then come out on the field. But don't stand behind the manager and do your talking."

ORLANDO CEPEDA: I said, "Hey, John, let's cool it. Juan is no picnic, you know. He's a tough guy, too. I would just leave him alone."

JIM LEFEBVRE: So that started it, right? That started the bad blood on Friday night. Then on Sunday afternoon, Marichal is pitching against Koufax.

Wills gets on, steals second, scores the first run. Next time Wills comes up, Marichal knocks him flat on his ass. Then Marichal decks Fairly. We go back to the dugout after the inning. Now it's simmering. The guys are saying, "Marichal's gotta go down! Marichal's gotta go down!"

MAURY WILLS: Roseboro walks over to Koufax by the bat rack. Roseboro says, "Fine, if Marichal wants to do it, we'll do it, too. When Marichal comes up, we'll let him have it."

Koufax said he didn't want do that. Roseboro said, "What do you mean, you don't want to do it? *He's* doing it to us."

They kept going back and forth. I was standing right there and I said, "Goddamn it, Sandy. *They're* doing it." So Roseboro, in disgust, finally says, "Okay, we'll do it like this."

JOHN ROSEBORO: We gotta retaliate, but Sandy is not gonna throw at anybody. Well, every winter back then, I had studied karate and kung fu. I was lethal at that time. I was a weapon.

So I said, "Don't worry, Sandy. I'll knock Marichal down from behind the plate. And if he says anything, I'll take him out of there."

Sandy threw the ball and I picked it up. Then I threw it back right by Marichal's nose. And he said, "You better not hit me with that ball!" Then I started out of my crouch and I saw the bat coming down. And I got my arm up, but, Jesus, he creased the side of my head and I forgot everything I learned in karate. I just started throwing punches.

JEFF TORBORG: The blood from the cut on his head had dripped down over his eye. It looked like his eye was gone. I mean, it was awful.

TOM HALLER: Tito Fuentes was in our on-deck circle, and *he* started swinging his bat. That's when all hell broke loose.

LOU JOHNSON: Now, usually a fight is just a fight. But then I saw the bats. That freaked me out. And I started going after Marichal.

JOHN ROSEBORO: I had slipped down while going after Marichal. And that was the picture that ran in *Life* magazine. Marichal has his bat up in the air. Fuentes has his bat up in the air. They're ready to give me the coup de grace.

I still don't know how they stopped it. But I remember my teammates pouring in. I remember Willie Mays. He was trying to get me to stop fighting. He said, "Your eye is out, your eye is out!" And I said, "Shit, I only hit this guy once. I've gotta go after him again."

JEFF TORBORG: Willie Mays was really the guy who got it stopped. John Roseboro still wanted to take on the world, and here his head was bleeding profusely. But Willie Mays got hold of John and pulled him away.

WILLIE MAYS: I was trying to help a friend, even though he was on the opposing team. So I got Roseboro right away out of the crowd, and I took him to their bench, and all this blood was running down his face. I said, "Rose, it looks like you got a big old gash there. Why don't you just sit down."

Then I got a towel and wiped him off, and under all that blood, the cut was not that bad. When he found that out, he called me all kinds of names. But by that time, everything had quieted down.

After San Francisco police finally controlled the 60-man brawl, Roseboro left with a two-inch gash on his head. Then umpire Shag Crawford ejected Marichal, play resumed after a 14-minute delay, and Mays hit a three-run homer off an obviously distracted Koufax. The Giants won 4–3 to split the series, and the Dodgers remained just a half-game in front.

In Los Angeles the next day, the press responded with anger when National League President Warren Giles fined Marichal $1,750 and suspended him for eight playing dates. "This was baseball's chance to prove that attempted murder will not be condoned in the major leagues, and baseball blew it," opined the *Los Angeles Examiner*. "Let a common citizen whack someone over the head with a bat and see what he gets," wrote the *Los Angeles Times'* Paul Zimmerman.

Considering the offense, Wills says most of the Dodgers considered the penalties "a slap on the wrist."

MAURY WILLS: And you know how you writers are? Going around and trying to stir things up? Well, this one writer got me to say it, and I said it. I said, "Warren Giles is a gutless son of a bitch."

In 1965, to use those words? They put it in the sports page with big, bold headlines: GILES IS S.O.B.—WILLS.

As the edgy aftermath continued, Marichal and Roseboro each received death threats. Roseboro filed a $110,00 battery suit against Marichal and the Giants before settling out of court for $7,500. Marichal was booed for years at Dodger Stadium, and Roseboro got the same treatment at Candlestick Park.

JOHN ROSEBORO: I guess my anger lasted about one year. After that, it was useless. It didn't make sense. Then Juan and I finally made friends. Our families spent time together in Santo Domingo. And then one day I got a call from Juan. He said, "I made the Hall of Fame. They voted me in." Then we both had a little cry on the telephone.

8

THE PROMISED LAND

OCTOBER 1965

WERE THE DODGERS AND GIANTS RATTLED BY THEIR BENCH-CLEARING BOUT on August 22, 1965?

Well, Los Angeles then lost three straight to the pitiful Mets, while San Francisco lost four straight to the Pirates. But if both California teams were shaken, they were still too tough and talented to fold.

In September the Giants won 14 straight games. Then, when the Dodgers seemed sunk, they won 13 straight and 15 of 16 to erase a 4½-game deficit. This hot streak thrust L.A. into the 1965 World Series, while the second-place Giants would have to watch on TV with everyone else.

The Dodgers were matched against the Minnesota Twins, whose powerful offense included the likes of Tony Oliva, Harmon Killebrew, Bobby Allison, and Don Mincher. Meanwhile, Jim Lefebvre and Lou Johnson each led the Dodgers with a whopping 12 homers apiece.

Still, Los Angeles boasted its customary array of speed and pitching. Wills entered the World Series with an electrifying 94 stolen bases. Drysdale had gone 23–12 with a 2.77 ERA. Claude Osteen had finished 15–15, but could have been 20–10 with more offensive support. Koufax had skidded off the charts, leading the majors in wins (26–8), complete games (27), ERA (2.04), and strikeouts (382), while also throwing his first and only perfect game.

Thus, the Dodgers were favored versus the Twins, but only by 7–5, because the bookies knew what everyone else did: Koufax wasn't pitching the first game of the World Series because it fell on Yom Kippur, the holiest day on the Jewish calendar. Which meant if the Series went the full seven games, Koufax would probably pitch twice instead of three times.

Koufax, though playing a sport with few Jewish stars, was not the first player to miss a game on Yom Kippur. Hank Greenberg and Al Rosen had both sat out before him. But those missed games had come in the regular season. In 1965, when the High Holiday fell on October 6, Koufax became the first man to refuse to play a World Series game on Yom Kippur.

LOU JOHNSON: Yeah, but you had to know Koufax. He always danced to his own music. And when his holiday fell on the opener, he put his faith first. Just like Muhammad Ali put his faith first.

So I would say our players accepted it. Plus, we also knew if we did lose that first game, we wouldn't lose the second. That would be Koufax's turn.

Almost to a man, his other Dodger teammates say the same thing: we respected Sandy Koufax. We supported his not pitching on Yom Kippur.

Only Dick Tracewski, one of his former roommates and still his close friend, admits to having a slightly different perspective.

DICK TRACEWSKI: There were three Jewish guys on our ballclub. There was Norm Sherry, Larry Sherry, and Sandy. So we used to call Norman the "Happy Jew." Larry Sherry was the "Rude Jew." And we had Sandy, who was the "Super Jew."

But it wasn't anything. I mean, there was no prejudice in these things. We were all close friends and they were great guys. But when Sandy didn't pitch on Yom Kippur? Well, I was a Roman Catholic. And if we happened to play the first game of a World Series on Christmas or Easter Sunday or Good Friday, I would play.

So I was kind of taken back when he wouldn't pitch that Yom Kippur opener. But it was Sandy's decision to make and I respected it. Everybody did. I really don't remember the guys being mad.

There were some people, however, who did find Koufax's actions somewhat puzzling, for he was not devout in his daily life.

MEL DURSLAG: I watched him for a long time, and he was never a religious guy at all. In fact, I never saw Koufax observe anything Jewish.

But he had a thing about this holiday: Koufax refused to pitch a game on Yom Kippur. And that made him a great hero among the Jews out here in Los Angeles. They really loved him.

ROGER KAHN: I wasn't aware of any particular religiosity about Sandy. So my reaction was, I never knew he cared.

But I do know it annoyed him when, for example, *Time* magazine said you can find him on the road with a portable phonograph listening to Mendelssohn's violin concerto. I remember Koufax said, "I listen to Sinatra a hell of a lot more than I listen to Mendelssohn."

So I think there was a sort of stereotyping of him as a Jewish person who liked Jewish composers and such. So Koufax just said, "Okay, I'll show them what being Jewish is. I won't pitch on Yom Kippur."

Rabbi Hillel Silverman, a prominent rabbi at Los Angeles Sinai Temple from 1964 to 1980, offers a more positive explanation. Moreover, he says it came from Koufax himself.

RABBI SILVERMAN: I met him a few times. And one time we talked about it. It was not a long talk. It was a brief talk. But I knew he was not that committed to formal religion. So my question was, "Why did you not pitch on the Day of Atonement?"

He answered, very humbly, that he felt he had a responsibility as a role model for many Jewish children. And being a role model, he wanted those children to know that it was important to respect their heritage. It was important for them to respect themselves.

That was the simple reason that he gave me. Which made him, in my eyes, a big man. Because this was big business, you know. The World Series. And it took courage to say, "Hey, I'm not pitching today."

Thus, explains the rabbi, Koufax became more than a source of ethnic pride in Los Angeles. He was a hero to Jews throughout the country.

RABBI SILVERMAN: Oh, yes. Absolutely. I must tell you that many rabbis, including myself, have referred to this many times on the Day of Atonement. We always say, "Here is a man who refused to desecrate the holiest day of the year by pitching in the World Series."

Then, of course, the Jews are like any other minority. When a member of their tribe is important in sports, it's a tremendous lift. Look at Sammy Sosa, who's from the Dominican Republic. He gets a parade every time he goes back there.

So naturally the Jews were very proud, and touched, that this great pitcher was of the Jewish faith. But as I'm sure you know, he was also respected by non-Jewish people.

MILTON BERLE: That's exactly right, and I'll tell you why. Did you ever take a good look at his curveball?

Not on October 6, 1965. With Koufax notably absent, Drysdale went to the mound for Game I of the World Series at Metropolitan Stadium in Bloomington, Minnesota. Then, after getting shelled for seven runs in a little over two innings, Drysdale reportedly quipped when Alston came out to yank him, "I bet you wish I was the Jewish one."

Still, after winning 8–2, now the underdog Twins would have to face Koufax, who figured to even the Series at I–I.

JEFF TORBORG: But we lost again, 5–I. And I remember thinking on our bus: "How can this great Dodger team be down two games to none? How could they beat Drysdale and Koufax?"

In Los Angeles for Game 3, Osteen came up huge in a 4–0 Dodger win. Drysdale then evened the Series with a 7–2 victory, Koufax threw a 7–0 shutout to put his team ahead, and Osteen lost 5–1 in Minnesota.

Now, Walter Alston had a decision to make. The seventh game of the Series fell on Drysdale's turn. He had his three days of rest, while Koufax had just two. But as Dodger coach Danny Ozark explains, Alston went with Koufax anyway.

DANNY OZARK: Alston had called a meeting of our coaches. And finally we decided that Sandy Koufax would be the logical guy because of all the left-handed batters on the Twins. Then Alston said, "Who's gonna go ask Sandy?" So I said, "I'll go ask him."

I found him and I said, "Sandy, would you pitch tomorrow?" And Koufax said, quickly, "Who's asking?" I said, "Forty guys." And Koufax said, "Yeah. Okay."

Of course, it was Alston and the coaches asking. But we all knew the players wanted Koufax.

CLAUDE OSTEEN: We had confidence in Drysdale, but let's face it. When Koufax pitched, it wasn't, did he win? It was, how many did he strike out, and did he pitch a no-hitter?

JOHN ROSEBORO: Drysdale was a good pitcher, but he had to work hard to win. So *we* had to work hard when Drysdale pitched. Koufax made it easy. He took the pressure off. If the other team got two hits, man, they were lucky.

But Sandy's arm was giving him problems in that last World Series game. He couldn't get his breaking ball over the plate. So I finally went out and said, "Sandy, what's going on?"

He said, "I can't throw the goddamn curveball." I said, "Well, what are we gonna do?" He said, "Fuck it! Let's just blow it by 'em!"

That's precisely what Koufax did in winning 2–0. On only two days' rest, and having already pitched 348 innings that season, Koufax threw a three-hit, ten-strikeout shutout in the seventh and final game of the World Series. And he did it without his curveball.

RON FAIRLY: When he didn't pitch on Yom Kippur, there were some people who criticized him. But I think they shut up when he was named World Series MVP.

Once Koufax had struck out the last two Twins he faced with nothing but fastballs, he was mobbed on the mound by his teammates and Alston. And now these had truly become the glory years. With their second World Championship in three years, and their third since moving to Los Angeles, the Dodgers had proven again that superior pitching and speed could bring home the grand prize and keep the fans rolling into Chavez Ravine.

Trouble was coming, however, for now their three biggest stars—Koufax, Drysdale, and Wills—wanted what they deemed their just rewards.

9

THE GREAT HOLDOUT

SPRING TRAINING, 1966

IN 1966 WALTER O'MALLEY WAS BASEBALL'S MOST POWERFUL OWNER. HE WAS charismatic, shrewd, politically astute. His team had won three World Series in Los Angeles, broken a number of attendance records, and firmly established itself as the sporting world's most profitable franchise.

Increasingly, in fact, it was now said that Walter O'Malley ran baseball. That he did most of the talking at owners meetings. That no commissioner could get appointed without his approval.

Or as the *New York Times'* Red Smith later put it, "When Walter O'Malley wants a cup of coffee, it is Bowie Kuhn who says, 'One lump or two?' "

In 1966 this was the man whom Koufax and Drysdale defied by staging the first joint holdout in baseball history. Then again, what other leverage did they have? In 1966 players were still restricted by the notorious reserve clause, which bound them to one team for as long as that team desired.

MEL DURSLAG: You didn't really have negotiations back then. You took what they offered or you quit.

I mean, look at Joe DiMaggio. He was a holdout every other season. But where was he gonna go? He was just screwing around. Then he'd squeeze a little bit more out of the Yankees, and they would reel him back in.

RON FAIRLY: Baseball back then? Are you kidding? How about Richie Ashburn back in the fifties? He wins a batting title. Gets over 200 hits. And they cut him $2,500 on his next contract. They said they were all singles.

In 1965, the year before their holdout, Drysdale had signed for $80,000 and Koufax $85,000. Then both went out and had terrific seasons, with 49 wins, 592 strikeouts, and three World Series victories between them.

That winter they negotiated separately with Bavasi, but they felt the crafty GM was playing them off each other. Then, in January 1966, Koufax and Drysdale asked for a collective $1 million over three years. At $166,000 per season apiece, this would make them baseball's highest-paid players.

According to Bavasi, the budget he got from O'Malley had room for Koufax to receive $100,000 and Drysdale $90,000. In other words, the two sides weren't even close.

Money wasn't the only problem, either. The Dodgers didn't sign players to multiyear contracts, didn't want players negotiating in tandem, and sure as hell didn't want to deal with an agent—in this case a Hollywood lawyer named Bill Hayes, whom Koufax and Drysdale hired to bargain for them.

"Baseball is an old-fashioned game with old-fashioned traditions," groused O'Malley. "I have never discussed a player contract with an agent and I like to think I never will."

TOT HOLMES: Obviously, Koufax and Drysdale were worth the money. But if O'Malley gave into "an agent," baseball's economic structure might change. O'Malley did not want to set that precedent.

Thus began "the great holdout" on February 26, 1966, as Koufax and Drysdale stayed home in Los Angeles while their teammates began spring training in Vero Beach. Jim Campanis, a rookie catcher that season and the son of future general manager Al Campanis, recalls the atmosphere at Dodgertown.

JIM CAMPANIS: These guys were 50 percent of our starting pitching. Not only 50 percent, but arguably the best two pitchers in baseball. So at first, our players were sure it would get handled. Then, as spring training went on, panic set in.

LOU JOHNSON: My feeling was: Shit, we don't get to repeat as world champs. Because this started looking serious.

JOHN ROSEBORO: My biggest concern was Maury Wills. I felt he should be paid as much as them. Matter of fact, he was probably more important. Because he played every game.

Wills, though eclipsed by the Koufax-Drysdale holdout, had also stayed home because of a contract dispute. In 1965, when he earned $60,000, Wills batted .285, his 94 stolen bases led the majors, and he had 11 hits in the World Series victory over the Twins. Thus in 1966, after several years of feeling underpaid, Wills wanted $100,000.

MAURY WILLS: I wanted what I figured Koufax and Drysdale would get. And Bavasi accused me of being involved with them! I said, "I'm not involved with Koufax and Drysdale!" Bavasi said, "Yes, you are. And Mr. O'Malley knows it. He's really mad at you. He's gonna run you out of the game."

They scared the hell out of me. So I said, "I'll be there tomorrow." Which I was. Then I signed for whatever they wanted me to sign for.

Wills settled for $85,000 three weeks into spring training, as the Koufax-Drysdale holdout remained a front-page story in L.A. Which according to a pair of close observers, didn't exactly devastate the Dodgers.

MEL DURSLAG: This was *great* publicity for them. And they understood the value. Especially Walter O'Malley. He was extremely cunning about PR.

BUD FURILLO: I was the sports editor at the *Herald* then. And I lived for stories like this. Like the time when Drysdale's wife, Ginger, told our writer,

"I'd go to work at Woolworth's before I'd ever let Don sign a contract for what they're offering." So next day we ran a headline in the paper: GINGER EYES JOB IN DIME STORE.

BUZZIE BAVASI: Walter O'Malley thought he was being cute. He would have someone find out when Drysdale wasn't home. Then Walter would call up and leave a message. Drysdale would call him back in Vero Beach. Then Walter would tell the press, "The boys are getting anxious. They called me again this morning."

MEL DURSLAG: It was all a joke, you see. Sure, they were holding out in tandem. But O'Malley was holding the trump card. Where the hell could they go?

MAURY WILLS: In those days, you had to be willing to quit. So the only leverage they had was if the Dodgers thought Koufax was capable of really quitting.

Well, Koufax did things his own way. He was a guy who could split. That may be the only reason why it ended.

Bavasi says he never thought Koufax would quit. But he did view the impasse far more seriously when opening day approached and his two best pitchers still had not reported.

BUZZIE BAVASI: That's when I flew back to Los Angeles. I thought the joke was carried on long enough. I told Walter O'Malley, "We have to sign them." Walter finally said, "I'll give you 225."

So I told Sandy and Don. I said I'd give Sandy 125 because people come out to see him break records. I said I'd give Don 100 because people come out to see him win ballgames.

Then I got to thinking. I said, "Damn it, that's not fair. Don, let me give you 110." Don said fine and that's what they ended up making—125 and 110.

In his autobiography, Drysdale put the figures at $125,000 and $115,000. Regardless, the two stars earned more than if they had bargained alone. But they also got nothing like their first demand: three years at $166,000 per man.

MAURY WILLS: I don't know if it was the money, but I think Sandy got bitter after that.

BUD FURILLO: He knew what he was worth. From 1961 to 1966, he was the greatest pitcher who ever lived. And Koufax was a very private person, who never forgave them for the embarrassment of that holdout.

MEL DURSLAG: He was very, very bitter over the holdout. He was bitter they brought him in for so small an amount of money. But that's how it was back then. Joe DiMaggio, Ted Williams, Willie Mays—none of them got paid much. And who was more famous than them?

BUZZIE BAVASI: I think Drysdale realized he did fine. Sandy, on the other hand, felt he deserved more. And he had a right to think that. If I had owned the ballclub, he would have gotten more, because every time he pitched, there were eight to ten thousand more people at Dodger Stadium. Sandy thought he should get a piece of the action.

And I have to agree with him. I can't fault Sandy for that. But he didn't know Walter O'Malley like I did. O'Malley wasn't about to give him anything.

So were there lingering consequences to the great holdout? Probably only Koufax knows for sure, but just seven months after it ended, he shocked the sports world by retiring at age 30.

When he said his reasons were purely medical, there were some who accepted his explanation. Others noted his eye-popping numbers that final season—27–9, 1.73 ERA, 317 strikeouts—and wondered if Sandy Koufax was once again keeping something from our view.

10

THE STUNNING EXITS OF WILLS AND KOUFAX

1966

PEACE AT LAST! THE HEADLINE IN THE MARCH 31, 1966, *LOS ANGELES TIMES* seemed to say it all. In fact, if you were a Dodger fan, you didn't even need to read the story to know that Koufax and Drysdale had finally ended their 33-day holdout.

But then, after missing virtually all of spring training, the two Dodger pitchers got vastly different results. Drysdale struggled to get in shape and had the poorest season (13–16) of his career. Koufax won his third Cy Young Award after leading the majors in wins (27), strikeouts (317) and ERA (1.73).

On offense, the 1966 Dodgers actually hit a few homers, as Lefebvre (24), Lou Johnson (17) and Fairly (14) all produced their career highs. Still, according to ace reliever Phil Regan, who went 14–1 that year with 17 saves and a sparkling 1.62 ERA, it was another tough pennant race for L.A.

PHIL REGAN: We didn't get into first place until around September 15. Then we won the pennant, literally, on the last day of the season.

We played a doubleheader on a Sunday. We only needed a split to win the pennant, but we got beat by the Phillies in the first game. So then we had to pitch Koufax the second game. Koufax won the game. We won the pennant. But it was a very difficult September.

Koufax, for the second straight year, had clinched the pennant for Los Angeles by winning a crucial game on two days' rest. Thus, after his 6–3 victory over the Phillies, none of his teammates suspected that Koufax had just won his final game.

The Dodgers were pitted against the Baltimore Orioles in the World Series. It was a young team with two future Hall of Famers—Frank Robinson and Jim Palmer—plus defensive greats Brooks Robinson and Luis Aparicio. Moreover, while the Dodgers had barely survived, the Orioles had finished first by a gaudy nine games.

Still, did anyone truly envision the 1966 Dodgers getting swept?

TOT HOLMES: No. That was a stunner. That was as big a stunner as the Dodgers sweeping the Yankees in '63. The Dodgers were not an overwhelming favorite, but they were certainly a favorite with the Koufax-Drysdale-Osteen bunch.

And except for the first game, when Drysdale got knocked around, the Dodger pitching was good that World Series. But their hitters didn't hit. They absolutely didn't hit a lick.

Not even a half-lick. In fact, after scoring two runs in the third inning of Game 1, the Dodgers didn't cross home plate again. That added up to 33 straight scoreless innings, which still remains a dubious World Series record.

Baltimore won 5–2 in the opener at Dodger Stadium, where Jim Palmer told reporters afterward, "You can beat the Dodgers with a fastball."

The 20-year-old rookie made this blunt observation after watching reliever Moe Drabowsky strike out 11 Dodgers in 6⅔ innings. Then, matched up against Koufax in Game 2, Palmer backed up his big mouth by throwing almost all fastballs in a four-hit, 6–0 victory.

JIM PALMER: It wasn't a Joe Namath. I really wasn't trying to psych them out. But somebody asked me a question after Game 1. And I had just seen Moe Drabowsky throttle them with high fastballs.

But that doesn't mean I didn't respect the Dodgers. I had tremendous respect. We were the underdogs. They were the defending world champions. They had won world championships in two of the last three years.

And here I'm 20 years old. I'm pitching against the best pitcher of the decade. And I don't expect to win. Nobody else beat Koufax. Why would I think I was going to?

As it turned out, I threw my first shutout. And Willie Davis dropped some fly balls for them in center. Then, after showing the world he had trouble catching the ball, he heaved one of his throws into the stands.

So I pitched the game of my life. And Koufax pitched very well. But they didn't score any runs, and they made some errors. So the Dodgers beat themselves, which they usually didn't do.

In the 6–0 defeat, Koufax had allowed just one earned run, but he was making his third start in eight days, and as Jack Mann pointed out in *Sports Illustrated*, "He looked tired, he was forcing his pitches, and he had Willie Davis behind him in the outfield."

Thus, Los Angeles fell behind two games to none. Then Osteen pitched superbly in Game 3, but still lost 1–0 as the Dodger offense continued laying goose eggs. This brief affair ended with Drysdale also losing 1–0, which set yet another humiliating record. Not since 1905 had a team been shut out in three straight Series games.

DANNY OZARK: The 1966 Series? I'm still trying to forget that one. But I do remember Mr. O'Malley's reaction. He was very irate that we lost four straight.

But if all of the Los Angeles Dodgers were irked and embarrassed, the next two months would only make them feel worse. The turmoil began right after the season with a series of exhibition games played in Japan, where Maury Wills ran afoul of Walter O'Malley and suddenly found himself traded to the Pirates.

JOHN ROSEBORO: They didn't make Koufax and Drysdale go to Japan. But the Dodgers said at least one superstar had to. So they made Maury Wills go.

Of course, he didn't last too long. Wills left Japan early without permission. And they had to prove a point, especially with a black player. So Walter O'Malley said, "You're out of here."

MAURY WILLS: My knee was torn up from all the sliding I did. So I didn't want to go, and I shouldn't have had to go. Koufax and Drysdale said they had previous business commitments. In 1966? Ain't no baseball players had any business commitments.

But the Dodgers said I wouldn't have to play. Just go wave to the fans, and sign some autographs. So I agreed to go under those conditions.

Then we're over there playing the Tokyo Giants. Well, the Dodgers put me in the starting lineup. Then I get on first base and 50,000 people are yelling, "Go, go, go" in Japanese.

So I say to Jim Gilliam, our first-base coach, "Don't they know my leg's hurt?" Gilliam shrugs his shoulders. So I figure I'll steal this one base and they'll be happy. So I steal it and, *wham,* I'm writhing in pain.

Now we go to Sopporo. Slick diamond, it's raining, and they played me again. I was rounding second base and felt something go *pop.* Now I'm on third base, down on one knee, in pain. That's when I decided to leave Japan.

So I went back to the hotel and tried to call Walt Alston. But I called Mr. O'Malley's room by mistake. I said, "I'm sorry, sir. I didn't mean to interrupt you. I was trying to call Walt Alston. But I need to go back to Los Angeles."

He started yelling, "No! No way you're leaving!" Then I hung up and went to the airport. But on the way back, my plane stopped in Hawaii.

JEFF TORBORG: He was supposed to be going back home to see his doctor. But he ended up playing his banjo in a nightclub in Hawaii. Walter O'Malley found out and he was infuriated.

BUZZIE BAVASI: I didn't go to Japan, because I didn't want to be away from my family for six weeks. So instead we took a cruise. While we're on board, I get a wire from O'Malley: GET RID OF WILLS, AND GET RID OF HIM TODAY.

BUD FURILLO: Will you stop this shit with O'Malley being the villian? Maury Wills cooked his own goose there. He knows that. He'd tell you that today.

MAURY WILLS: Mr. O'Malley took it personally. He felt like I slapped his face. So, yeah, I guess I probably had it coming. But I still cried like a baby. Man, I didn't want to leave the Dodgers.

The Wills trade was announced on December 1. Two weeks earlier, on November 18, with most of the other Dodgers still in Japan, the franchise received an even greater jolt when Sandy Koufax announced his shocking retirement at the age of 30.

Don Sutton heard about it in Mississippi, where he'd gone back to college after completing his rookie year in Los Angeles. Sutton, the Hall of Famer who won more games (324) than any man who pitched for the Dodgers, recalls how he reacted to the news.

DON SUTTON: I was living in a dorm and there were some guys who couldn't understand why I was standing there with tears in my eyes. But with the impact Sandy Koufax had on baseball, the class he brought to every relationship, and his influence on me my rookie year, I was just really stunned and disappointed.

Also, of course, I never saw it coming.

Neither did millions of other Koufax fans. But as he explained to reporters during his packed news conference at the Beverly Regent Hotel, "The decision was based partly on medical advice and partly on my own feeling. . . . I was getting cortisone shots with pretty good regularity. And I just feel like I don't want to take a chance on completely disabling myself."

So it wasn't the pain itself, which Koufax had felt for years in his arthritic left elbow. It was the risk of causing permanent damage. Moreover, as Koufax said, he was fed up with all the pain pills and anti-inflammatories, which made him feel "half high" out on the mound.

Still, hadn't he just won 27 games with a 1.73 ERA? Wasn't he still performing at his peak? So could there be other reasons behind his stunning decision to hang up his spikes at age 30?

BUD FURILLO: He certainly felt some bitterness over his holdout. But that had nothing to do with him retiring. If he hated the Dodgers so much, why would he pick Vero Beach as a place to live?

BUZZIE BAVASI: I sure hope it had nothing to do with the holdout. But I can't say for sure, because he's a loner and keeps his thoughts to himself.

But I have to think it was just because of his arm. Dr. Kerlan, our great orthopedist, told me that if Sandy played much longer, he wouldn't be able to golf, go fishing, go bowling. Why would Sandy want to take that chance?

JIM CAMPANIS: He was definitely damaging his arm. In fact, his left arm was two inches shorter than his right arm. It just wouldn't straighten back out.

Still, though, I was shocked when I found out. The best pitcher in baseball is retiring? But I'll tell you what my father thought. He thought Dr. Kerlan scared him to death. He told Sandy he might end up a cripple. That's why my father thought Sandy retired.

JEFF TORBORG: You should have seen his arm after he pitched. There was so much swelling, it looked like somebody pumped it with an air pump. So I know he took painkillers before and after each start. And I know Sandy didn't like the feeling.

TIM McCARVER: I had played with Sandy that year in the All-Star Game. He was the starting pitcher in St. Louis. I walked into the training room before the game, and he was using this ointment called Capsolin. This stuff is used to loosen up the joints. But most guys mix it with cream because it's so hot.

Sandy used it full-strength right out of the tube. His elbow, his shoulder, his back—he must have used half a tube. I'll never forget it. His skin was beet red. And I thought, My God.

Now, it was insufferable weather in St. Louis. Two people had heart attacks that day. And so I figured if Sandy needs this going out on the field with 105 degrees and all this humidity, well, he could be done. And sure enough he announced his retirement at the end of the season.

CARROLL BERINGER: I can tell you exactly how hot Capsolin is. One day I pitched batting practice in St. Louis. It was hotter than hell and I was sweating. So I ran inside to change sweatshirts. My number was 52 and Sandy's was 32, and I got on his sweatshirt by mistake.

I wore that sucker back onto the field, until I brought a little more sweat, and that Capsolin kicked in. It burned like fire, man. It set me afire. I couldn't get back in the clubhouse quick enough.

So I asked Bill Buheler, our trainer, "How does he stand that?" And he said, "Well, that's what he's got to have."

So Sandy pitched in pain. And, remember, he always pitched a lot of innings. And I think Sandy quit because he really feared that he'd lose the use of his arm later in life.

JOHN ROSEBORO: They were also shooting his arm with cortisone, and he was in good shape financially. So he figured, why take a chance on being a cripple?

That's what I heard back then. And I haven't heard differently in many years.

Maybe so, but what about what the great Jim Murray wrote in the *Los Angeles Times* in 1998? After noting the Dodgers "played hardball" with Koufax and Drysdale during their spring training holdout, Murray wrote, "History tells us lingering bitterness played a part in Koufax's decision to retire that winter (after a 27–9, 1.73 ERA season, no one could believe him when he said it was because his arm hurt)."

JEFF TORBORG: I know he was in extreme pain. But you have to remember Sandy's personality. He's a very private guy, very deep and intelli-

gent. And when Sandy and Don held out, some people acted like it was sac-
rilegious. How could they band together and do this to the Dodgers?

So it became a very public negotiation. And I can see where Sandy would
be very bothered by that. And it could be that it hurt him. It could be that
it stuck with him.

MAURY WILLS: Sandy was in pain, yeah. But guys like Roberto Clemente
used to walk back shaking their heads after striking out against him. "How
in the fuck can he say he's got a sore arm? Jesus, sore arm, my ass."

So while Sandy had pain in his arm, I think he could have gone on. It
was a combination of pain and being unhappy with his environment. There
was some resentment over his holdout. There was some indifference.

I don't know if it was toward Walter O'Malley or the Dodgers or baseball. But that was all part of it, yeah.

Did that strange thing called fame play a role, too? Did the glare of the
public spotlight help drive Sandy Koufax out of baseball?

KEVIN KENNEDY: I've been friends with Sandy for almost 20 years.
And after knowing him all this time, and talking about certain things, I feel
that his arthritis, that his arm could be crippled someday if he didn't quit,
was definitely a part of it.

But I also believe the lifestyle, the notoriety, was not Sandy's thing. I think
he had enough of all the limelight. I think he was ready for some distancing.

The left elbow, the holdout, the increasingly fierce desire for privacy—it is
difficult to determine precisely why Koufax walked away so young. But after
his five straight ERA titles, four no-hitters, and three World Series rings, was
it somehow better this way? That Sandy Koufax left us wanting more?

This idea was presented to Bob Costas, the fabulous broadcaster for
NBC who lived most of his childhood on the East Coast, except for almost
two years in Los Angeles, where he saw Koufax pitch in the Coliseum.

BOB COSTAS: I think what made him important to people was the
combination of greatness and style. You know, results are one thing, but his

style was so elegant and compelling. To combine that kind of power with that kind of grace is really something that stirs the imagination.

My perspective on his retirement at age 30? He probably could have continued to be one of the best pitchers in the league, if not *the* best, for at least a few more seasons after that. But as he himself said at the time, he didn't want to risk permanent damage to his arm.

And then, as you look at it from more than 30 years down the road, his leaving when he did actually enhanced his reputation. They talk about Joe DiMaggio walking away. Or Jim Brown walking away. Or Rocky Marciano walking away. But I can't think of anyone in sports who left closer to his peak than this guy. And from everything I could see then, and everything I've heard since, he has always carried himself as a gentleman. On the field and off the field as well, Sandy Koufax has always had grace.

11

THE LEAN YEARS

1 9 6 7 – 6 9

No one expected the Dodgers to win their third straight pennant in 1967. But even with Sandy Koufax suddenly and shockingly done with baseball, Maury Wills shipped off to Pittsburgh, and Tommy Davis traded to the Mets, did anyone believe they would tumble all the way from first place to eighth?

PHIL REGAN: What did we finish that year—28 games out of first? Well, Sandy won 27 games the year before. And Maury always won a lot of games every year.

So we just weren't the same team in '67. Take away Koufax and Wills, and what team would be?

The swift decline continued in 1968. Young starting pitcher Bill Singer, who would win 20 games in 1969 and throw a no-hitter in 1970, recalls a Dodger team that batted just .230, scored a measly 2.9 runs per game, and had a guy named Al Ferrara batting *fourth* on opening day.

BILL SINGER: In 1968 our entire team hit about 65 homers. But we also had a third baseman who made 50 errors! So it wasn't only the loss of Koufax and Wills. Scouting, player development, trades, whatever—a great Dodger organization hit a rough spot.

Still, one man performed magnificently. As the 1968 Dodgers finished tied for seventh place—giving them successive losing seasons for the first time since 1937–38—Don Drysdale threw six consecutive shutouts. His scoreless streak finally ended at 58⅔ innings, breaking a record held 55 years by Walter Johnson.

On August 11, 1969, Drysdale retired from baseball with a torn rotator cuff, and although the Dodgers improved to 85–77 that season, nobody missed the poignancy of his departure.

DON SUTTON: He was like my big brother when I came up. So it felt like my big brother walked away. That's about the best way I can put it.

TOT HOLMES: Yeah, that was tough for them. He was the only Dodger player left from Brooklyn. And happening when it did—in the midst of bad times—you knew the jig was up for them for some time.

JIM LEFEBVRE: Drysdale was the heart and soul of the last generation. When he left, an era ended. Then it was only a matter of time for the rest of us.

Buzzie Bavasi, in fact, was already gone. After 30 years in the Dodgers' organization, including the past 17 as general manager, he had left in June 1968 to become president and part owner of the new expansion franchise in San Diego.

BUZZIE BAVASI: Why I left? Oh, well, that's easy. There was no problem there. But young Peter O'Malley was getting older. And Peter was a good man. But I could see the handwriting on the wall.

Also, it was a good opportunity for me. Arnholt Smith, the owner in San

Diego, gave me 30 percent of the ballclub. Well, I never got a piece of the club with the Dodgers. Nobody got a piece but Walter O'Malley.

It should be emphasized that Bavasi says this without any sign of bitterness. And yet, according to several longtime observers, O'Malley actually gave Bavasi a shove.

"There was a rift at the end," says a veteran Los Angeles reporter. "Buzzie resented Walter for bringing in Peter as an executive. That caused some bad blood. Which led to Walter finding a franchise in San Diego for Bavasi and easing him out of the Dodgers. That's why Buzzie left for San Diego. He'll never tell you that, though."

BUD FURILLO: He was the best general manager in baseball, and the Dodgers never paid him what he was worth. But it wasn't just Bavasi. Walter O'Malley lowballed everybody.

After Bavasi left in June 1968, Fresco Thompson served as general manager until his death of cancer that November. Then the powerful GM position went to veteran scouting director Al Campanis, whose protégé was an exuberant minor league manager named Tommy Lasorda. Meanwhile, Walt Alston now lost his own mentor in Bavasi.

In 1969 Peter O'Malley became executive vice president of the Dodgers. A graduate of Penn and its Wharton School of Finance, he had previously run the Dodgers' spring training camp in Vero Beach, then the Dodgers' minor league team at Spokane, and finally operations at Dodger Stadium. In 1970, at age 32, he was named team president, as his father made himself chairman of the board.

JIM LEFEBVRE: Walter O'Malley had that booming voice. He had that dynamic presence. He was "the man" in the National League and probably all of baseball.

Peter was much quieter than Walter. But Peter was a very bright guy, too. And Peter always had his mother, Kay. Talk about a sweetheart of a person. Everyone in baseball loved Kay O'Malley.

ROGER KAHN: The last time I ever talked to Sandy Koufax, he said he thought Peter O'Malley combined some of his father's good sense with his mother's kindness.

JEFF TORBORG: Walter O'Malley was the man who took the game national. He was above the game in many ways. So Peter O'Malley had a tough act to follow. But he didn't just walk in there. He paid his dues.

JIM CAMPANIS: This was a baseball family, remember. And what Walter did with his son—which was amazing, and which you don't see today with baseball's corporate structure—is send Peter down to the minors.

Well, it's very hard to send your kid away. It's hard for the kid to leave the big-league atmosphere. But Peter went down there and learned the business. And he became a great minor league executive.

So in one way, the end of the sixties were tough for the Dodgers. The franchise was in transition—both the players on the field and the front office. And there were those terrible seasons in 1967 and 1968.

But Peter was getting prepared to one day become the owner, and Walter was still very powerful and active. The minor league system was strong, and they had signed a killer group of young kids—Garvey and Lopes and Cey and Buckner and Russell. And, of course, Tommy Lasorda was managing them in the minors, and they were winning pennants at every level.

So you could see it coming. The Dodgers were gonna be great as soon as these kids grew up.

PART III

———

THE SEVENTIES

12

TWO BRAZEN PLAYERS
AND ALSTON

1970–72

It was the year Janis Joplin died of a drug overdose. President Richard M. Nixon announced the U.S. invasion of Cambodia. Four unarmed college students were killed by National Guardsmen during an antiwar demonstration at Kent State.

In baseball in 1970, Jim Bouton published *Ball Four,* which enraged the establishment and delighted millions of fans with its raucous account of life in the big leagues. Commissioner Bowie Kuhn suspended Denny McLain for 90 days for associating with known gamblers. Curt Flood filed a lawsuit challenging baseball's reserve clause, which would result in Flood losing but also paving the way for free agency.

As the 1970s unfolded, the mustachioed Oakland A's would win three straight World Series and contribute some much needed color to a sport being heavily challenged by pro football. The first World Series night game would be played. The American League would adopt the designated hitter. The role of the bullpen "closer" would turn crucial.

Henry Aaron would become the all-time home run king, Frank Robinson the first black manager, and Catfish Hunter the first de facto free agent. This in turn led to the death of the reserve clause, the birth of million-dollar salaries, and even more heated relations between the owners and players. In April 1972, in fact, the fans got an ugly glimpse of baseball's future when every major league player went out on strike—the first strike in American sports history.

Two years earlier, the 1970 Dodgers finished second, returning to the first division for the first time since 1966. They even discovered some offense, tying the first-place Reds for the highest team batting average (.270) in the majors.

However, Los Angeles only hit 90 homers, while Johnny Bench and Tony Perez hit 85 homers alone for Cincinnati. Thus in December 1970, the Dodgers acquired Dick Allen, their first genuine power hitter since Frank Howard.

Still, the deal surprised a lot of baseball people. During six stormy years in Philadelphia, Allen built a reputation as an outlaw. He frequently skipped batting practice, sometimes drank on the job, and once nailed his teammate Frank Thomas with a left hook.

On the other hand, the enigmatic Allen could flat-out play. In 1966, with the 42-ounce club he called a bat, Allen hit .317 with 40 homers. In 1970, the year before coming to Los Angeles, he hit 34 homers with 101 RBIs.

In 1971 his 23 home runs, 90 RBIs, and .468 slugging percentage all topped the Dodgers. So why did they dump him after only one season?

All-star catcher Tom Haller, who came to Los Angeles from hated San Francisco, says Allen "never fit the Dodger image."

TOM HALLER: They were a very publicity-conscious team. But Richie Allen never cared about PR. He was kind of the Lone Ranger.

BILL SINGER: Most of the players loved him, but he was the kind of free spirit who would drive a manager nuts. I mean, he would drink a little too much. Sometimes even right up until game time.

JOE MOELLER: Walt Alston never wanted him in the first place. That was an Al Campanis move all the way. So 1971 was kind of strange, because Richie Allen had his own work schedule. He would show up 20 minutes before the game. He'd skip fielding practice. Then he'd go out and make two errors at third base.

TOM HALLER: Consequently, the Dodgers got rid of him, which was a heck of a lot easier than kowtowing to him.

Not everyone in the clubhouse felt that way. Bobby Valentine, the controversial manager of the Mets who began his baseball career as a promising young shortstop with the Dodgers, says he was sorry to see Dick Allen go.

BOBBY VALENTINE: That was my rookie year, and he stood alone as their only power hitter. He was their only real stick. But I don't think he and Walt Alston ever talked. I remember Dick saying, "Maybe today's the day he'll talk to me."

So Dick knew he would be gone after that season. He told me point-blank on our plane, "I'll lead this team in every category. Then I'll be traded when the year's over, because the old man doesn't like me."

Turned out he was right. They couldn't wait to get rid of him, in fact.

In 1971, with much of the power supplied by the lame-duck Allen, the Dodgers produced their best record (89–73) since 1966 but still finished one game behind the Giants in the third year of baseball's divisional play (both clubs played in the National League West).

In 1972 Valentine had his own problems with Alston. In 1968 Valentine had been the Dodgers' No. 1 draft choice before teaming up in the minors with the equally brash and confident Tommy Lasorda. By 1970 they were the two shining stars of their Triple-A farm club in Spokane. Valentine batted .340 and won Player of the Year in the Pacific Coast League. Lasorda won Minor League Manager of the Year as Spokane led the PCL by an eye-popping 26 games.

In 1971 Lasorda remained in Triple A while Valentine made the Los Angeles Dodgers' roster. Valentine was everyone's next "phenom," and major league stardom seemed certain. But Alston had little use for his cocky young shortstop.

BOBBY VALENTINE: I was loud and energetic, and I was Tommy's guy, and I made no bones about it. And I'm sure I said some things that got back to Alston about Tommy doing a better job if he got the opportunity to take over.

So I never really had a relationship with Walt Alston. For the two years I was there, he called me Bill.

By 1972, his second big-league season, Valentine felt he should be the team's starting shortstop, but Alston gave the job to Bill Russell, another young up-and-comer produced by the Dodgers' strong minor league system.

BUD FURILLO: The truth is, Bobby Valentine was ticketed to be the next great Dodger shortstop after Maury Wills. But Alston didn't like Bobby because he was so extroverted.

So Alston got rid of him, and that's the way Bill Russell got the job. Then Russell kept it for, what, the next 20 years?

BOBBY VALENTINE: As I envisioned things, Garvey would be the Dodgers' next third baseman, Buckner would be the first baseman, Lopes would be the second baseman, and I would be the shortstop. Because that's the way we all came up together.

But Bill Russell happened to be exactly what Walt Alston liked. They were from the same mold—quiet, reserved kind of guys who did their hunting and fishing. Not that it's good or bad. But Russell was so much like Alston, and I was the antithesis of Alston. I was much more fiery, like Tommy, and Tommy and Alston had this rivalry going.

So after the 1972 season, I met with Alston about his plans for shortstop. I said, "I'd like to come to spring training and have a chance. I think there should be a competition."

Walt said he had no plans to play me at shortstop. If I was going to be on the team at all, he would play me at second base. So I said, "Well, I guess I should be traded."

Two months later, I was. They traded me to the California Angels. And so, regretfully, I never played for Tommy Lasorda in the big leagues.

In 1972, Valentine's final season with the Dodgers, they finished a distant third behind the first-place Reds, who were now the powerhouse in the National League. But the glory years in L.A. were hardly over. Led by a famous infield that would remain intact for a record eight years, the Dodgers would soon regain their previous luster.

13

"IRON MIKE" AND
THE WORLD SERIES

1973–74

WHEN YOU THINK OF LOS ANGELES DODGERS AND "THROWING PROBLEMS," the name that comes to mind is probably Steve Sax. But how many recall Steve Garvey's own major bout with errant throws a decade before Sax's famous ordeal?

Denis Anthony does. A 45-year-old salesman for a restaurant equipment distributor, he is a lifelong Dodger fan who used to work at their stadium selling tickets.

DENIS ANTHONY: When Steve Garvey first came up, he played third base. And he was a pretty good fielder. I mean, he could catch the ball. But Garvey had trouble finding the first baseman. His throws would go to the right or go to the left. Or he would bounce them in.

Sometimes his throws went over the first baseman's head. In fact, a lot of the balls went into the stands. So there was this little joke that went around: When Steve Garvey played third, it was Ball Night at Dodger Stadium.

But you also knew this guy could hit. That was obvious since he was a rookie. So that became the big question: "Where are you gonna play Garvey?" Because if he ever found the right position, you could tell this guy would be a star.

In 1972, when Garvey made a whopping 28 errors in only 85 games, a majority of them came on wild throws. Garvey believes he knows why, even though throwing problems are always a little strange and mysterious.

STEVE GARVEY: I had always had a strong arm. And then my freshman year at Michigan State, I separated my shoulder playing football. It was enough of a separation that I never quite threw the same again after that.

But it may have been partly psychological, too. Because if I had to make a quick throw, if it was a quick play, boy, it would be on the money. Give me time and who knows where it would be going.

So in the fateful summer of 1973, how did he make the transition from a scatter-armed third baseman to a budding superstar playing first base?

That depends on who you ask. Garvey says Alston simply decided to move him to first. Garvey's ex-wife, Cyndy, has said that she gave Alston the idea. Bill Buckner, the incumbent first baseman, says the suggestion to Alston came from him.

Bobby Valentine has yet another interpretation. He says fate intervened on Garvey's behalf.

BOBBY VALENTINE: In 1973 Bill Buckner was playing first base for the Dodgers. That was rightfully so, because Buckner batted .300 wherever he went.

Garvey was on the bench, because they finally decided he couldn't play third base. Then in June of '73 the trade deadline was approaching and the Dodgers were getting ready to trade Garvey. But Von Joshua, the left fielder, got injured. Manny Mota, the fourth outfielder, pulled a hamstring.

So the next logical candidate was Garvey, because he had played some left field. But instead of putting Garvey in the outfield, Alston moved Buckner to left and put Garvey at first.

That's how Steve Garvey became the Dodger first baseman. Then he owned the position for ten years.

Garvey debuted at first base on June 23, 1973. By then Ron Cey was already starting at third, Davey Lopes at second, and Bill Russell at shortstop. Garvey, Lopes, Russell, and Cey would play together for the next eight seasons. They would help win four pennants and one World Series. They would also, at times, not be terribly friendly toward one another.

That mostly came later, though. On July 1, 1973, the young and talented Dodgers were being called "the Mod Squad" and leading their division by a flashy 11 games. But unable to hold off the powerful Reds, they ended up finishing second, even after winning 95 games.

In 1974, determined to pull ahead of Cincinnati, the Dodgers dealt Willie Davis to the Expos for relief pitcher Mike Marshall. To many, including Marshall, the trade was bizarre, for Davis was clearly declining while Marshall was now the best reliever in baseball. In 1973 Marshall had led the league with 31 saves, posted a 1.78 ERA, and pitched in a big-league record 92 games.

MIKE MARSHALL: I was very surprised when Montreal traded me. I was even more surprised for *whom* they traded me. I expected them to get players like Cey and Lopes—a couple of really talented young guys.

Instead they got a guy who was on his way out. In fact, Los Angeles pretty much slammed the door behind him. So I was quite surprised about the whole trade. But I had, a long time ago, stopped trying to figure out the geniuses who ran baseball.

Well, that probably explains it. He didn't exactly sugarcoat his opinions. He could be condescending toward the big shots. Which can get a man traded in pretty much any business.

And yet, above all, says Dodger pitcher Al Downing, what set Marshall apart were his radical ideas about how frequently a human being could pitch.

AL DOWNING: Mike felt the more he threw, the stronger his arm would get. But what baseball people didn't realize is that Mike had already done the research on this. For years he studied kinesiology. Then later he ended up getting his Ph.D.

Now, in 1974, Mike pitched in 106 games for us. But he only had 21 saves. So he was pitching a lot of those games, I think, basically to try and prove his theory.

Did that help us or hurt us? That's hard to say. But either way, Mike was gonna be maligned. That's what baseball does to guys who are different.

MIKE MARSHALL: I *finished* 83 games! How the hell do you finish 83 games and only get 21 saves? Because at the time, they had a ridiculous save rule. They have since changed it back, but it was bullshit. If not for that damn rule, I would have the save record and every other damn record in relief pitching.

That's why those 21 saves mean absolutely nothing. I did the job that year. The Dodgers would have been nowhere if I hadn't been there.

BILL BUCKNER: Mike was very, very opinionated. And I think he really tried to BS some people. He talked about that health stuff all the time. Then I'd see him go up to his room at two in the morning with six bags of McDonald's.

RON CEY: Mike was a different breed. When he played for Montreal, he was the guy who pitched in shirt sleeves even when it was 20 degrees outside.

In 1974, when "Iron Mike" broke his own record by pitching in 106 games, he won 15 of them, saved 21 others, and appeared in a truly remarkable 208 innings, which was more than any reliever before or since.

In addition to Marshall, impressive performances came from Garvey, Sutton, and Jimmy Wynn. Garvey won his league's Most Valuable Player award with a .312 batting average, 21 homers, and 111 RBIs in only his first full season at first base. Sutton went 19–9, including 13 wins in his last 14 decisions. Wynn, the other great player acquired that year in a trade, led the Dodgers with 32 homers and 104 runs scored.

For the second straight season, Los Angeles started fast and built a ten-game lead by early July. And once again the Reds came charging back, but this time the Dodgers had the stronger finish. In fact, they produced their best record (102–60) in 21 years.

Los Angeles won its first pennant since 1966 by next defeating Pittsburgh in the playoffs. Then the Dodgers faced the mighty Oakland A's in the first all-California World Series.

Exactly how formidable were the A's? They were trying to become the first team besides the Yankees to ever win three consecutive World Series. They boasted an array of stars, including Reggie Jackson, Catfish Hunter, Rollie Fingers, Joe Rudi, Sal Bando, Ken Holtzman, and Vida Blue.

But exactly how harmonious were the A's? As Ron Fimrite pointed out in *Sports Illustrated*, "There have been more fistfights in the A's clubhouse this year than in Madison Square Garden." And even the World Series wasn't sacred. On the day before Game I, Fingers received five stitches in his scalp after a brawl with Blue Moon Odom in the visitors' clubhouse at Dodger Stadium.

In charge of this colorful crew was owner Charles O. Finley, the garish and meddlesome maverick whose innovations included orange baseballs, green and gold uniforms, paying his players $300 each to grow facial hair, and making a mule named "Charlie O" the team mascot.

Joe Rudi, the Oakland left fielder who would play a crucial role in the 1974 World Series, calls Finley the type of owner "you just don't see in baseball anymore."

JOE RUDI: Remember when he was signing players like Catfish Hunter and Blue Moon Odom? He was also passing on guys who *didn't* have good nicknames. Then, of course, with Vida Blue, Finley tried paying him to change his name to True.

That to me sort of epitomized Charles Finley. He was a circus promoter who owned a baseball team.

AL DOWNING: The A's were probably one of the best teams ever. But most people in baseball didn't like Finley. They thought he was nuts. So the A's never got the credit they deserved.

STEVE GARVEY: They were an interesting team for us to play. They had donkeys and colored balls and mustaches. But they were also a veteran team, and we were still pretty young. And they beat us pretty quickly, in five games.

The 1974 World Series was hardly a rout, though. Three of the Dodger defeats came on 3–2 scores, and as Roger Angel noted in *The New Yorker,* the deciding factor was experience. The older A's "knew how to *execute,*" while the younger Dodgers were prone to "little mistakes, nearly forgivable errors or youthful lapses of judgment."

The most famous sequence came in the fifth and final Series game. The score was tied 2–2 in the bottom of the seventh when Buckner took his position in left field, where he was targeted for some comments he'd made about Oakland after Game 3.

JOE RUDI: Buckner said the Dodgers had a much better team than the A's. He said there were only two guys, Reggie and Catfish, who could even make their team.

Buckner doesn't recall his exact words. But he'll never forget the response from the maniacs in Oakland's left-field stands.

BILL BUCKNER: I got hit in the head with a whiskey bottle. I was really stunned, and they delayed the game for 15 minutes.

In reality, the delay was perhaps eight minutes as the fans showered the field with other debris. Now, eight minutes is still long enough for a pitcher to ordinarily keep throwing. But as the *Los Angeles Times'* Ross Newhan explains, pitching for the Dodgers was Mike Marshall.

ROSS NEWHAN: Marshall was a beauty. Marshall was a classic. And Marshall didn't warm up. That was his arrogance. He didn't need to warm up. That was Mike Marshall saying, "I know more about my body and staying warm and making quality pitches than anyone else."

Marshall's catcher that day was Steve Yeager, a longtime Dodger respected for his toughness and smarts behind the plate.

STEVE YEAGER: When you have a delay that long, you gotta throw a few pitches, just to get familiar with the mound again, and familiar with the strike zone. Every pitcher in baseball would do that. But Mike didn't want to.

So I was telling him to throw from behind the plate. Lopes and Cey and Wynn were yelling at him. But what are you gonna do? Put a gun to his head and make him warm up?

JIMMY WYNN: I called out from center field, "Continue to throw! Stay warm!" Mike turned around and said, "I'm already warm!"

Ron Fimrite, the national baseball writer for *Sports Illustrated* during the 1970s, picks up the story from there.

RON FIMRITE: Joe Rudi was the first hitter for Oakland. And Rudi figured out that since Marshall hadn't warmed up, Marshall wouldn't try any breaking stuff. Undoubtedly, his first pitch would be a fastball.

JOE RUDI: I didn't know much about Marshall. Just what I read in the paper—that he was a hell of a pitcher, and he was a little eccentric.

Well, when all that junk was being thrown at Buckner, the umpires walked out to short left field. Marshall walked out there also, I guess to put his two cents in. Then even when he came back, he never threw a pitch.

I figured since he hadn't loosened up, he wasn't going to throw a breaking ball. So I looked for a fastball. That's what Marshall threw, and fortunately I hit it pretty well.

BILL BUCKNER: First pitch, boom, Joe Rudi hit a home run.

JIMMY WYNN: They went up 3–2 in the bottom of the seventh. That turned the Series back in Oakland's favor.

STEVE GARVEY: Probably, yeah, that was the crushing blow.

STEVE YEAGER: Again, what can you do? You can't force a guy to warm up. Maybe he learned his lesson. I don't know.

MIKE MARSHALL: If I needed to warm up, I would have warmed up. This is twenty-twenty hindsight nonsense. I threw the pitch I wanted to throw, and Rudi, based on some convoluted thinking, guessed the right pitch and hit it out of the ballpark.

Joe Rudi did a nice job. I give him credit. But there wouldn't have been anything wrong with my team scoring a run or two. I *did* come into that game in the sixth inning. But if I come in when we're tied 2–2, and we don't score any runs in my three innings, we cannot win the game. Right?

In fact, just moments after Rudi's homer, the Dodgers had a chance to tie the score when Buckner led off the eighth inning with a single that squirted past Bill North in center field. Buckner hustled to second, but rather than playing it safe, headed to third. He got thrown out on a close play, the Dodgers lost 3–2, and Oakland won its three straight World Series.

Fimrite, in his cover story for *Sports Illustrated*, called Buckner's dash for third base "the final Dodger boo-boo of the year."

AL DOWNING: He was right if he wrote that. Buckner made a boner on that play.

RON CEY: Of course, Bill Buckner is known for the ground ball that went through his legs when he played for Boston in the World Series. But in 1974, he also made a serious mistake when he tried going to third and got thrown out.

There is one man, of course, who disagrees.

MIKE MARSHALL: I thought Buckner was safe. I *said* I thought he was safe, and their third baseman Sal Bando called me a liar. I don't see how that makes me a liar. I just thought he was safe.

14

ONE BIG HAPPY FAMILY

1975

IN 1975 THE DODGER FAITHFUL WERE STUNNED WHEN THEIR BELOVED TEAM was barely heard from. How could a club win the pennant, hang tough against Oakland in the World Series, and then finish 20 games back in its own division?

Players and journalists cite three main factors:

- An extraordinary performance by the Reds, who went an implausible 64–17 at home, 108–54 overall, and defeated the Red Sox in that year's World Series.
- Key injuries to Mike Marshall, Bill Buckner, and Jimmy Wynn.
- Clubhouse issues. In particular, Steve Garvey issues.

Of course, some journalists had played a part themselves by showering the handsome young Garvey with praise. In October 1974 *The New Yorker* called him the Dodgers' "shining new star." Then came *Sports Illustrated* in April 1975, noting that Garvey "smiles at everybody, gives autographs like a garage gives calendars and is a known gentleman." *Sports Illustrated* also explained that he grew up in Tampa, where he had once been the team's batboy during spring training. Thus the gentle article's flattering headline: BORN TO BE A DODGER.

In 1975, the year after Garvey won the MVP award in the National League, becoming a media darling had its rewards. Garvey started to land bigger endorsements and more lucrative speaking engagements than his teammates. But as the legendary Jim Murray pointed out, the 26-year-old Garvey paid a price.

"His teammates couldn't believe it was all true," wrote Murray in his memoir. "They gnashed their teeth and changed the subject when Garvey's name was mentioned. Finally, one day, they unburdened themselves to a female reporter from San Bernardino. The word 'hypocrite' came up. A lot."

The explosive story ran on June 15, 1975, in the San Bernardino *Sun-Telegram*. The reporter's name was Betty Cuniberti, and she quoted several Dodgers blasting Garvey.

STEVE GARVEY: Some of them were quoted anonymously, and that's what probably bothered me the most. If you don't want to stand up and put your name behind it, then you're just hiding behind the First Amendment.

But two of his fellow infielders weren't hiding. Ron Cey was quoted as saying, "If he wants to go out of his way to be the clean-cut kid, that's fine, as long as he doesn't interfere with my style.... Basically everyone knows he's a public relations man." Davey Lopes said Garvey viewed baseball "more as a business" than as a game.

Naturally, the story got huge play. Garvey was rapidly becoming an icon and this was the public's first glimpse of the animosity felt toward him by teammates. Moreover, the story shot holes in what *Sports Illustrated* called "the myth of Dodger camaraderie."

ROSS NEWHAN: The tension just kept building after that. Because everywhere the team went, the relationship was probed.

STEVE GARVEY: There was a feeling of being watched. Not just on the field, but in the dugout. There were binoculars on us. Watching me and watching other guys. "Garvey is sitting there. Where are they sitting?"

So it was a difficult education for me. I was shocked that anybody would criticize his own teammate like that. Because then it becomes this media event. And then the fans become polarized, you know? And I think the majority of fans were on my side.

DAVEY LOPES: We're not gonna go out to dinner, but I always respected Steve Garvey as a player. And that's all I needed to do. Whether I liked him or not is irrelevant.

But, yeah, at one time we had our differences. We almost came to blows a couple times. Once was that article. But it wasn't what I said that caused the tension. Somebody else made a reference to his wife, and Garv went on a mission all of a sudden.

We were playing in San Diego. Garv came up at batting practice and said, "I know it was you that said that stuff about Cyndy." I said, "You know I said that?" He said, "Yeah." I said, "Then someone's a liar. And I'll tell you what you should do. You bring that person down here in front of me. Then have them tell me to my face that I was the one who said that."

Then I said, "Listen, Garv, you don't ever have to worry about one thing. Whenever I say something, my name will be next to it. Now, I am telling you I didn't say it. But if you want to try and kick my ass, go ahead."

Because he was angry. He was upset. So I said, "Hey, we can go right here right now." He just made a gesture with his hands. And that was the end of it.

But people kept harping and harping on that stuff. It got to the point where you're saying, "I don't want to hear about this shit anymore. I'm here to play baseball. Forget about talking all this Peyton Place crap."

Mark Cresse also recalls the turbulent summer of 1975. He was just getting started as a bullpen catcher before serving as bullpen coach for 22 seasons—the longest tenure of any coach in Dodger history.

MARK CRESSE: Sure, I remember that season. I remember them all. What do you want to know?

Why was a player so talented, so reliable, and so enormously popular with the fans, the most controversial man inside his own clubhouse?

MARK CRESSE: Steve was a great player. He had a great work ethic. But he was also great at politics. He always knew exactly what the people needed to hear to create an image. It's nothing bad about Steve. He's a smart guy, and it worked. People loved him. Mom, apple pie, and Steve Garvey. But some of the players wondered if he was too good to be true.

DON SUTTON: Because he wanted to be. That's it. He wanted to be.

He wanted to be *what?* Controversial?

DON SUTTON: That's it. Any more questions won't do you any good. He wanted to be exactly what he was. And that's the end of my take on that.

MIKE MARSHALL: We all knew how Mr. Sutton felt about Garvey. That was obvious a few years later when they fought.

ROSS NEWHAN: I believe a lot of it was envy. The amount of publicity Steve got really weighed on those guys.

One year, as I recall it, Steve's locker was right between Sutton and Cey. And they never talked to Steve. They talked over or around him.

RON CEY: Right now I work with Steve in marketing and community affairs. So we're probably much closer now than we were back then.

But there's no question that Garv was in fact around the cameras. There was no doubt about it. He knew exactly what was going on.

DAVEY LOPES: Steve had his own agenda. He wanted to be Mr. Dodger. And there was some bullshit involved, to be honest with you. There was a lot of favoritism from the Dodgers. Special favors were given to Steve, special favors to his wife, Cyndy.

Just stupid little shit, when you look back on it. But I think you get caught up in the atmosphere. You're in Hollywood, you forget who you are, what you do, and you just get carried away with the whole scene.

Ken McMullen offers another perspective. McMullen, the Dodger third baseman whose job was taken by Cey when McMullen got injured in 1973, says he was friendly with all the players involved.

KEN McMULLEN: Steve was getting it done out on the field. But he was also out there kissing babies, and getting all of the press and the publicity.

They would have liked that, too, but those other guys just weren't cut out for that. Cey was very withdrawn. Davey was very shy. Bill Russell didn't care one way or another. Sutton, it just kind of rubbed him the wrong way.

The other thing was, they all lived close together. They all lived in the Valley, and their wives were out there, too. And sometimes wives can create jealousy, also. Sometimes wives can bicker about their husbands. I'm pretty sure some of that was happening, too.

Pretty sure? The Dodger wives were so famous for bickering, Steve Yeager forbid his new bride from telling him what transpired in the family section at Dodger Stadium.

STEVE YEAGER: I said, "Whatever the hell goes on in section 105, I don't want to know. You can handle it up there. If I got a problem with a guy, I'll handle it down here."

The *San Francisco Chronicle's* Scott Ostler used to cover the Dodgers in his award-winning columns for the *Los Angeles Times*. Ostler presents his own view of Steve Garvey and his relationship with his teammates.

SCOTT OSTLER: I tend to be a pro-Garvey guy. And I think some of the players were jealous of him. Garvey was kind of a god in Southern California. He was very, very popular with the fans.

I remember traveling with the Dodgers. The bus would pull up to a hotel at 11 o'clock at night in New York and there might be 30 autograph seekers waiting. Everyone from the bus would brush past these autograph seekers except Garvey. Garvey would always stop and sign for them.

Now the anti-Garvey faction took the basic position that he was a kiss-ass. He's out there trying to make points. My position would be, what kind of point is he going to make at 11 at night in New York with a bunch of scruffy autograph seekers?

I just think Garvey liked people. Maybe it was something in his background, where he had this need to be nice. I never saw that as a bad thing. But a lot of the players saw that as a kind of sucking up and kissing ass.

Here's my impression of Steve Garvey: He was like that guy in high school who wants people to like him. So maybe sometimes he tries a little too hard. Because he's hoping to get asked to join this club, and he's worried they won't think he's cool enough.

15

ALSTON'S FINAL DAYS

1976

ON SEPTEMBER 27, 1976, THE DAY WALTER EMMONS ALSTON ANNOUNCED HIS retirement, the baseball world was saddened but hardly surprised. The 64-year-old Alston had managed the Dodgers for 23 straight seasons.

"I simply feel I've been at it long enough. Now I can get away to ride my motorcycle and my horses, to shoot pool and skeet, and to play a little golf," Alston said at his farewell press conference.

Don Sutton was 20 years old when he started pitching for Alston in 1966. He calls Alston's retirement "gut-wrenching."

DON SUTTON: It was the same feeling I got when Koufax and Drysdale quit. Maybe a little more so, because Walter Alston was so much like my father. They could have been from the same family. And so when Walt retired, it ended a working relationship that I valued very much.

MIKE MARSHALL: There was nothing underhanded about the man. He didn't glad-hand you, he didn't bullshit you. He was the best manager I ever played for.

TIM McCARVER: Walt Alston was a cool guy. He was smart and confident, he knew his players very well, and I always got the feeling that Alston engineered games. Especially in the Koufax-Drysdale years, when the Dodgers didn't have a lot of hitting, but they still knew how to manufacture runs. So I always gave Alston a lot of credit for that. As a matter of fact, I don't think Alston really got enough credit over the years.

Yes, and here is another frequently overlooked part of the Alston era: He may not have retired voluntarily. In fact, several prominent Dodgers say he got pushed.

This much is known for sure: In 1976, Los Angeles finished second to Cincinnati for the fifth time in seven years. This time the Dodgers finished 10 games back—10 games closer than 1975—but that was still pretty depressing for the most storied franchise in the National League.

This much is also sure: Sixteen of the current Dodgers, including the entire Garvey-Lopes-Russell-Cey infield, had played for Tommy Lasorda in the minors. Furthermore, Lasorda had won five pennants in only seven years at Ogden, Spokane, and Albuquerque.

By 1976 Lasorda was in his fourth summer as Dodger third-base coach. Thus, as that season began, the issue wasn't who would succeed Walt Alston. It was how long would Tommy Lasorda have to wait.

BUD FURILLO: Oh, God, poor Tommy. How bad he wanted that job. And Walter O'Malley knew it. In fact, one day Walter told me, "Tell your friend Lasorda just be patient."

But, see, the Braves wanted Tommy Lasorda. The Yankees wanted Tommy. But I said to Tommy once, "What do you want to do? Go manage the Braves for a year and then get fired? I told you Walter O'Malley said you'd be the manager here." Tommy said, "Yeah, that's right. *You* told me, not him."

TOMMY LASORDA: Sure, I had opportunities to go elsewhere. There were three or four different ballclubs that wanted me. But there I was in 1976, coaching third base for about $20,000 a year and turning down enormous amounts of money to manage another team and also be the captain of·my own ship.

I did it because I wanted to manage the Dodgers. But nobody promised me I'd get the job. I was just banking and betting that I was gonna get it. And it turned out to be exactly the right move.

In 1976 Chris Mortensen covered the Dodgers for the Los Angeles *Herald Examiner*. He is now a highly respected correspondent for ESPN television. Joe McDonnell was just getting started that year as a Los Angeles–based radio reporter. McDonnell is best known today for being caustic, but he also has excellent sources and a comprehensive knowledge of the Dodgers.

CHRIS MORTENSEN: Most of the players that season had experienced Tommy Lasorda in the minors. So they knew how much fire he would provide. But they also knew Tommy would be a roller coaster. So you had this struggle within the Dodger organization. Do we really want to see Walt Alston go?

JOE MCDONNELL: There were a thousand rumors in 1976. Alston was going to quit. Alston was going to be forced out. I think, at the end, he was tired of it all and wanted out. But I also think the Dodgers were scared they'd lose Lasorda. He was a hot commodity right then. So I think they said, "Walt, this would be a good time for you to go."

CHRIS MORTENSEN: Yeah, I think there was a nudge. Al Campanis was general manager then. And Al Campanis was ready for Tommy Lasorda.

RON CEY: I think Alston got pushed. And it seemed to really hurt him a great deal. I remember in his press conference when he stepped down. He was very emotional.

STEVE YEAGER: You could see it on his face. I'm sure he got some coaxing from upstairs.

In 1976 Dodger pitcher Tommy John had just come back from a radical operation in which a tendon from his right forearm was transplanted into his left elbow. Known today as "Tommy John surgery," it rescued John's career and has since been used on dozens of pitchers' elbows.

John remembers Alston's final days.

TOMMY JOHN: Up until Bill Russell got fired, the Dodgers historically never fired their managers. Walt Alston managed there for 23 years. Then Tommy Lasorda managed for 20 years.

But I do think that Peter O'Malley and Al Campanis felt it was time for Alston to move on. They probably felt the game had passed him by. I know our players did.

John raises a valid question. If Alston in fact got his pink slip, was it the best decision for the franchise? After 23 years in Brooklyn and Los Angeles, four World Series titles, seven pennants, and 2,040 victories, more than all but five managers in baseball history, had Alston stayed too long?

BILL BUCKNER: He was getting older. And as we all know that's when you have a tendency to forget things. So it was obviously time for Walt to get out. And it was time for Tommy to get in there.

TOT HOLMES: I recall a bit of that Casey Stengel thing. You could sometimes catch Walt on the bench with his eyes shut. So, yes, it was probably time.

JOE MCDONNELL: There were so many of those indications. He would ask for a relief pitcher who hadn't played for the Dodgers in five years. That made the players say, "Hey, now wait a minute."

MARK CRESSE: It was a no-brainer. Most of those guys played for Tommy in the minors. They won pennant after pennant. So Tommy had more control over them than Walt did.

Starting pitcher Doug Rau, who won 16 games in 1976, feels Alston had "lost contact with that era's players."

DOUG RAU: The generation gap had grown. Walt sat in meetings and said, "I can't believe this. I've never managed a cockier bunch of guys in my entire career." Because most of us came from the Tommy Lasorda school of baseball. You're good. You know you're good. You'll never say die.

Our players fed off that cocky attitude. But Walt had a different style. He came from a different era. It was time.

That sentiment was echoed, albeit anonymously, in a profile of Lasorda in *Sports Illustrated*. "It was time for Walt to retire," a front-office man was quoted. "He was starting to let things slide among the players and becoming too conservative on the field. We needed Tommy's fire."

STEVE YEAGER: Oh, I don't know . . . when is it time to change? Walt Alston was pretty successful. We played in the World Series in 1974. Then the Reds did everything right in 1975 and 1976. So, tell me, what's the panic?

MIKE MARSHALL: No, no, no. I couldn't disagree more. Alston never lost charge of the clubhouse or the players. He was not conservative on the field. I thought he was brilliant on the field.

As for Tommy's fire and all that hugging nonsense, we were professional ballplayers. We went out there and played as hard as we could. It wasn't because we were looking forward to a hug from Tommy. I think you know how Bill Russell felt about that.

Marshall is referring to Russell's famous statement in 1998, a season that began with Russell the manager and Lasorda the vice president of the Dodgers. Then, after Russell got fired by president Bob Graziano on June 21, he nonetheless appeared to blame Lasorda.

"Tommy's just vicious when he wants something," Russell reportedly told Doug Krikorian of the Long Beach *Press Telegram*. "He did the same sort of thing when he was a coach under Alston and wanted Alston's job. Tommy's been second-guessing me ever since I took over for him. Why? I don't know. All I know is that we haven't spoken for months."

Responded Lasorda, "That's ridiculous, a lie, and you can tell Russell that. I haven't been in town this much that season, and no way I've been campaigning for any job."

The Lasorda-Russell rift will be covered later. For now the question is put to Lasorda himself: Did Russell have any basis for saying he undermined Alston?

TOMMY LASORDA: How the hell can he say that when I never did? I worked for Walter for four years as a coach. When did I ever undermine him? The guy was a legend. I played for Walter Alston for six years. Why in the hell would I ever undermine him?

Russell's a liar. He's a big fat liar. And you can print that. I want you to print that. I want him to know how much that hurt me.

TOMMY JOHN: No. The answer is no. I never saw Tommy do anything like that.

RON CEY: When you're an everyday player, you don't know everything that's going on. Tommy was in the dugout when I was playing third base. When I was in the dugout, Tommy was coaching third base.

But there were still plenty of times when I was with Tommy. And I just didn't see that.

DAVEY LOPES: No. I was never aware of that. But let me tell you something: When you're the manager, you will be second-guessed by your players, by your coaches, by 55,000 people in the stands, every media person, and anyone who thinks they know anything about this game. It goes along with the job.

BOBBY VALENTINE: At the end of Walt's career, there were a lot of people questioning Walt—and Tommy wasn't one of them. I think Tommy "undermining" Walt was Tommy out there throwing batting practice, Tommy working extremely hard, Tommy telling the players they had to believe in themselves.

I mean, we all stray once in a while. Because we're all human. So I'm sure there were times when Tommy spoke to the young guys he was close with, guys who might be sitting on the bench, guys having a rough time, and Tommy probably consoled them. He probably would say, "You'd be playing if I was managing."

Is that undermining? I don't know. That's a pretty broad word. It's one of those broad strokes I really dislike. But they happen to get thrown around Tommy a lot.

MARK CRESSE: I can't say he undermined him, no. But he definitely outworked him. Tommy was awesome. He threw batting practice for hours. He hit fungoes forever. If you call that undermining, yeah, he undermined. He worked his ass off.

It should be noted that Valentine and Cresse are both loyal supporters of Lasorda. Here are the comments of two staunch Alston men.

MIKE MARSHALL: Lasorda used to say, "Oh, you should have heard Walt today. He told Jackie Robinson to go and get ready to hit."

Bullshit. Walter Alston was the most lucid, intelligent baseball man I ever played for.

DON SUTTON: I don't know that undermine is the right word. But I don't think he was as supportive as a right-hand man is supposed to be.

As for Bill Russell himself? After his quotes led to such an uproar, he repeatedly declined to comment on them. Now, in a rare interview on the subject, he denies making the statements attributed to him in the *Press-Telegram*.

BILL RUSSELL: That basically came from Doug Krikorian. He came into my office and made a lot of statements to me. A lot of statements that I didn't deny, but I didn't say anything. Doug's the one who made all the statements, and he wrote that I said that, which is not right. I didn't. Doug's the guy who did all that.

Krikorian has not replied to numerous requests for an interview. But since Russell is talking, what does he say now about Lasorda's relationship with Alston?

BILL RUSSELL: I was just a young player coming up. And as far as I know, he was a loyal coach. That's all I know.

As the author Tobias Wolff once said, every memory has its own story to tell. So maybe it's all point of view. Or maybe as baseball author Roger Kahn says, "How about normal office politics?"

Whatever, Lasorda deserved it when the Dodgers named him their manager on September 29, 1976. His five minor league pennants, his bottomless work ethic, his ability to pump up his players, and his contagious enthusiasm for baseball—putting asses in the seats, in other words—all made Lasorda the right man for the job.

Walter Emmons Alston? He went back home to Darrtown, the small farming town in southern Ohio. Then in 1983, just ten months before he died, Alston ended up where he belonged.

The Hall of Fame in Cooperstown.

16

LIFE WITH TOMMY

1977

Tommy Lasorda grew up in Norristown, Pennsylvania, the small working-class town to which his parents had emigrated from Italy. He was only 17 in 1945 when he signed as a minor league pitcher for the Phillies. Lasorda was 20 when he was sold to the Dodgers, the organization he would spend most of his life with.

A scrappy little left-hander with a good curveball, he once won 20 games in Triple A, but he appeared only briefly in the majors. With Brooklyn and Kansas City, he went 0–4 in 58 innings between 1954 and 1956.

Finally, in 1960, Lasorda hung up his spikes after 16 years of toiling in the minors. Then the Dodgers hired him as a scout, a minor league manager, and a major league coach before he succeeded Alston at age 49.

Just how different in style and temperament were they?

STEVE YEAGER: You got 180 degrees difference there. Walt was very quiet, and Tommy is very loud, flamboyant, and enthusiastic. Tommy yelled and screamed. Tommy blew up. Tommy cursed. Most of the time we laughed. We had grown up with Tommy in the minors. Tommy was just Tommy.

ROSS NEWHAN: Tommy was hugging players after they did something good. Tommy knew the first names of everyone's wife and kids. So the spotlight was suddenly on this very gregarious personality. And that took some of the pressure off the players.

TOMMY JOHN: Walt Alston had no confidence in me as a pitcher. Every time I got into the sixth or seventh inning, and I'd get guys on base, boom, I was done. Alston would take me out.

First time I got in that situation with Tommy? He came out and said, "Look at the bullpen." I said, "There's nobody in it." Tommy said, "That's right. And I'm not Walt Alston. You're gonna pitch yourself out of this jam."

Then he walked away. Tommy had confidence in me.

DOUG RAU: One of the key things Tommy did was connect with Reggie Smith. Reggie had problems in Boston. He had problems in St. Louis. But when Reggie came to us, Tommy made him feel like "the man." And Reggie became "the man." Even Steve Garvey knew it. Reggie was really our MVP for a while.

REGGIE SMITH: Lasorda came to me and said, "I need you." No one in baseball ever said that to me. So how could I let him down?

The other thing that stood out was his attitude. Tommy was willing to fight at the drop of a hat. That kind of spirit suited me just fine.

TOMMY LASORDA: I brought a whole new philosophy of managing into the major leagues. I hugged my players. I ate out in restaurants with my players. Even Al Campanis said, "You can't do that. You can't eat with your players. Managers don't do that."

I told him I didn't care. Because I wanted my players to know I needed them. I wanted them to know that I appreciated them. I wanted them to know that they were responsible for whether I'd even stick around or not.

Mike Littwin of the *Rocky Mountain News* and Mark Heisler of the *Los Angeles Times* both covered the early Lasorda years for the *Times.* They give their perspectives on a man they each refer to as "unique."

MIKE LITTWIN: Here's a Lasorda story that Al Campanis told me. It was at Vero Beach around 1951. Lasorda was there for spring training, but he was still a pitcher in the low minors.

There are two large groups of Dodgers in this hall. In the middle of one group, telling stories, is Chuck Connors. He was, of course, the ex-Dodger who became a movie star. In the middle of the other group telling stories is Tommy Lasorda, who is a Class A pitcher. And not even a very good one.

So here is a guy who is competing with Chuck Connors, while surrounded by Jackie Robinson, Duke Snider, Roy Campanella, and half the Hall of Fame. And Lasorda is the center of attention.

Then, of course, he becomes a coach with the Dodgers. And when he's still a coach, *not* when he's manager, he becomes a friend of Frank Sinatra, becomes a friend of Don Rickles, he gets miked up by NBC for a national TV game. He becomes a minor national celebrity, becomes a Hollywood darling, becomes a fixture in Los Angeles long before anyone should have any idea of who this guy is.

I've never seen anything even close to this. You'd be hard-pressed to find an analogous situation. Here is this guy in one of the legendary sports franchises who had accomplished nothing before 1977. Yet within the organization, he is already semi-legendary.

MARK HEISLER: There was a real energy coming from Tommy. He was really a force. But he was also this amazing chameleon. He would be talking with baseball players and every third word would be a profanity. I mean, if you weren't used to Tommy, it would just blow you away.

But the funny thing about Tommy was all of a sudden, you know, the context would change. A nun would walk into the room. And Tommy would, boom, go into this other thing. He would never swear once. And it wasn't because he slowed down his delivery. He was still being Tommy without the swearing.

One time they showed him dancing when he was managing in Albuquerque. All these black guys were on the dance floor, looking cool and whatever. And here is Tommy. He's throwing himself out there, looking like Tommy would, but he doesn't care. He thinks he's doing great.

Tommy just had this incredible confidence. Tommy just keep thrusting himself forward.

MEL DURSLAG: He was dynamite from the start. He's a very engaging guy, Lasorda, and he seemed to know the entire Hollywood crowd. And, of course, he developed a friendship with Sinatra. That was a hell of a credential for him.

MIKE LITTWIN: Frank Sinatra sang the national anthem before Tommy's first game as manager. That's how the Lasorda era started.

Yet not everyone embraced the extroverted rookie manager. The most glaring exception was Sutton, an Alston loyalist who had made his position clear even before the Dodgers appointed Lasorda. When a reporter asked Sutton who he thought should replace Alston, Sutton said his former teammate Jeff Torborg. Of course, Lasorda was miffed, since he was obviously the heir apparent.

DON SUTTON: The question was posed to me, "What do you think about Walter Alston retiring?" And I said, "I'd rather he didn't." Next question was, "Who would you pick to manage the Dodgers?" And I said, "Jeff Torborg," because I saw in him a lot of Walt's qualities.

And that probably was purely selfish on my part, because I didn't want any change in the atmosphere.

Did this color his early relationship with Lasorda?

DON SUTTON: It didn't color my end of it, but I can't speak for Tommy. And whether or not it did is irrelevant. I wasn't going to change the way I did my job. I grew up on a farm. I grew up working my butt off. I could have played without a manager.

TOMMY LASORDA: I didn't feel we were as close as we should be. But we got along. It never got to the point where we weren't on speaking terms.

But one thing about Don Sutton. He kept himself in great shape. Great work ethic. Good clean-living young man. So, it was just a feeling that we had, but I think it simmered down and we became closer.

DOUG RAU: They knew how to handle things professionally. But off the field, I'd say things were somewhat strained. Don had come up through the Alston school. Then Tommy took over. And guess what? Don didn't go for Tommy's "bleeding Dodger blue" stuff. Don thought it was an act. He made no bones about that.

But when it really mattered to Lasorda, on opening day of 1977, there was Sutton on the mound as Sinatra sang the anthem before an electrified crowd at Chavez Ravine. Then Sutton got tagged for a homer on the first pitch and Chavez Ravine turned into a library. But Sutton settled down and won 5–1, and the Lasorda years got started with a triumph.

The 1977 Dodgers just kept smoking. Led by Ron Cey, the hottest hitter in baseball, their 22–4 start was the third fastest in big-league history. Meanwhile, the powerful Reds, who had won the previous two World Series, were struggling a few games below .500.

So why didn't Sparky Anderson seem more concerned?

"The Dodgers' lead doesn't bother us. They always come back to us every year in July. Don't ask me why, but they always come back," declared the Cincinnati manager.

To which Lasorda responded, "Sparky's got a right to his opinion. They're like rear ends—everybody has one." Then Anderson called Lasorda "Walking Eagle. He's so full of it he can't fly."

Authentic feud or simply gamesmanship? Regardless, it first went public at a banquet held for Alston and Lasorda before the start of the '77 season. "This is the year Los Angeles finds out how good a manager Walter Alston is," Anderson told the crowd. Lasorda stewed in silence for the moment, but as center fielder Rick Monday recalls, the verbal battle was on.

RICK MONDAY: We started doing this thing under Tommy that season. All eight of our starting players would run in the outfield together before the games.

Well, then we went to play against the Reds. And someone said, "Hey, Sparky, look at those guys running." Sparky said, "Yeah, but wait until September. They'll be running in eight different directions."

Tommy said, "Yeah, that's right. They'll be running to eight different banks to cash their World Series checks."

JOE McDONNELL: I don't think they particularly liked each other. But I don't know if Tommy liked anyone he managed against. He was so damn competitive. And he was really bad when he was young. They would lose a game and he would absolutely lose his mind.

RON FIMRITE: It was unusual for Sparky to comment about another team in that manner. That was a little out of character for him. But, of course, Sparky grew up in Los Angeles. I think Sparky probably would have liked to manage the Dodgers. So there may have been a tinge of jealousy there.

MARK CRESSE: Neither one of them was a great player in the major leagues. They were minor league guys who each probably had a chip on his shoulder. And they were both raised in the Dodgers' organization.

As far as managing against each other, I do know there was respect there. That's why they wanted to beat each other so badly. In fact, it got to the point where Tommy wouldn't let us wear anything red. If Tommy saw you in red, it meant you got fined.

Tommy trained us to hate the Reds. And it worked. Whenever you played the Reds, it was exciting. You just lived for those games. So did the fans.

ROSS NEWHAN: The baseball itself was terrific. You had Rose, Morgan, Bench, Garvey, Lopes, Cey, Reggie Smith, and on and on. Then you had two strong managers in Tommy and Sparky. So the rivalry in the seventies between the Dodgers and Reds was probably the best in the major leagues.

TOMMY LASORDA: We won the pennant in 1974. We finished 20 games behind them in 1975. We finished 10 games behind them in 1976. So in 1977 when I took over, I knew the Reds were the team we needed to beat.

I wanted our players to know it, too. So I wanted them to hate the color red. I wanted them to hate the Cincinnati Reds. So in order to do that, we *created* a rivalry between me and Sparky. I was once his teammate. I was his friend. But when he put that red uniform on, the friendship ceased.

SPARKY ANDERSON: I was very tight with Walter Alston. And I did have fun with Tommy, just joking and kidding. But that's all it was to me—just fun and games. I always respected him as a manager.

The Dodgers always had tremendous enthusiasm. Their enthusiasm was their strength. And part of that was Tommy. Maybe 100 percent of that was Tommy. No question about it. You can't win every year. Nobody does. But Tommy Lasorda was able to maintain that high level of enthusiasm. That rubbed off on his players. That's one of the reasons he's in the Hall of Fame.

In 1977, Lasorda's rookie season, it was the Reds who finished 10 games behind the first-place Dodgers. So whether or not Anderson, also a Hall of Famer, had been kidding, he had gotten it wrong at that preseason banquet. This was the year Los Angeles discovered how good a manager Tommy Lasorda was.

There were plenty of other heroes that rock-and-roll summer at Chavez Ravine, where 2,955,087 passed through the turnstiles, breaking the big-league record set by the Dodgers themselves in 1962. Steve Garvey hit 33 homers, Reggie Smith 32, Ron Cey 30, and Dusty Baker 30. And this made baseball history as well, for no other four teammates had ever hit 30 homers apiece in one season.

After defeating Philadelphia in the National League playoffs, Los Angeles faced New York in the 1977 World Series. When last these teams had met in the postseason, it had been 1963, Koufax had been overwhelming, and the Dodgers had swept the Yankees in four games.

In October 1977, according to *Sports Illustrated*, this World Series pitted THE GOOD GUYS AGAINST THE BAD GUYS. Ron Fimrite, in his cover story, quoted Lasorda as saying, "I believe in togetherness. I believe a team is like a family." Wrote Fimrite, "The Yankees, too, are a family. A family like the Macbeths, the Borgias and the Bordens of Fall River, Mass."

RON FIMRITE: I'm sure New York fans saw it differently. But I think the fans around the country saw the Yankees as the embodiment of big-city evil and brashness.

And the Dodgers really did have that homespun look to them. People like Billy Russell looked like the guy next door. The Yankees, of course, had Billy Martin. You can't have a homespun look with Billy Martin as your manager.

This was the famous Bronx Zoo. They were known for their internal warfare, and the cast included not just Billy Martin, but George Steinbrenner, Reggie Jackson, Thurman Munson, Graig Nettles, Lou Pinella, Goose Gossage, and Sparky Lyle.

STEVE GARVEY: Those guys reminded me of the old Oakland A's. They had that soap operaesque type of thing going. Which, of course, was perfect for the New York tabloids.

STEVE YEAGER: Thurman Munson was still alive in '77. Thurman was their captain, and when Thurman opened his mouth, they listened to him. But I don't think a lot of them liked Reggie Jackson. Not because of his playing ability. But maybe because of his antics and attitude.

RON CEY: They were not a happy group of guys. And Graig Nettles was part of it, too. From everything I've heard, he and Reggie didn't get along, either.

Cey is putting it gently. As everyone in the baseball business knows, Nettles and Jackson once got into a fistfight at a party.

But what about the Dodgers? How did their players view Reggie during the 1977 World Series?

STEVE YEAGER: I viewed him as a real hemorrhoid the night he hit three homers on three straight pitches. That was a hell of a feat.

Yeager is referring to Jackson's fabled performance in the sixth and final game. By then Los Angeles had gone 1–1 at Yankee Stadium and 1–2 at Dodger Stadium to trail the Series 3–2. Back in the Bronx for Game 6, the Dodgers led 3–2 in the fourth inning on Reggie Smith's third homer of the Series.

Then the other Reggie took over. First he pushed the Yankees ahead 4–3 with his two-run homer off starting pitcher Burt Hooton. Then he two-run homered again off Elias Sosa. Reggie's third home run, with nobody on, was positively crushed, and he provided all the power himself, because it came off knuckleballer Charlie Hough.

TOMMY LASORDA: What stands out about that moment? That's a moment that I don't want to remember. I want to forget it. The guy hit three home runs in one Series game. Man, that guy destroyed us.

ROSS NEWHAN: That was truly electric. And I don't know if it will ever happen again.

Jackson's three consecutive dingers on three pitches gave the Yankees an 8–4 win and their first World Series victory in 15 years. Moreover, Reggie had homered his last time up in Game 5, meaning he'd hit four home runs in four straight at bats. This set a new World Series record, as did his five total homers, his 10 runs scored, and his 25 total bases.

REGGIE SMITH: I got upstaged by a namesake. And I hated losing. But after the Series ended, you just had to marvel at his performance.

MARK CRESSE: He was brash. He bragged a lot. But the guy was hot as hell. He backed up everything. He was Mr. October.

17

DODGER BLACK AND BLUE

1978

It was another interesting year for the carefully polished image of the Dodgers. The debunking began, oddly enough, on Mother's Day 1978 when a reporter asked Lasorda what he thought of Dave Kingman's performance after he hit three homers against the Dodgers.

It probably wasn't the most intelligent question, and Lasorda knocked it right out of the ballpark. "What do I think of Dave Kingman's performance? What the——do you——think I——think of——Dave Kingman's performance?"

Lasorda's entire response is much too long and profane to catalog here, but it will never be forgotten by those who have heard it. In fact, it quickly became the hottest undergound tape in Los Angeles.

But if the secret was out—Tommy, the warm father figure, had an edge—what happened later that summer did far more to bury the myth of the Dodgers as the sunshine boys of baseball. The stars of this episode were Sutton and Garvey, who didn't much like each other, teammates say, but managed to keep it in-house until Sutton came out blasting in an interview with the *Washington Post*'s Tom Boswell.

"All you hear about on our team is Steve Garvey, the all-American boy," Sutton told Boswell. "Well, the best player on this team for the last two years—and we all know it—is Reggie Smith. Reggie doesn't go out and publicize himself. He doesn't smile at the right people or say the right things. . . . Reggie's not a façade or a Madison Avenue image. He's a real person."

Sutton's cutting remarks were picked up in newspapers around the country. Then on August 20, in the visitors' clubhouse at Shea Stadium, Garvey asked Sutton if he'd been quoted correctly. Sutton said yes, he had, and tempers flared. But it might have ended there, according to Garvey, had Sutton not made reference to Garvey's wife, Cyndy. That's when Sutton and Garvey got into a grappling match on the clubhouse floor.

Sutton declined to comment on the subject. But Garvey and others will talk about about one of the game's most famous clubhouse fights.

STEVE GARVEY: It could have been a similar situation to Lopes and Cey. I mean, the amount of attention that I was getting. Am I positive about this? No. Is it possible? Yes. There may have been some resentment. Because Don was a premier pitcher. He had been there quite a while. And when he said "Madison Avenue," he was essentially saying that I was self-promoting.

REGGIE SMITH: I knew Sutton's remarks would cause a problem. And I felt, quite possibly, that I was being used to make a dig at someone else. Because even though you like the compliment from one player, you know it's criticizing the other guy. And I didn't need to be in the middle of that.

MARK HEISLER: The players resented the fact that Garvey was so good at promoting himself. Much better than any of them. And the guys who really minded it the most were the guys that wanted the popularity.

The number one guy was Sutton. He was another guy who had some phony in him. But he wanted to be popular, and Garv was popular. And Sutton really resented Garvey for that.

TOMMY JOHN: I really don't know the details, because I didn't live near those guys. All those guys that were having those problems all lived out in the San Fernando Valley.

I lived in Orange County. I stayed completely away from the Valley. In fact, Claude Osteen told me when I got there, "Don't move out to the Valley." I asked him why, and he said, "Trust me. You'll see."

Dusty Baker, who is now the much-admired manager of the San Francisco Giants, was an All-Star left fielder for the Dodgers in the late 1970s and early 1980s.

DUSTY BAKER: Garvey and Sutton lived a few doors down from each other. They never drove together to the park, never socialized, nothing. There was no love lost even before they fought.

RON CEY: There was a lot of anxiety that season. We had struggled up to that point. And Garv was always a politician. He was very good at handling interviews and getting people on his bandwagon.

Then Sutton said Reggie Smith was our most valuable player. Garvey took that to Sutton, and there had always been this animosity about Cyndy anyway. Well, I think there's only so long that you can hold things in. Then something has to go.

REGGIE SMITH: I was in the clubhouse when it happened. There was a lot of grappling and scratching. I didn't see any punches. It's just that they were locked up, and it took us a few minutes to pull them apart.

TOMMY JOHN: I was in the clubhouse signing baseballs. They were wrestling, scratching, hitting—all real close. Someone yelled, "Stop the fight!" And Joe Ferguson said, "Let 'em go. Maybe they'll kill each other."

MARK CRESSE: I was in the bullpen. But there's no doubt in my mind that if they got in a real fight, Garvey would break him in half. I like Don Sutton, but physically Garvey was an ex–football player and built real well. And what I heard is that everybody grabbed Garvey to keep him from killing Sutton.

STEVE GARVEY: It was, did you say this? And if you did, why? Then he started to bring her into it. I said, "This is not about her. There's no reason to bring her into it."

Then he poked me in the chest and that was it. All of a sudden we were pushing and shoving. It wasn't much of a fight. I got scratched in the eye. Cornea got scratched a little bit. Fortunately, neither one of us was hurt. There were no broken bones or anything.

TOMMY JOHN: The Dodgers were very PR-conscious, so the last place you'd want it to happen is New York. I mean, everybody just swooped down on us.

DUSTY BAKER: It happened on a lot of good teams. It happened on the A's. It happened on the Yankees. But all these New York reporters were sitting in Lasorda's office at Shea Stadium. Lasorda and Al Campanis were talking about how we were all a family. Then it comes out these guys are fighting in the clubhouse.

MARK CRESSE: It was kind of funny when we got back to L.A. There was a big press conference called before the game, and all the guys who were pro-Sutton couldn't wait, because they figured Sutton was going to use the media to just bury Garvey. Then Sutton ended up apologizing! And all the guys could not believe their ears.

But as Geoff Witcher explains, it wasn't the type of apology Garvey expected. Witcher is the former host of *Dodger Insider*, a pregame show carried by XTRA Sports 1150, the Dodgers' popular flagship radio station.

GEOFF WITCHER: Sutton apologized to the Dodgers. He apologized to the fans. And Sutton even broke down while he was talking. But he never apologized to Steve Garvey. And Garvey said, "Well, that's nice, but he hasn't apologized to me."

STEVE GARVEY: It was a media moment. I had met with Peter O'Malley after it happened. Then Don had met with Peter after me. So there was supposed to be a public apology. But, no, he never quite apologized.

Thus Garvey and Sutton still weren't speaking when the Dodgers went out that night and defeated the Phillies. Then, when Sutton pitched the following game, Garvey had a home run and three RBIs in a 6–5 Dodger victory.

JOE McDONNELL: The Dodgers were never one big happy family. These guys did not get along. I knew that the minute I started covering them.

But that was a truly professional baseball team. Once they stepped on the field, all that other stuff was left inside the locker room.

In fact, after their intramural fisticuffs, the Dodgers won 21 of their ⟍ next 32 games, climbed from third place to first, and became the first team in the majors to clinch its division title.

STEVE GARVEY: There's nothing like a great personal controversy to pick up the energy level. And that's what happened. We started to get hot.

TOMMY LASORDA: Who knows? Who knows what the answer is on things like that? But we did get real hot.

They stayed that way through the playoffs, eliminating the Phillies in four games as Lasorda became the first National League manager in 37 years to win pennants in his first two years on the job. This set up a World Series rematch with the Yankees, who had trailed the Boston Red Sox by 14½ games before charging back to beat them in a one-game playoff on Bucky Dent's improbable home run.

While George Steinbrenner's Yankees entered the Series in their trademark style—manager Billy Martin had just been fired for ripping Steinbrenner, Bob Lemon had been hired, then Martin had been rehired, but only to manage again in 1980—the Dodgers came into the Series mourning the death of their longtime first-base coach Jim Gilliam.

Once a gifted second baseman for the Dodgers, he had replaced Jackie Robinson at that position in 1953 and then gone on to win four World Series rings in Brooklyn and Los Angeles. Gilliam was only 49 when he died of a brain hemorrhage two days before the World Series opened.

DUSTY BAKER: He was one of the most honest guys I've met in this game. Then one day he didn't show up at the ballpark. I said, "Where is he?" They said, "He's in the hospital. An aneurysm."

I didn't know what an aneurysm was. Then a few days later he was dead. That really hurt. And we dedicated that World Series to him.

DAVEY LOPES: When I was a little kid, Jim Gilliam was one of the first black Brooklyn Dodgers. Then he was one of our coaches when I came up. We both played second base. It was an immediate attraction.

In Game I of the 1978 World Series—played in Los Angeles just a few hours after Gilliam's burial—Lopes slugged two home runs, Baker homered once, and the Dodgers crushed the Yankees 11–5. Then Cey hit a three-run homer and rookie pitcher Bob Welch struck out Reggie Jackson with two outs in the ninth to save a 4–3 victory in Game 2.

JOE McDONNELL: The Dodgers hadn't won a World Series since 1965. But now they were up 2–0, and people were saying no way they could lose.

In fact, Burt Hooton did a radio interview with Jerry Coleman. Hooton sat down, kind of smiling, and Coleman said, "Well, you guys got this thing wrapped up now."

They never won another game.

The third game, at Yankee Stadium, turned into a showcase for Graig Nettles, who made several great plays at third base in a 5–1 Yankee win. Then came unforgettable Game 4—and one of the most crushing losses in Dodger history.

Still ahead in the Series 2–1, Los Angeles led 3–0 on Reggie Smith's three-run homer in the fifth. The Yankees scored in the sixth to make it 3–1, and with only one man out, they still had Reggie Jackson on first and Thurman Munson on second.

Lou Pinella then hit a liner to shortstop Bill Russell, who dropped it, picked it up, stepped on second base to force out Jackson, and threw to Garvey for the double play.

But Jackson, standing 15 feet off first, stuck out his hip. Or did he? Regardless, Russell's throw struck him and bounced past Garvey while Munson scored from second to cut the Dodger lead to 3–2.

Lasorda and his players went ballistic. They screamed interference, insisting that Jackson got hit by the ball on purpose. But at Yankee Stadium, in the heart of the big bad South Bronx, first-base umpire Frank Pulli refused to reverse his decision.

The Yankees tied it 3–3 in the eighth. Finally, in the tenth, they won 4–3 on Pinella's RBI single. That knotted the Series at two games apiece, and the controversy was bubbling.

BURT HOOTON: That was a horrible call. And everyone in Yankee Stadium knew it.

DAVEY LOPES: Yeah, he stuck his hip out. Anybody with any kind of vision would have seen that. But obviously Frank Pulli didn't see it.

STEVE GARVEY: But the umpire with the best view wasn't Frank Pulli. The umpire with the best view is the second-base umpire. And you can see it on the replays: The second-base umpire *sees* him stick his hip out.

So he sees it. But he says, "I didn't see it." He doesn't want to get involved. So what are you gonna do?

TOMMY LASORDA: The umpires made a terrible, terrible call. He moved into the ball. That's interference. And neither one of them had the courage to call it.

SCOTT OSTLER: I thought Reggie Jackson made a great play. It was obvious he did it on purpose. And to be able to think that fast? And then deflect it with your hip, when you could get hit in the nuts with it instead?

It was a moment of great instinctive genius. It was one of the all-time great plays in the World Series.

CHRIS MORTENSEN: Reggie had gotten under their skin again, only in a very different way. In 1977 he did it with his bat. This time he used his hip.

MARK CRESSE: He made a smart play. No question. But he still got away with murder.

GEOFF WITCHER: Losing that game broke their heart. And that play, specifically, turned around the entire World Series.

Roger Angell felt the same way. "Game four was the fulcrum," he wrote in *The New Yorker.* "When it was over, the weight of this strange World Series had shifted irreversibly."

The Dodgers' next loss, in Game 5, was just plain ugly. Their box score showed one wild pitch, two passed balls, and three errors, but there were also several "hits" that smashed off the shins of Dodger infielders. The Yankees won, 12–2, raising the question: Were the Dodgers still demoralized from the last game?

RON CEY: I don't know about demoralized, but obviously we didn't recover well. We didn't handle the situation well. Luckily, I don't think I got many plays. That may be the only good thing that happened to me. I wasn't involved with all those bonehead plays.

STEVE GARVEY: No, I wouldn't say demoralized. But you've lost your momentum. You feel like you've been cheated. Then you have to deal with it in the press—New York press, Los Angeles press. So then you go out the next day, and you're probably a little flat.

RICK MONDAY: Angry and frustrated? Yes. We had a pivotal play taken from us. But did it have an impact the next game? Not at all. Not with that group of guys.

MARK CRESSE: That's baseball. That can happen. A lot of teams look good one day and lousy the next. It's the way you play over the course of the season that makes you a good ballclub. And that was a good ballclub.

Still, it had been a grim weekend in Gotham. The Dodgers arrived leading the Series 2–0. They flew home trailing 3–2, with a few Dodgers grumbling about the New York writers, the New York fans, and even New York City itself. Of course, this only invited more criticism, for as Angell pointed out, it wasn't "the press or the fans who beat the Dodgers . . . it was the Yankees."

The 1978 World Series ended in Los Angeles, where the Dodgers lost 7–2 for their fourth defeat in a row. They had also dropped their fourth straight World Series—in 1966, 1974, 1977, and now this one.

STEVE YEAGER: Hell, yeah, it weighed on us. You're starting to feel like a bridesmaid instead of a bride.

DUSTY BAKER: Most of us didn't leave our house for a week or two. Because in L.A., if you don't win it all, you are considered a failure. You choked.

JOE MCDONNELL: That was a great Dodger team. They had Garvey, Lopes, Russell, Cey, Baker, Monday, and Smith. They had Yeager and Ferguson at catcher. But they were in danger of becoming the best team never to win a World Series.

TOT HOLMES: They almost dropped back into the Brooklyn mode. We can win the pennant. But oh my God, we can't go anywhere else.

GEOFF WITCHER: It was very much like Brooklyn. The Dodgers could beat anybody but the Yankees. Then in 1955, they finally broke through.

Those were the Alston years. But what about Lasorda? Did he ever lose hope after his back-to-back losses to the Bronx Bombers?

TOMMY LASORDA: Nope. I used to say in my prayers, "Dear God, if you could see it in your heart to put me and my team into another Fall Classic, please let it be against the Yankees."

I wanted them real, real bad.

18

THE WAR ZONE

1979

JUST HOW BAD WAS THE CRASH OF '79?

Johnny Carson needled the Dodgers on *The Tonight Show.* Howard Cosell asked Davey Lopes on national television whether Tommy Lasorda should be fired. *Sports Illustrated* wrote, "A team that had once represented itself as the soul of suburban affability, Los Angeles snarled and grumbled as churlishly last year as such curmudgeonly clubs of the past decade as the Yankees and the A's."

Of course, getting on each other's nerves was nothing new to the 1970s Dodgers. But as longtime beat writer Gordon Verrell of the Long Beach *Press-Telegram* explains, the workhouse tensions were fanned by losing that season.

GORDON VERRELL: Tommy's first year on the job was pretty much bliss. The second year there were some problems. They struggled in their division, and then you had the Sutton-Garvey thing in August. But they still won the pennant.

In 1979, they were in last place at the All-Star break. And there was a lot more sniping inside their clubhouse.

JOE MCDONNELL: They had just gone to hell. They were horrible the first half of the year. It was almost like a war zone in there.

How did a powerhouse collapse so quickly? Especially with Lopes, Cey, and Garvey all hitting 28 homers?

There were important injuries to Reggie Smith and Rick Monday, but the single biggest factor was a pitching staff razed by Doug Rau's torn rotator cuff, Terry Forster's elbow surgery, Bob Welch's sore arm and descent into alcoholism, the loss of Tommy John to free agency, and sub-par seasons from the usually reliable Don Sutton (12–15) and Burt Hooton (11–10.)

DOUG RAU: Our pitching staff was decimated. So we were behind the eight ball. What looked like a wonderful team was in last place.

Then the press takes hold and the nit-picking starts. What's wrong? Is it Lasorda? Is it the players? Is it dissension? Well, it's all of the above and injuries.

At one point, a Los Angeles newspaper polled its readers on whether Lasorda should be fired. Since his first two teams had won pennants, this was ridiculously premature, and Lasorda won the poll in a landslide.

TOMMY LASORDA: When you saw how many pitchers we lost that year? I couldn't understand why they would do that. But I just tried to remember what my father told me. He said, "Every knock is a boost." I just happened to overcome them all for 20 years.

Yet it couldn't have been fun when even Johnny Carson got into the act. Performing his Karnac routine on *The Tonight Show*, he first gave the answer: "Send in the Clowns." Then he gave the question: "What are they playing at Dodger Stadium instead of the National Anthem?"

DAVEY LOPES: We were so horseshit that year, everybody was saying get rid of Tommy. It finally got to the point where I made statements on his behalf to Howard Cosell. Howard asked me on national TV, "Do you think Tommy Lasorda should be fired?"

This was on live TV, and I said, "Absolutely not." Then I gave my reasons why. But that's how horseshit we were in '79.

CHRIS MORTENSEN: I'll tell you when it got the ugliest. They were in last place at the All-Star break and one of their players was quoted, anonymously, calling some of the other players "cancers" and "dogs." Then they called a team meeting to find out who made these statements. And there was almost a fight in the locker room.

Then somehow that meeting seemed to awaken the team. They never made a run, but they played much better from that point on.

TOT HOLMES: They had the best record in the National League in the second half. Which was a truly remarkable turnaround. But they dug themselves such a hole, they still ended up under .500.

In fact, Los Angeles (73–89) produced its first losing record since 1968. But still it had been a strong decade for the franchise. In addition to winning three pennants in 1974, 1977, and 1978, the Dodgers became the first team in history to attract three million fans in a single season (3,347,845 in 1978).

Sadly, however, 1979 also marked the death of Walter O'Malley. He lost his fight to cancer on August 9, ending the very large life of the man who brought the Dodgers to Los Angeles, helped nationalize major league baseball, and imposed his will on the sport almost until he died at age 75.

PART IV

——

THE EIGHTIES

19

WORLD CHAMPIONS—
AT LAST

1980–81

In 1980 more than 50 American citizens continued to be held hostage in Iran. The United States hockey team shocked the powerful Soviet team at the Winter Olympics. John Lennon was shot and killed outside his apartment building in New York City.

In baseball that year, George Brett went into September batting .400 before finishing at a remarkable .390. The Phillies finally won their first World Series after 97 years of frustration. Yankee owner George Steinbrenner paid a record $16 million for coveted free agent Dave Winfield.

But as the new decade continued, the ancient struggle between labor and management resulted in a bitter strike that interrupted the 1981 season and sent salaries shooting up almost 50 percent in the next two years. Then, in the next big squabble of the eighties, the owners were found guilty of collusion—an illegal conspiracy to stop bidding on free agents—and were ordered to pay the players $280 million in lost wages.

Meanwhile, baseball discovered that a number of its wealthy players used cocaine. In addition to Steve Howe's troubles in Los Angeles, 23 players were named in the 1986 criminal trial of a longtime cocaine dealer named Curtis Strong. It was a public relations disaster for baseball, followed by yet another in 1987 when the Dodgers' general manager Al Campanis made racially-charged remarks on Ted Koppel's *Nightline.*

Back in Los Angeles in 1980, the most surprising preseason moves were the signings of free-agent pitchers Dave Goltz and Don Stanhouse. Though free agency was in vogue throughout the majors, the Dodgers had always relied on homegrown talent from their strong minor league system. But now, desperate for pitching, they purchased Stanhouse and Goltz for $5.1 million.

Stanhouse, supposedly the team's new closer, injured his back and saved just seven games. Goltz won only seven as a starter. Thus, it would be eight more years until the wary Dodgers would sign their next free agent—a scowling ex–football player named Kirk Gibson.

But even without much help from Goltz and Stanhouse, Dodger pitching bounced back in 1980. Jerry Reuss went 18–6 with a no-hitter. Sutton was 13–5 with a league-leading 2.21 ERA. Brash reliever Steve Howe won Rookie of the Year. Fernando Valenzuela, another new young pitcher, showed sensational glimmers of things to come by allowing no earned runs in 10 relief appearances in September.

When Los Angeles and Houston both ended up 92–71, it forced a one-game playoff and thrust a key decision on Lasorda. Should he entrust Goltz or Valenzuela, who would be making his first big-league start? Lasorda went with Goltz, who got shelled in a season-ending 7–1 loss.

In 1981, at least until the strike, Valenzuela was baseball's biggest story. He wasn't supposed to start on opening day, but with Reuss and Hooton injured, the chubby 20-year-old shut out the Astros. By the night of May 14—when he was 8–0 with five shutouts and an ERA of 0.50—"Fernandomania" had gripped the public.

SCOTT OSTLER: It was the perfect story. This kid grew up in a tiny Mexican village that had no plumbing or pavement. Then he just starts mowing down the opposition.

TOMMY LASORDA: When he first came up, he didn't have a suit. So that's the first thing I did. I took him out and I bought him a suit.

MARK CRESSE: The first time we ever saw him, we were staying at a fancy hotel in Atlanta. I saw him walk into the lobby. He had a scruffy haircut and terrible clothes on.

I could speak pretty good Spanish, so I went over to welcome him. Then I said goodbye and came back through the lobby an hour later. Fernando was still sitting in the same chair. He was waiting for his suitcase. He had no clue what a bellman was, or that his suitcase was already in his room.

He was green as grass. The next thing you knew, he was this big star.

MIKE LITTWIN: Not only did he have this phenomenal start, not only was he this mythical character from no place, he was also fat, and he had this mysterious windup where he gazed up to the sky, as if he was getting his strength from God himself.

And then of course it happened in Los Angeles, which was the perfect setting for Fernandomania.

MARK HEISLER: The Hispanic population was huge in Los Angeles. Then all of a sudden, boom, Fernando opened that market for the Dodgers.

GORDON VERRELL: At first everyone thought he was a fluke. A guy just doesn't show up and start throwing shutouts. Then he kept winning and winning, and he would go into a city, and these press conferences were becoming gigantic. They were holding them in hotel ballrooms!

Fernando's interpreter and almost constant companion was Jaime Jarrin, the Hall of Fame announcer who has broadcast the Dodgers games in Spanish since the team moved west in 1958.

JAIME JARRIN: It was always a madhouse. In Chicago, for instance, the tickets were sold out as soon as they announced that he was pitching. And Chicago was the first game he didn't finish. He got hit hard. We lost.

Then after the game they said, "Please, Jaime, take Fernando back out on the field." Because the people didn't want to leave. It was almost two hours since he had left the game in the sixth inning, and 25,000 people were chanting, "Fernando, Fernando." So he went out, waved, said good night, and people left.

He was popular in every city. And of course he was very popular with Latins. In the early sixties, the Hispanics coming to Dodger Stadium were probably eight percent of the crowd. When Fernando came on, that eight percent went up to about 28 percent.

Now it's about 38 percent of Hispanics who come to our park. Same thing in Chicago, in New York, in Miami. And that's because of Fernando Valenzuela. In my honest opinion, he created more baseball fans than anyone in the game.

We even went to the White House together that season. When we walked upstairs to the dining room, the Marine Corps Band was playing the most exquisite Mexican songs. Beautiful arrangements. And Fernando was really, really impressed by that.

Then, after the luncheon, there was a line of great people waiting to shake Fernando's hand and get his signature. People like George Bush, who was then the vice president; Caspar Weinberger, the secretary of defense; Alexander Haig, the secretary of state. People who had the world in their hands were in line waiting to get a signature of this Mexican kid, 19 years old, who couldn't speak any English. That is one thing I will never, never forget.

STEVE YEAGER: Well, he said he didn't speak English. But you'd call him a couple names and he knew what the hell you were talking about.

RICK MONDAY: He was very childlike in the clubhouse. He used to carry this lariat with him. He would lasso guys as they walked by. He thought that was hysterical.

MARK CRESSE: He would rope you around your leg. Then he'd pull the rope and you'd fall on your butt. He thought that was great.

RICK MONDAY: But on the mound? We used to marvel. Never seemed to get flustered. Always seemed to be focused. A runner would get on first base, and he would think he was getting a real good jump off him. Then Fernando would very casually pick him off.

MARK HEISLER: Fernandomania was the most incredible thing you ever saw. I mean, this guy was on Swedish television. But Fernando was for real. He was a real ballsy kid. He *never* wanted to come out of a game.

TOMMY LASORDA: That's true. When a lot of pitchers look to the bullpen in the seventh, eighth, and ninth innings, they're looking for help. This guy never even knew we had a bullpen.

GORDON VERRELL: Even New York went crazy for Fernando. He was the biggest thing, by God, to happen to major league baseball in some time. Then the strike came in. And that screwed up everything.

The 1981 labor war was fought over one key issue. When a free agent signed with a new team, the owners wanted more compensation for his former team. Those teams currently received an amateur draft choice, but now the owners wanted a major league player. The powerful players union flatly said, No, we fought hard to win free agency. Now the owners are trying to grab it back.

Dave Stewart was a rookie reliever that season. Already nicknamed "Smoke" for his 95-mile-per-hour fastball, he wouldn't become a star until he played for Oakland, where he won a Cy Young Award and had four successive 20-victory seasons.

DAVE STEWART: That was a tough year to be a rookie. Everybody kept saying this was for us—the strike was going to benefit all the young players. Well, that's really tough to see when you sit out two months, not doing something that you've been dreaming of doing.

It was tough financially, too. I was married, with a child, living in Los Angeles. I think minimum salary was $21,500, and we missed almost two months during the strike. Heck, I even went to work at a hardware company. I made nine dollars an hour. Just trying to make ends meet.

The players walked out on June 12 in the first midseason strike in baseball history. During the subsequent 50 days and 712 games that were lost, most teams remained surprisingly unified. But in Los Angeles, several Dodgers were irked at Steve Garvey for reportedly getting paid during the strike through a guaranteed-money clause in his contract.

In fact, Davey Lopes criticized Garvey in the papers. Then, after the owners blinked and baseball resumed, Lopes found himself getting booed by Garvey supporters at Chavez Ravine.

DAVEY LOPES: What I said was right. But if 50,000 people didn't agree, they had the right to boo me. But I won't say it didn't hurt. Because it did. It shocked the hell out of me, to be honest with you.

STEVE GARVEY: I don't remember being paid. I'm not saying that I didn't, but I don't remember getting any checks.

MIKE LITTWIN: The strains within that team had never gone away. But you don't have to like each other to perform well. Look at the Dodgers and Yankees during that time. They were both tremendously dysfunctional families. And yet they dominated that period in baseball.

On August 10, 1981, when the fractured season resumed, the Dodgers were declared the first-half winners of the National League West based on their half-game lead over the Reds when the strike began. This secured them a spot in the NL West "mini-playoffs," no matter how poorly they played in the second half.

Then the Dodgers got complacent, slipping all the way to fourth as Houston edged Cincinnati by just 1½ games. Thus the furious Reds sat out the playoffs, even while having baseball's best overall record (66–42).

STEVE GARVEY: That was the irony. The Reds ended up not going anywhere.

DAVEY LOPES: I didn't care about the Reds. I could care less what they thought. We had a tough team, and we showed that in the playoffs and World Series. We kept fighting back from adversity.

They began in the "mini-playoffs" against Houston, trailing two games to none before sweeping three straight. Then, facing the Expos in the National League Championship Series, they fell behind 2–1 before winning in Montreal to even the series. In the fifth and deciding game, also in Montreal, the score was I–I in the ninth inning when Rick Monday hit a dramatic two-out homer. The Dodgers won 2–I and then flew straight to New York for another chance at redemption versus the Yankees.

TOMMY LASORDA: My father taught me a saying when I was a kid. He said, "Because God delays does not mean that God denies."

Well, He delayed, but He didn't deny. We got the Yankees again.

STEVE YEAGER: We really felt we had to do it that year. Not only because of the Yankees, but we also knew our team would start breaking up. That team had been together for so long.

Still, history and the bookies favored the Yankees. They had defeated the Dodgers in 1977, in 1978, and in eight of their ten World Series meetings. Los Angeles, in contrast, had not won a World Series since 1965 in the Koufax era.

MIKE LITTWIN: The '81 Series was strange because of the strike. I mean, the Dodgers didn't even have the best record in their division. The Reds had the best record.

So as that World Series got started, some questioned whether the Dodgers even belonged. And they certainly didn't appear to after losing the first two games at Yankee Stadium.

MARK HEISLER: They came back to Los Angeles down two games to nothing. And everybody in New York was calling Steinbrenner "the Boss." Even the papers were calling him the Boss. I know you have tabloids there, and they will be colorful. But it was pretty disgusting. I mean, they were really smooching his butt.

STEVE YEAGER: Then suddenly the Series turned around. Fernando pitched Game 3, and he was in trouble all game. But Tommy just stayed with him and stayed with him. Finally, he won.

After this monumental 5–4 victory, the Dodgers won 8–7 in Game 4 as Jay Johnstone hit a crucial pinch-hit homer. Then Reuss took the mound with the Series tied 2–2, and even without his best stuff, he gave Los Angeles a three-game sweep at home with a gritty 2–1 decision over the formidable Ron Guidry.

JOE MCDONNELL: That was also the game when Cey got hurt. He got hit in the head by a Goose Gossage fastball. That was pretty damn scary.

RON CEY: It hit me in the helmet, and the helmet just exploded off my head. Then I remember falling in slow motion. My wife thought I was dead.

JOE MCDONNELL: Cey was walking around after the game. He had this big towel on his head, which was filled with all this ice. Then someone asked him, "Will you play in Game 6?" Cey said, "It's the fuckin' World Series. Of course, I'm going to play."

Meanwhile, his eyes are rolling back in his head. But there was no way Ron Cey was going to miss the chance to win a World Series. And that goes back to your theme, that this was their last chance.

With the Dodgers now ahead 3–2, the sixth game would be played in the South Bronx. But first came the World Series' oddest moment: George Steinbrenner's allegation that he punched out two drunken Dodger fans inside a Los Angeles hotel elevator.

Of course, not everyone bought the Boss's story.

RON FIMRITE: He showed up with a bandaged hand and claimed he'd been in a fight while defending the Yankees' honor. I never did believe that. He may have hurt his hand, but I don't think it happened fighting off angry Dodger fans. That's not conceivable.

JOE MCDONNELL: Oh jeez. Come on. He probably punched a door.

SCOTT OSTLER: That was great! I loved that story! But the general perception was that he made it all up. Maybe he ran into a couple of guys who gave him shit, and he barked back at them. But if there was a real fight, I think the guys would have surfaced. Wouldn't they rush out and tell their story? Hey, George punched us out! Hey, we kicked his ass!

MIKE LITTWIN: No one believed that story. It was like the Dan Rather–Kenneth mugging. And among the Dodger family, it was considered to be quite funny. They got a lot of mileage out of that.

RICK MONDAY: I thought it was amusing that George would want to take the limelight and say he punched two guys out. My question is, Who held them?

STEVE GARVEY: Who knows what happened? We just beat them three straight. Maybe George created this stuff to create some energy. Some enthusiasm. I'll fight for my guys and all that stuff. You can't put it beyond him. This guy wanted to win the World Series.

But you can't always get what you want. And on a cold October night at Yankee Stadium, where they were so used to getting kicked around, the Dodgers closed out the 1981 World Series with an easy 9–2 victory in Game 6. Making it even more poignant, the winning run was driven in by Ron Cey.

TOMMY LASORDA: They were tremendous guys. They loved to play. And, boy, they believed in themselves. The Yankees had beat us in two World Series. Then we played the mighty Yankees again, and we were two games down, and they figured we couldn't bounce back. And we beat them four straight.

And how did George Steinbrenner react? Rather than congratulate the Dodgers, who had just won their first World Series in 16 years, he irritated them when he immediately issued a public apology to the citizens of New York for his team's performance.

RON CEY: We just won the World Series. Why not give somebody credit? I thought it was very unprofessional.

RICK MONDAY: I won't tell you the two words that went through my mind. But the second word was "you."

RON FIMRITE: That was typical George Steinbrenner back then. He liked upstaging his team. But in this case, he also humiliated them.

SCOTT OSTLER: His apology came out about a half hour after the Series ended. I was standing by Reggie Jackson's locker and some PR guy came around handing out these mimeographed copies of Steinbrenner's apology. Reggie's eyes sort of got as big as pie plates. Then I think he just went off on Steinbrenner.

STEVE YEAGER: Well, I didn't appreciate it, either. But the point is, I like Steinbrenner. I really do.

But I still considered it a horseshit comment. He's apologizing for a team that he felt shouldn't have lost the World Series. There's nothing wrong with him feeling that way. But he apologizes 20 minutes after we win? Bullshit. Wait till the next day. Wait till we're out of town.

But you know what? I didn't care later that night. I didn't really give a shit what George was apologizing for. I was flying back to Los Angeles, drinking champagne with the guys, and we were world champions. And that was such a great feeling. Because everyone knew this might be our last year together.

DUSTY BAKER: We were conscious of that all season. We even had a slogan during the World Series: If we win, they can't trade us all.

RON CEY: In the last game of the 1981 Series, the first four hitters in our lineup were the four infielders. It was Lopes, Russell, Garvey, and myself.

I felt that was significant, because we had played so long and so well together. We deserved it, and finally we did it, and we knew the end was in sight.

DAVEY LOPES: I played poorly in that World Series. And I knew it was my last game as a Dodger. Gut feeling. Just knew. Things were being said, and things were being denied. But I just knew.

20

THE LAST WALTZ

1982

DAVEY LOPES WAS RIGHT. WHEN THE DODGERS BROKE UP THEIR FAMOUS infield—after a record eight full seasons, four pennants, and one World Series title—he was the first to leave Los Angeles.

In 1981 the oft-injured Lopes had batted just .206. His six errors against the Yankees set a World Series record for second basemen. Then, on February 8, 1982, the Dodgers sent him to Oakland for a minor league second baseman named Lance Hudson.

Though Hudson would never play in the big leagues, he was also never expected to replace Lopes. That role fell to Steve Sax, a fiery, confident 22-year-old who had jumped straight from Double A to the Dodgers in August 1981.

GORDON VERRELL: The Dodgers called up Sax after the strike. And as soon as Sax walked in, Al Campanis started comparing him to Pete Rose. He said, "This kid is exciting! This kid runs to first base on walks!"

Was that meant to light a fire under Lopes? I don't know. But either way, Davey knew his time was coming.

DAVEY LOPES: There were business aspects of it that I understood. But the real truth is, I didn't want to leave. The Dodgers were all I knew. So yeah, I was hurt. But I just sort of hid it. Put a barrier around it. And went to Oakland.

The proud and intense Lopes departed with 418 stolen bases, second only to Maury Wills in franchise history. He also had more power than most second basemen, hitting 28 home runs in 1979, and 99 in his ten-year Dodger career.

In 1982, even with Sax on his way to winning Rookie of the Year, the defending world champions started slowly. Soon the Dodger front office was criticizing its veterans, saying they might be replaced by the slew of minor league stars in Albuquerque. This naturally irked veterans like Cey, who told *Sports Illustrated*, "I don't care how old you are if you can still do the job."

RON CEY: We finished one game out in '82. Had they left us alone, we would have won. I really believe that. All the meetings they had, all the comments they made, found their way into our clubhouse. That became a distraction. Players were saying, "Did you hear what they just said?"

On July 30 the 1982 Dodgers were 10½ games behind the Braves. They surged into first place in August, faded in late September, but still had a three-game lead with ten games to play. On the season's final day, Los Angeles needed to win at hated San Francisco in order to force a playoff with Atlanta. But it lost 5–3 on a crushing three-run homer by Joe Morgan.

That marked the end for the blunt-talking Cey, who went in a trade to the Cubs for two minor leaguers. In 1984, when critics said he was washed up, his 25 home runs and 97 RBIs helped the Cubs win their first division title. Today he trails only Eric Karros for most home runs by any Los Angeles Dodger (Cey had 224 to Karros's 241).

RON CEY: Once I got over my personal emotions and understood that it was nothing more than a business transaction, then it became much easier to handle.

But yeah, I was very upset with it. I felt like I could have stayed here longer, kept producing longer, and all of us could have been together longer. Maybe won a couple more World Series.

MARK HEISLER: That was Branch Rickey's influence on Al Campanis. Al Campanis worshiped Branch Rickey. And it was Rickey who made the famous statement: "It's better to get rid of them one year too soon than one year too late."

STEVE GARVEY: That was historically the Dodger Way. But I've always felt they broke us up too soon. Probably four or five years sooner than they had to. Because we all played pretty good baseball for other teams.

STEVE YEAGER: I could never figure it out. Why do you win the World Series and then disassemble your champions? Maybe the front office felt they wouldn't skip a beat. Well, they did skip a beat. They couldn't find a third baseman after Ron Cey. And Greg Brock was no Steve Garvey.

When it came to Garvey's somewhat bitter exit, the speculation began even before the 1982 season, which was the last year of a six-year, $2 million contract that seemed lucrative when Garvey signed it, but had since left him, according to Jim Murray, "the most underpaid player in the National League."

Thus, after six 200-hit seasons, a .303 lifetime batting average, and 945 consecutive games played, Garvey wanted a new deal by opening day of 1982. When the Dodgers wouldn't talk until July, he wondered if they truly meant to keep him.

On October 9, the normally stoic Garvey got choked up when the fans stood up to cheer him after the last Dodger home game. On November 3, he turned down the team's best offer of $5 million for four years. On December 21, he signed with the Padres as a free agent for $6.6 million over five years (with incentive clauses that could pay another $2 million).

Mike Scioscia, who was then a gritty young Dodger catcher, recalls how he reacted to the news.

MIKE SCIOSCIA: It wasn't like when Cey and Lopes left. Those guys were huge. But Garvey was a legend in Los Angeles. He was someone you really felt was going to end his career here.

Then he went to San Diego and led them to a World Series, too. So he still had plenty of baseball left in him.

SCOTT OSTLER: Part of it was what I'll call the Joe Montana–Steve Young syndrome. If the 49ers didn't have a backup quarterback that was worth a shit, they would have tried to eke more out of Montana, even when his career was on the decline. Keep him around not only for box office, but because he's still a pretty good quarterback.

But they had Steve Young there, who looked like he had the potential to be a pretty damn good quarterback. Well, the Dodgers had that same deal with Greg Brock waiting in the wings for Garvey. And that was one of the specialties of their front office: Al Campanis could take a Greg Brock and make him sound like the second coming of Babe Ruth.

JOE MCDONNELL: It goes back to the 1982 season. Greg Brock was pumped up all year long by the Dodgers. Then they brought him up in September. When Brock got his first hit, the crowd went crazy because of all this hype. And I remember telling the guys in the press box, "Say goodbye to Steve Garvey."

MARK HEISLER: The Dodgers did try to sign him, but only to a point. Garv wanted five years and the Dodgers offered four. So there was money involved, and when it came to negotiating money, nothing with the Dodgers was ever easy.

The Dodgers wouldn't budge off of five years. Garv wouldn't budge, either. He looked like a teddy bear, but he was an extremely stubborn guy.

STEVE GARVEY: I wanted to spend the rest of my career there. But there were no negotiations until midseason. And there was a lot of pressure from the press. "Are they going to re-sign you? What's going to happen?"

So now it becomes public. It's a controversy. And the negotiations linger and linger. Finally both sides said, "Let's just wait until the season's over."

Well, I had been struggling somewhat. But then I started hitting. We started winning. But they were always pretty rigid in their philosophies. They had the Dodger Way and they stuck to it. Probably because they felt Greg Brock could step in and do the job.

Now, you gotta remember I was once a bat boy for them in spring training. Then I got signed by them. Then I played first base like my idol, Gil Hodges. The Dodgers were a significant part of my life. Not to be part of them anymore was a shock.

21

WILD TIMES IN L.A.

1983

IF THE 1983 DODGERS WERE BESET WITH PROBLEMS, MAKING BOX OFFICE MAGIC wasn't among them. For the third time in four seasons under Lasorda, the team attracted more than three million fans. No other franchise had done it even once.

Moreover, in 1983, the fans' loyalty would be tested in ways not even the gloomiest imagined. The struggles began in spring training, when Los Angeles looked truly inept, finished only 11–17, and cast legitimate doubt over how this team would perform without its veteran stars Garvey and Cey. The answer came quickly enough. The 1983 Dodgers could still hit and pitch. They just couldn't field.

The Dodgers made 166 errors, and 91 of them came from their rebuilt infield. Third baseman Pedro Guerrero (30) and second baseman Steve Sax (29) made an amazing 59 errors all by themselves.

JERRY REUSS: How many? 59? Is that right? Well, Guerrero never wanted to play third base. He was really an outfielder.

SCOTT OSTLER: Cey was gone. They needed a third baseman. And it didn't seem like a terrible thing to ask a guy. But Guerrero made it sound like they were asking him to skydive naked without a parachute. I mean, I don't think anyone ever accused him of trying to learn the position. His great ongoing quote was: "I can fucking hit."

DUSTY BAKER: Someone asked him in an interview, "What were you thinking about late in the game?"

Pedro said, "I was thinking, Don't hit the ball to me because I might not catch it. And please don't hit it to Sax because he might throw it away."

W hich leads us to Sax's famous throwing problems. But first let's establish how good a young player he was. In 1982 the hustling Sax had stolen 49 bases, batted .282, won Rookie of the Year, and been called "the next Pete Rose" by *Sports Illustrated*.

In 1983 Sax had another robust offensive season, batting .281 with 94 runs and 56 stolen bases. But on defense he suffered from a strange condition. He could not even make the routine throws to first.

GEOFF WITCHER: I'd never seen anything like that. He was playing second base. It wasn't a long throw. And some of the balls were going into the stands.

MIKE SCIOSCIA: Of course, I remember it. I lost about 15 pounds running from behind the plate to back up first base.

KEVIN KENNEDY: I was one of their minor league coaches then. Now I work with Steve at Fox. He said, "Kevin, they would blindfold me at practice. I could turn double plays blindfolded at practice. Then I would get in the game . . ."

DUSTY BAKER: That was also the year his father died. He died of a heart attack. He was only 42. So it was a shock. And watching Sax go through those throwing problems, and then with his father dying . . . well, that was terrible. I really felt bad for him.

C an Sax trace the problem back to its beginning?

STEVE SAX: Yeah. A game in April against Montreal. I took a relay from the outfield. I didn't need to throw the ball to home plate. But I did anyway, and I threw it hard, and it got away from the catcher. It was a senseless error and a run scored.

Then I made an error the next day, and then pretty soon it just stuck in my head. I lost my confidence. I'd wake up in the night sweating. It was the worst thing I ever went through in my life besides losing my parents.

JOE MCDONNELL: I was pretty close with Sax. And he always had a pretty good sense of humor about it. You could kid him about it, and he wouldn't take offense. Because he was a really good kid.

But you could tell that it bothered him. There were a million jokes, you know? "Who's the only guy who could overthrow the ayatollah? Steve Sax."

DUSTY BAKER: One time we played in New York and they had a banner with a bull's-eye on it. This is in the upper deck. They were yelling, "Throw it up here. We need a souvenir."

MARK HEISLER: Once, the Braves were in town and I happened to be sitting in their dugout before the game. Sax was on second base practicing throws. He was missing a lot of them, and throws kept rocketing into the Braves' dugout. Finally Gene Garber yelled, "Save it for the game."

Todd Moulding, the team's bullpen coach from 1983 to 1994, recalls what happened to Sax when it was the Dodgers' turn to play in Atlanta.

TODD MOULDING: When we walked in, they had put a net in front of the whole dugout. And I'll never forget poor Steve Sax. You could just see in his face he felt terrible.

I thought that was kind of in bad taste. But that's how the game was played. If a third baseman had a pulled hamstring, well, you bunted on him. That was just major league baseball. It could be heartless.

What about Sax's teammates? How did they react to his errant throws?

STEVE SAX: I'm sure deep down they were pretty pissed off.

RICK MONDAY: You don't know how to approach it. Do you approach it from a lighthearted standpoint? Or do you approach it from "Hey, come on, get your ass in gear"?

MIKE SCIOSCIA: One day some of the players printed a memo. It said it was Batting Helmet Day. They were giving out batting helmets to the fans sitting behind the first base dugout.

JERRY REUSS: Johnstone was merciless. He got some police tape and cordoned off a section and put up a sign: "Beware. This is a Sax throwing area. You could be the next target."

STEVE HOWE: One day I was coming in to pitch. There were bull's-eyes all over the place in Philadelphia. I came in and I said, "Saxie, if they hit the ball to you, flip it to me real fast and I'll throw them out."

Sax went ballistic. He said, "Oh shit! You had to mention it!" But I wanted to make light, because he looked like he was about to fall over.

MARK HEISLER: I don't know about Tommy. He might have been pissed off. Remember, Tommy himself was very confident. Very assertive. So he was a little intolerant of any head stuff. Now all of a sudden some guy is paralyzed by his own mind? That wasn't the kind of thing that Tommy dug.

JAY JOHNSTONE: There was a game in St. Louis. Tommy said to Sax before the game, "Go with me for a walk around the field."

So he and Sax started walking. Tommy said, "How many people in this country can play big-league baseball? How many big leaguers can hit .280? How many big leaguers can steal 40 bases?"

Sax kept saying, "Not many." Then Lasorda said, "How many women can throw the ball to first base? Every fucking one of them! So why the fuck can't you throw the ball to first base?!!"

STEVE SAX: Yeah, I recall that. And he was right. In fact, Tommy was great. He kept putting me in the lineup. He didn't bench me.

TOMMY LASORDA: Certain people, even Al Campanis, told me to take him out. I said, "I'm staying with him. I'm not gonna destroy his confidence."

Then I just kept talking to him, working with him, and making him believe. Finally, he worked through it.

Sax had made 25 errors by August 7. Then he committed just four the rest of the season. None came on errant throws.

JOE MCDONNELL: It just shows you how mentally tough this kid was. This kid went through torture, with everybody making fun of him. And yet, he came out of it. He became an All-Star again. And one of the better second basemen in the game. He was a tough kid.

Sax's travails were painful, but Steve Howe had even more harrowing problems that season. One of baseball's best relievers the past three years, he had a 95-mile-per-hour fastball, a wicked slider, and the seemingly fearless swagger of many great closers. Howe also had a nasty cocaine habit.

MARK HEISLER: Steve was very macho. He was very cocky. And underneath very cocky is generally scared.

STEVE HOWE: I was scared even when I pitched in high school. Scared of not being perfect. Scared to fail.

In 1977 he snorted his first line as a college sophomore at Michigan. He was still using sporadically in 1980, when he earned 17 saves, breaking the Dodger record for rookie relievers. That November, he received a phone call.

STEVE HOWE: They said, "You got 20 minutes to make it down to Little Joe's. You have been made Rookie of the Year."

Uh? What? The mad scramble was on. Then I walk in a room. There are cameras and lights and the hugest lineup of reporters I'd ever seen. But there was only one chair, and that was for me. You want to talk about scared to death? I started to get dry heaves.

I went into the bathroom. Am I going to make a fool of myself? Am I going to sound arrogant? One of our players comes in. "You nervous, kid?" "Yeah." "Here, try this." What do you think it was?

The next day the paper said they loved me. I made a connection. Every time I felt uncomfortable, every time I felt fear, I could take this. I was 21 years old. My problem really wasn't on the field. The problem was everyday life. I couldn't cope.

In 1981, when the Dodgers defeated the Yankees in the World Series, Howe got the win in Game 4 and saved Game 6 to nail down the Series. On the triumphant flight back from New York, he kept telling his wife, Cindy, he had to pee. "Must be all the champagne," Steve said. Of course, he was packing his nose.

In 1982 he snorted two grams per day. *During the season.* Yet he still went 7–5 with a 2.08 ERA and 13 saves. Then, at the urging of Cindy and the Dodgers, his addiction became public when he entered a drug treatment center in November.

On May 28, 1983, after not allowing a single earned run all season, he got dangerously high and missed a home game. He checked back into rehab the next day, and when he rejoined the Dodgers one month later, Commissioner Bowie Kuhn fined him $53,867. That was Howe's salary for the month he was suspended and the largest player fine in baseball history.

At the time Bill Dwyre was in his third year as sports editor of the *Los Angeles Times.* In 1996 he won the prestigious Red Smith Award for his contribution to sports journalism.

Here he recalls how *Times'* readers reacted to Howe's now-public struggle with cocaine.

BILL DWYRE: Most of the letters said, "This guy is a bum. He had all this opportunity, man, and look what he did. If I could go out there and pitch for that kind of money . . ."

It was typical guy-at-the-corner-bar reaction. But in those days, there was not a lot of tolerance for this being any kind of illness or disease. It was seen as a weakness. And Tommy may have led the way in that.

TOMMY LASORDA: Steve Howe broke my heart. We were very close. But why in the hell would you take drugs? It's against the law. It's harmful to your body. It will lead you down the path of destruction.

You can't tell me it's a disease. I never believed that. Never did, never will. How can it be a disease when you deliberately put something inside your body? That, to me, is a weakness. I don't care what anybody says.

STEVE HOWE: Tommy was very frustrated and angry at me. Tommy used to make this statement: "I'd look at a pack of cigarettes and ask who's stronger—the cigarettes or me?" Then he'd say, "That's how I quit smoking."

That tells you a lot about why he'd be angry. If he could put that down, then why couldn't anyone else?

In September 1983 Howe was suspended again for missing a team plane. That ended his season—right in the midst of a tight pennant race with Atlanta. Now, almost 20 years later, Howe is asked: Did he ever feel he was letting down his teammates?

STEVE HOWE: My guilt and my remorse and my shame go beyond that. Unless you have ever been in that position, it's beyond the scope of what you could even imagine.

RICK MONDAY: Let the team down? Yeah. He let himself down, I think, even more.

MIKE SCIOSCIA: There were a lot of emotions going on. The first thing was, we wanted Steve to get better. We felt sick inside that he had a problem.

But sometimes we said, "Damn, this guy is a huge part of our club. And he makes a choice like that?" Because if Steve was healthy, who knows how many more championships we could have won?

TOT HOLMES: That was their biggest flaw in the 1980s. They couldn't find a big-time closer to replace Howe. And, in their search for one, they traded away a number of quality players.

BURT HOOTON: Well, it was kind of maddening that somebody would get caught up in drugs. But my wife and I helped take care of his wife and their new baby. So we kind of got a little more involved. And there was a lot of sadness in it, too. This thing had its hooks in him. And he had a devil of a time getting them out.

JOE MCDONNELL: You also need to put it in perspective. Howe was the one who got caught, but he wasn't the only player doing coke. Are you kidding me? In the early 1980s? A lot of players were doing coke then.

MARK HEISLER: With the players who *didn't* do drugs, they were not particularly sympathetic to Howe. And it typically tended to be a black-white thing. A lot of the white guys were doing alcohol, which was "okay." And some of the black guys, back then, were more likely to be doing coke.

Now, alcohol was fine. It was legally sanctioned. And the other one was prescribed. So one was part of the all-American life. And one of them was evil. It was just Looney Tunes.

MARK CRESSE: I kind of feel like I let *him* down. My dad was a Navy captain. I was so straitlaced, I never smoked a cigarette in my life. So I had no clue about drugs. And I was his bullpen coach. Maybe I could have helped him. But I was oblivious.

I just thought he was a hyper kid. I could hardly ever watch a game without him either choking me around the neck, or pumping me in the ribs with his fingers, or aggravating me. He was *always* messing with me. So I thought he was just hyper. Obviously, he was 30,000 feet up there.

But Howe says he was not high during games. He also denies the published reports that said he snorted cocaine in the Dodger bullpen.

MARK CRESSE: That, I don't know anything about. As far as being high during games, maybe he wasn't. But I'm sure there was some residue. You can't be that big an annoyance all the time.

STEVE HOWE: Was I coming down when I went to ball games? Yes. Was I taking it down in the bullpen? That's not true. There's no way I could throw a 95-mile-per-hour fastball at somebody not having control of my senses. No way. I would have killed somebody.

Sports *Illustrated*'s Richard Hoffer profiled Howe in February 1992. By then he had played for the Dodgers, Twins, Angels, and Yankees. He'd been suspended from baseball six times, and banned from baseball once.

Yet Howe was still in the big leagues, having been reinstated in 1990.

RICHARD HOFFER: He was pitching for the Yankees. And he still had a lot of bravado. I remember when I went to Montana to try to track him down. He lived there in the off-season. And Howe let it be known that anybody who tried to track him down up there was in for some big trouble.

And then, when you talked to him, he really seemed interested in turning his life around. But, my God, how many times was he suspended? Six or seven? If he wasn't such a great pitcher, I can't imagine him getting that many chances.

MIKE SCIOSCIA: That's the reality of it. If you can get guys out, or hit 30 home runs, baseball doesn't care what baggage you drag in.

MIKE LITTWIN: Well, of course! That's the hypocrisy of every sport. Lawrence Taylor gets chances. Darryl Strawberry gets chances. The guys who can play will get invited back.

RICHARD HOFFER: It's almost unconscionable. But in a way, for Steve Howe, it worked out for him and for everyone involved. He seemed to have straightened himself out at the end, and was useful to himself and to his family.

In 1983 the Dodgers had more problems to accompany Howe's struggles with cocaine. There were the fielding mishaps of Sax and Guerrero.

Yeager's broken wrist. Scioscia's torn rotator cuff. The deflating rookie year of first baseman Greg Brock, who hit 20 home runs but batted just .224. Which is why you had to give Lasorda his due. He cursed and hugged and held his team together. He used more than 100 different lineups. And in what was expected to be a rebuilding year without Garvey and Cey, Los Angeles stole the National League West.

The playoffs looked promising as well, since the Dodgers had beaten the Phillies in 11 of 12 games during the season. But now the Phillies were baseball's hottest team, winning 25 of their last 32, and they defeated the Dodgers three games to one.

GREG BROCK: What an emotional season. There were so many ups and downs for all of us. But welcome to the big leagues.

22

"WHY DIDN'T YOU WALK JACK CLARK?"

1984–85

TOMMY LASORDA'S WINTER STARTED NICELY. FOR HIS SUPERB MANAGING JOB IN 1983, the AP and UPI named him National League Manager of the Year. Then, amid rumors that George Steinbrenner wanted to hire him, Lasorda signed with the Dodgers for a reported $1 million over three years. Thus, Lasorda made club history: No other manager, including Walter Alston, had ever been given the job for more than one season.

But within a matter of weeks, Lasorda's feeling of calm evaporated. First came the announcement from Bowie Kuhn that he was suspending Steve Howe for the entire 1984 season. Howe's relapse in September, Kuhn explained, had violated his probation. Now Kuhn was suspending Howe in order to protect "the image of baseball."

Then came the 1984 season itself. As the Dodgers slipped badly, going from first place to fourth (79–83), they suffered a string of major injuries. But still Lasorda's critics ran headlines like this one: LASORDA MANAGES THE DODGERS FARTHER INTO FOURTH PLACE.

In May 1985, observed *Sports Illustrated*, the Dodgers were "the laughing-stock of baseball, committing errors in such bunches that they threatened to set records for ineptitude." Nine of those errors were made by Pedro Guerrero, still laboring mightily to play third base.

Finally, on June 1, with the Dodgers just 23–24, they either made a great move or corrected their own blunder by moving Guerrero back to left field. His war with third base over, he hit a record 15 home runs in the month of June. Then Guerrero batted .460 in July, the rest of the offense joined in, and the Dodgers—a team most experts had dismissed—won their fifth division title under Lasorda.

JAY JOHNSTONE: The media was all over him. They were saying Tommy should step down. He didn't have control of the team. And all this other BS. But Tommy refused to panic. Everyone panicked *except* him.

In baseball's first best-of-seven playoff series, the Dodgers and Cardinals split the first four games. Then, in the ninth inning of Game 5, little Ozzie Smith hit a rare home run to give the Cardinals a stunning 3–2 victory. The reliever he homered off was Tom Niedenfuer, trying to fill the void left by Steve Howe, whom the Dodgers had finally released when he failed to appear for a game that June.

Back at home in Game 6, with the Dodgers leading 5–4 going into the ninth, Niedenfuer was on the mound again. When St. Louis put runners on second and third with two outs, Los Angeles was one out away from forcing a seventh game in its own ballpark. But first Lasorda faced a huge decision: let Niedenfuer pitch to Jack Clark, the Cardinals' best hitter, or walk Clark and pitch to the less dangerous Andy Van Slyke. The odds said pitch to Van Slyke, batting .091 during the playoffs. But Lasorda was a gambler who managed by instinct. He let Niedenfuer pitch to Clark, with a playoff batting average of .381.

On Niedenfuer's first pitch, a fastball straight down the middle, Clark crushed a three-run homer deep into the left field pavilion. The Dodgers lost 7–5, Chavez Ravine fell deathly silent, and the jubilant Cardinals went to the World Series.

As the great Jim Murray once wrote, baseball is "the citadel of the second guess." In this case, here's how Mike Downey started his column in the *Los Angeles Times:* "He should not have pitched to him. That is all there is to it. He should have walked Jack Clark, or hit Jack Clark in the ribs with a change-up, or offered Jack Clark several billion dollars to leave the bat on his shoulder. Anything but pitch to him."

Cardinal manager Whitey Herzog said, "I've always figured that if I can pitch to a guy making $1.3 million a year or a guy making $100,000 a year, I pitch to the guy making $100,000."

Of course, Lasorda also had supporters. "Lasorda's decision, although it didn't work out, was unquestionably the correct one," wrote the highly regarded Bill James. "To load the bases with a one-run lead to let a right-hander (Niedenfuer) pitch to a left-handed hitter (Van Slyke) would have been lunacy."

But what James failed to note is that had Lasorda walked Clark, Niedenfuer probably *wouldn't* have pitched to Van Slyke. Lasorda more likely would have called on Reuss, a left-hander who was normally a starter, but who Lasorda had throwing in the bullpen.

JERRY REUSS: In a meeting we had before we faced the Cardinals, Tommy spent more time on Jack Clark than anybody. He said, "If we get in a situation with the game on the line, we're not pitching to Jack Clark. He's the only guy on this team that can kill you with a home run. And this guy has a flair for the dramatic."

So then I was down in the bullpen warming up. When I saw what was happening, I looked at Kenny Howell, who was there with me. I said, "Unbelievable. He's gonna pitch to him. Didn't we say in the meeting we wouldn't do that?"

I remember the ball being hit, the crack of the bat reaching us, and the arc of the ball. Guererro throws his glove down. Howell and I look at one another. I said, "What the hell were we talking about? The series comes down to this, and we get beat by Jack Clark?"

STEVE YEAGER: Hell, yes, I'd have walked him. First base is open and Clark's a fastball hitter. Next is Andy Van Slyke, who couldn't hit water if he fell out of a boat. Make the kid beat you. The kid ain't done anything. You know Jack Clark can beat you.

BOB COSTAS: One of the things that's most interesting about Lasorda is that he's one of the last managers that did not embrace the modern techniques. Lasorda didn't look at computer printouts. It was all by his own experiences, his own instincts, his own feel. That's how he managed every game.

But in this particular scenario?

BOB COSTAS: Still don't understand it. Clark was the most dangerous hitter in their lineup. And, damn, you don't want to face him in that situation. You know, the scouting report on Clark was first-pitch-fastball hitter. So Niedenfuer throws him a first-pitch fastball that still hasn't come down.

Niedenfuer could not be reached for comment on his famous gopher ball, but Clark seems pretty happy to discuss it. He grew up in Los Angeles, by the way, where he dreamed of becoming a Dodger but wound up getting drafted by the Giants. In July 1985, his first year with the Cardinals, he had a savage home-plate collision with Mike Scioscia. In fact, Clark knocked the Dodger catcher unconscious.

Here he recalls the dramatic ninth-inning homer that knocked Los Angeles out of the 1985 World Series.

JACK CLARK: When I saw Lasorda go out there, I thought they were going to walk me. But I also knew the Dodgers' history as far as challenging people. And I'd seen Lasorda go out there and tell his pitchers, "Go right at them. We're not backing down from anyone."

So I wasn't sure what to expect. But I was having a really good series. I was swinging the bat really well. And so when they pitched to me, I kind of felt that they were trying to show me up. I thought they were trying to show Whitey Herzog up. And so it was real important for me to come through for Whitey and for the city of St. Louis and for myself. But I honestly wasn't trying to hit a home run. I was just thinking about what my old hitting coach, Hank Sauer, had told me. He said, "Always be ready for fastballs. And if you get a good one, try not to miss it."

STEVE SAX: Jack Clark crushed that ball. It's probably still going. But I don't think you can really fault Tommy for that. I mean, he went with his closer. He went with his best reliever. And if he strikes him out, it's a great move.

TOMMY LASORDA: Why would I want to walk Jack Clark? For what, huh? I'm not gonna walk Jack Clark. Because the time right before that, I walked Tommy Herr to get to Jack Clark. And Jack Clark struck out. Who do you think struck him out? Tom Niedenfuer.

Hey, I didn't feel like I made a mistake. If I'd have known the guy was gonna hit a home run, I wouldn't have done it. But I didn't know he was gonna hit a home run. I wish somebody would have told me he was gonna hit a home run *before* it happened. Not *after* it happened.

Hey, a second-guesser is someone who doesn't know anything about the first guess. The second-guesser is someone who needs two guesses to get one right. Hell, I'm not gonna walk that guy. Why should I walk him?

TODD MOULDING: You know what? He made the right move. We just didn't execute it right. Because Lasorda went out there and told Tom Niedenfuer, "Don't give this guy anything to hit."

JAY JOHNSTONE: What you want him to do is swing at a couple bad pitches. Then you throw him a few more bad pitches and maybe he strikes out. And if he doesn't swing at bad pitches, then you just walk him.

So now Niedenfuer pitches. He sees the target way on the outside corner. And his mind says outside corner. But his arm throws it right down the middle. That's why Tommy Lasorda got second-guessed. Why didn't you walk him before the home run? Well, that wasn't the plan. The plan was to keep the ball away from him, and see if he'll swing at bad pitches. But it didn't turn out that way. It was one pitch and boom. We lost. No World Series.

MARK CRESSE: Tommy actually deserves a lot of credit. When the media came in, it would have been easy to say, "Hey, don't ask me. Ask him. I told him to keep the ball away from Clark."

But Tommy never did that. He took a lot of heat and he didn't pass the buck.

TOMMY LASORDA: Hell, I'll take the blame. I didn't want that to fall on Niedenfuer. He just threw the ball down the middle. And I asked him why and he said, "He was probably thinking I wouldn't give him anything good to hit, and I tried to fool him." I said, "Christ, you fooled yourself."

JACK CLARK: I never asked them about it, because I never really cared what they thought. But I managed a team this year in the minor leagues, and there were a lot of times when I went out and said to the guys, "Pitch around him. Don't give this guy anything to hit."

Then the first pitch is right over the plate. You just scratch your head, like, what did we just talk about?

JOE MCDONNELL: All the Dodgers were stunned after that game. But Niedenfuer was crushed. And he still came out and answered every question. He was unbelievable.

GORDON VERRELL: He never changed his tune. He never put the heat on anyone else. And he could have. He could have said, "Talk to Lasorda. He makes the final decisions."

He could have said, "If Steve Howe wasn't sniffing that stuff, I wouldn't have been out there every other day all season."

But he never did. Niedenfuer was a stand-up guy.

As for Tommy Lasorda, who also faced wave after wave of probing reporters? His voice cracked when he told them, "We'll be back. We'll be back. You can count on it, we'll be back."

23

THE AL CAMPANIS AFFAIR

1986–87

TOMMY LASORDA WAS RIGHT. LOS ANGELES WOULD RECOVER FROM JACK Clark's crushing home run. But first the team would struggle through two losing seasons, one of them charged with racial controversy.

In 1986, the more benign year, the Dodgers suffered again from a spate of injuries and awful fielding. They ended up in fifth place (73–89), their worst showing since 1967.

In 1987 the turmoil began on opening day. Shortly after the Dodgers lost at Houston, their longtime general manager Al Campanis appeared from the Astrodome on ABC's *Nightline*. The show had been planned to honor the 40th anniversary of Jackie Robinson's rookie year with the Brooklyn Dodgers. Campanis had played with Robinson one year before that, in 1946, for the Dodgers' Triple-A farm club in Montreal. In fact, Campanis and Robinson roomed together.

Thus, for the *Nightline* staff, booking Campanis made a lot of sense. Robinson's old friend and the current Dodger GM could talk about the man who broke the color line in big-league baseball. But the interview, for Campanis, was a disaster. When asked by anchor Ted Koppel why baseball had no black managers or general managers, Campanis seemed to say that blacks were simply unqualified for such jobs.

KOPPEL: Just tell me why you think it is. Is there still that much prejudice in baseball?

CAMPANIS: No, I don't believe it's prejudice. I truly believe they may not have some of the necessities to be, let's say, a field manager, or perhaps a general manager.

KOPPEL: Do you really believe that?

CAMPANIS: Well, I don't say all of them . . . but how many quarterbacks do you have? How many pitchers do you have that are black?

KOPPEL: Yeah, but I got to tell you, that sounds like the same garbage we were hearing forty years ago about players.

CAMPANIS: No, it's not, it's not garbage. . . . Why are black men, or black people, not good swimmers? Because they don't have the buoyancy.

Many who knew Campanis couldn't believe it. An educated man, a graduate of NYU who spoke five languages, he had no history of racism. In addition to befriending a young Jackie Robinson, he had signed and promoted hundreds of minority players in his 40 years with the Dodgers as a minor league manager, scout, scouting director, and general manager. *Sports Illustrated* once called him "one of baseball's most notable equal opportunity recruiters."

But none of that could save Campanis now. Within 24 hours of his shocking comments, the Dodgers were under pressure from civil rights groups, presidential candidate Jesse Jackson, baseball commissioner Peter Ueberroth, and reportedly Rachel Robinson, Jackie's widow. Later that same day, Campanis issued an apology. The next day, his career ended when Peter O'Malley asked him to resign.

Today, almost 25 years after what Jim Murray called "probably the nadir of the Dodger organization," the Al Campanis episode is still baffling. How could a man with a reputation for fairness make such seemingly bigoted observations?

Those who knew him well—and one man, Ted Koppel, who would not meet Campanis in person until several years later—give their perspectives on the single biggest controversy in Dodger history.

TED KOPPEL: The whole thing was unexpected. That show was never intended to make news. I'm not a huge baseball fan, and I certainly didn't know who Al Campanis was before I interviewed him. But I knew that we had invited him on the program because he had once roomed with Jackie Robinson.

So my impression of him was, here's a white ballplayer, rooming with a black ballplayer, back in the forties. Which I figured could not have been easy in those days. So my predisposition was, here's a good guy.

BUD FURILLO: I was sitting near Al in the Houston Astrodome press box. This was right before he did *Nightline.* Well, people have accused him of being drunk. What drunk? He was drinking Coca-Cola.

GORDON VERRELL: I was sitting next to Steve Brener, the Dodgers' publicity man. Somewhere around the third inning, Brener said kiddingly, "Hey, Al is going on TV tonight."

But Brener didn't know that Campanis was going on *Nightline.* He thought he was doing the postgame show with Vin Scully. Then when Brener found out, he just went nuts. He didn't want Al to go on there.

STEVE BRENER: It was about the fifth inning. The guy from *Nightline* came up and asked if I knew where Al Campanis was sitting. Then I went over to Al. I said, "What was that all about?" He said, "I'm going on *Nightline.*" I said, "Are you sure? I wouldn't go on there." He said, "Don't worry about it. They talked to me last week."

I'm just not a *Nightline* fan. So I kept telling him I wouldn't do it. Al kept saying there's nothing to worry about.

GORDON VERRELL: So now the game is over. I look down at the field and it is the eeriest scene I can ever recall in a ballpark. The Astrodome has all the field lights off. Everything is dark, except home plate, where Al is sitting on a wooden stool with one TV light on him.

I said to someone, "My gosh! The Chief looks like he's sitting in the electric chair." And then, of course, you find out out later he was.

BUD FURILLO: That poor devil is sitting down there in that chair with an earplug on. He can't see Koppel, who is sitting in a studio in Washington, D.C. He can't see that damn Roger Kahn, who is also being interviewed, but from New York. And now the questions start coming.

JIM CAMPANIS: They asked my father to go on the show to talk about his friend Jackie Robinson. Then very little was said about Jackie Robinson. They started right in with all the other stuff.

So he was ill-prepared to answer those questions. And what I really think happened is this: You have a 72-year-old guy. He's got an earphone in his ear, talking to a camera at 11 o'clock at night. And he's tired. And he is trying to defend baseball. And in trying to defend baseball, he did himself in.

My father had never shown any prejudice. In his office for 20 years he had three pictures. He had a picture of Sandy Koufax, who is Jewish, a picture of Roberto Clemente, who is Latin, and a picture of Jackie Robinson. In a way, that summed up my dad. Only thing he cared about was if you could hit, run, field, and throw.

TED KOPPEL: First of all, you gotta understand why I even asked him the question. Rachel Robinson had been interviewed and was part of the setup piece. And someone had said to her, "What do you think? How much progress has there been since Jackie's day?" And Rachel said something to the effect of "There's been a lot of progress on the field, but there hasn't been much progress in the front office."

So I just said to Al Campanis, "What do you think? How come there aren't more black managers, more black coaches?"

That's when he started giving that labored response about blacks not having the necessities. At first I thought he maybe had misunderstood, or was using the word necessities in some way that I didn't quite understand. So I re-asked the question, and then it was quite clear. He was saying what I thought he was saying.

Then I tried again to give him a chance to back away from it. I said, "Look, we're gonna take a commercial break. And when we come back, I'm gonna give you a chance to dig your way out of this thing."

And he just dug himself in even further, because then he started getting into all the physical differences and how blacks don't float and that's why they're not good swimmers.

MARK HEISLER: It was really the saddest thing. It was just tragic. Al was a very sweet guy. He was never even close to being a hater.

But he had a way of mangling the language. And I even wrote this one time. As much as I liked the guy, he would go off the point and say something weird so often, people actually wondered if he was senile, or just pretending to be that way to confuse them.

I remember talking about this to George Vescey, who is not the kind of guy to carry a racist. George and Al were close. They almost collaborated on a book. And Vescey just couldn't believe it. Al Campanis a racist? That was the very last thing you could imagine.

GEORGE VECSEY: He has an earplug popped in his ear. He hears the disembodied voice of Ted Koppel. And Al tended to bumble anyway. He tended to be a little circuitous and use the wrong word. So Al didn't need this disjointedness to bumble.

But what the hell did he mean by "necessities?" It's a meaningless word. He wasn't saying qualification, he wasn't saying aptitude. He found this meaningless word, necessities. And he found it while he was live on national television.

I spent a lot of time with him, and I'm sensitive to this stuff, and I never saw anything like bigotry in him. He had such admiration for Jackie Robinson. And Al wasn't just waving the bloody flag, covering himself in glory. This was his life, this was his career. That he had been Jackie Robinson's roommate. And it was a claim to fame, but a legitimate one.

TOMMY LASORDA: They hung an innocent man. And it just broke my heart. He was my mentor, he did everything to help me. And to see him suffer like that? That was the worst thing that could happen to a man.

And I'll tell you something else. I would never talk to Ted Koppel for what he did to Campanis. He shouldn't have let that happen. I don't care what he tells you, he should never have allowed that to happen.

TED KOPPEL: Look, Al gave me a call years later. He heard that I was out in Los Angeles and he asked if he could come see me and I said, "Sure." So we had a cup of coffee and a piece of cake together and talked for about an hour and a half. He really seemed like a very nice man.

And I have often thought that Al Campanis got himself into terrible trouble that night in large measure because he's a man from an older generation who was still saying the kinds of things that I guess white ballplayers

Ebbets Field was sacred to Brooklynites who came to worship their Dodgers.

Small and intimate, Ebbets had just 32,111 seats. This charmed most Dodger fans, but irritated team owner Walter O'Malley.

Walter O'Malley enraged Brooklyn and delighted Los Angeles when he moved the Dodgers out West in late 1957.

Walter Alston managed the Dodgers for 23 straight seasons. And yet, his job always seemed in jeopardy.

Their first four years in town, the Dodgers played in the Los Angeles Coliseum—an enormous stadium designed for football.

Since 1962, when beautiful Dodger Stadium opened its turnstiles, the franchise has routinely set attendance records.

Duke Snider, a Dodger legend, was sold to the lowly Mets after Los Angeles blew the pennant in 1962.

The magnificent Sandy Koufax throwing one of his five career no-hitters.

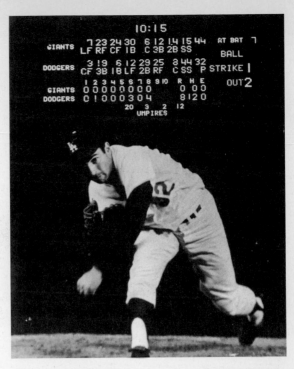

Maury Wills brought speed and daring back to baseball when he broke Ty Cobb's stolen-base record in 1962.

Don Drysdale was an enforcer who never met a hitter he wouldn't brush back.

In 1974 "Iron Mike" Marshall earned his nickname by pitching in an amazing 208 innings out of the bullpen.

Steve Garvey was nearly traded by the Dodgers before becoming a cornerstone of the franchise.

In 1977 and 1978 Tommy Lasorda guided Los Angeles to the World Series in his first two seasons as a major league manager.

Don Sutton clashed with Steve Garvey and Tommy Lasorda, but he was a true professional on the mound.

Davey Lopes was smart, intense, and willing to state his opinion. No wonder the Dodgers voted him their captain.

Ron Cey ended the Dodgers' third-base problem when he took over the job and kept it for ten years.

In 1981 Fernando Valenzuela seemingly came out of nowhere to captivate the fans and dazzle the hitters.

Tommy Lasorda exults as the Dodgers finally triumph over the Yankees in the 1981 World Series.

Steve Howe had a blazing fastball— and a cocaine addiction that ravaged his career.

In 1987 general manager Al Campanis was fired after his controversial comments on Ted Koppel's *Nightline*.

The talented but moody Pedro Guerrero was traded in the middle of a pennant race after a clubhouse incident with Kirk Gibson.

Kirk Gibson scared his own teammates, intimidated his opponents, and sparked the Dodgers to the 1988 World Championship.

In the thrilling 1988 season, Orel Hershiser broke the major league record by throwing 59 consecutive scoreless innings.

There were huge expectations when Darryl Strawberry came home to Los Angeles, but he made more headlines off the field than on it.

In 1997, when he sold the Dodgers to Fox, Peter O'Malley relinquished control of the team his family had owned since the Brooklyn era.

Mike Piazza spurned an offer that would have made him the highest-paid player in baseball. The Dodgers soon traded him in the most controversial deal in their history.

Bill Russell played in Los Angeles for 18 years. He managed there for less than two full seasons.

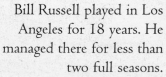

Amid all the tumult and change, hard-hitting Eric Karros was a steadying influence for the franchise.

Davey Johnson came to the Dodgers as a proven winner. He was fired after only two seasons.

and front office professionals were saying in locker rooms and bars and restaurants to each other back in the fifties.

And back in the fifties, that wasn't considered remarkable or particularly bigoted stuff. But in the context of the eighties, it sounded horrible. And it was sad that this happened to Al, because I think there are a lot of genuine bigots in this country and a lot of genuine bigots in professional sports, and I'm sure there are a lot of genuine bigots in professional baseball. I don't think Al was one of them.

BUD FURILLO: Al was not a racist. But the statements he made were indefensible. And I can tell you where he got them from. Everything he said came from William Shockley's book. This was an accomplished anthropologist, saying things like blacks aren't as smart and they can't swim. I had already warned Al about this. He was throwing around these quotes from Shockley's book.

BILL DWYRE: A lot of people said, "He didn't have a racist bone in his body." Well, there's a difference between racism and malicious racism. So what those people meant was, he didn't have a malicious bone in his body. I would agree with that. Al was like everyone's grandpa. But his thought process was of a day and age that was long gone.

Four minority players give their viewpoints. Franklin Stubbs and Chris Gwynn played on the 1987 Dodgers. Davey Lopes and John Roseboro were respected team leaders and All-Stars. Lopes is now the manager of the Milwaukee Brewers—a level, many believe, that Lopes would have reached much earlier if he was white.

FRANKLIN STUBBS: To this day, I don't think Al was a racist. He probably did more for black and Latin players than most people in this game. He helped my career. He stayed in my corner. It never crossed my mind that he was a racist.

CHRIS GWYNN: I was still in Triple A the night it happened. I actually watched the telecast, and I was shocked. I was shocked and I started thinking: How much success can I have in this organization if he feels that way?

But then again, in spring training, Mr. Campanis had always been cordial. He always asked how I was doing, and anything he could help with. So when I saw him on *Nightline*, I felt confused. Very confused, you know?

DAVEY LOPES: I had the utmost respect for Mr. Campanis. And I backed him up when it happened. Because he never said anything that was racist before. He never showed any favoritism. If he could have nine black faces on that field and win, then I think he would have done it.

But I didn't like what he said. And even to this day, there are people in the game who think that way. They think we as minorities have a smaller brain, we're less articulate, we're less intuitive, we're less creative, we're just a little better than an animal.

Al wasn't that brash in what he said, but he said that we lack necessities. All he was saying was we are not smart enough. Necessity was a nicer way to say it. So he was just making a statement that was made by a lot of people for a long time.

JOHN ROSEBORO: The Dodger front office, baseball's front office, professional football's front office . . . well, I shouldn't say all, because that's not right. Most of them had the same subconscious thoughts. Years ago, you couldn't have a black quarterback. You couldn't have a black catcher. Pitchers don't want a black catcher, he can't think.

I think that stuff was all in Campanis's subconscious, and alcohol brought it out. And this bullshit about him being Jackie Robinson's roommate? What came out on that show was what was in his mind. And in the minds of a whole lot of people still today.

As Bud Furillo mentioned earlier, *Boys of Summer* author Roger Kahn was also a guest on that famous *Nightline*. When Campanis began self-destructing, and Kahn chose not to defend him, Kahn enraged many of those who knew Campanis. But in retrospect did Kahn truly do wrong?

JIM CAMPANIS: Yeah, he was a bastard. He goaded my dad into trying to defend baseball. How can one man defend baseball?

BUD FURILLO: Roger Kahn knew Al Campanis as well as anybody. He could have said, "Wait a minute. This isn't really Al Campanis talking. This isn't the guy I know." But Kahn just jumped on Al. He didn't help him at all.

TOMMY LASORDA: Roger Kahn could have helped Al. He could have helped him a great deal. But he didn't. And I have never spoken to Roger Kahn since.

But another view is presented by Bill Dwyre, the *Los Angeles Times* sports editor who is friends with both Kahn and Lasorda.

BILL DWYRE: Roger was furious. He was offended and furious. Roger has so much history with this team, with Jackie and the Boys of Summer, and I think Roger handled himself correctly. If you watch the show, there is controlled outrage there. Here is Al, a guy he's known forever, and yet this guy is offending Roger's obvious sensibilities. Not only his obvious sensibilites, but he is a Jewish man who has felt these kind of things. So I think Roger was remarkably restrained. And I'm glad he was.

ROGER KAHN: They called and said, would I go on for the 40th anniversary of Jackie? I didn't want to be like Howard Cosell—everyone's my best friend. But Jackie and I were quite close. I ghosted pieces for him for a black sports magazine, and we were pretty good buddies. And he was always nice to my children and so forth.

Well, they called me earlier that day. They said, "What do you think we ought to ask you?" So I said, "Why don't you ask me what Jackie would think about the state of blacks in baseball today?" They said, "Good, that's what we'll ask you."

So I had all this time to think. And I felt there were two answers, one of which is Jackie would be happy that marginal black players are now on major league rosters. Whereas when he was playing, you were either a star or you were in the minors.

But the second point, the real point, was that Jackie was a Republican and believed in capitalism, and he would be very annoyed that there are no black owners and no black general managers and no black managers. And I figured that's what I'd say, because it is true to the spirit of what Jackie believed in.

So then I'm in New York. I'm in an ABC studio with a plug in my ear. Koppel's in Washington. And when I got asked the question, I gave them my answer. Then Koppel said to Campanis, who was in Houston, "Mr. Campanis, is Mr. Kahn's statement true, and if it is true, why aren't there more blacks in management?"

That's when Al said they lacked the necessities. Koppel nearly fainted and soon went to a commercial. When Koppel came back, he gave him another chance. And Al basically repeated what he said. Then Al said blacks can't swim because they lack buoyancy. And Koppel said, "How about lacking access to pools?"

Finally, I'd heard enough. I said, "I get it, Al. Blacks have enough intelligence to work in the fields—the cotton fields, the ball fields—but they do not have enough intelligence to manage a baseball team."

So that was how it happened. And if I could have helped the guy, I would have. If he made some mistake on something less important than equal employment under the United States Constitution, I would have helped him. But this was just so jarring. So I didn't give an inch. I stayed right with my loyalty to Robinson.

What about the Dodgers themselves? Could they have done more for Campanis *after* his racial blundering on *Nightline?* He'd been in the Dodger family, after all, since 1943.

Some say Peter O'Malley had no choice. With the credibility of his franchise at stake, he had to dismiss Campanis. Others, including even Roger Kahn, don't believe the punishment fit the crime.

ROGER KAHN: I don't think he needed to be fired. I think you do a statement the next day saying there are too few blacks in leadership positions in baseball, and this is a terrible thing, and we dedicate ourselves to remedying this from this day forward.

That's what I would have done. Then I would have fined Campanis $10,000 or so. Because the things that Campanis said were probably things being said in a lot of front offices. He just forgot that he was on television.

GEORGE VECSEY: It was the start of the '87 season. It was the 40th anniversary of Jackie Robinson's rookie year. So given the political timing, it was untenable. Something certainly had to be brokered or handled.

So the Dodgers did what I think was expedient, but not necessarily the right thing. They forced him out. They hunkered down for a day or two, and then he was gone.

TED KOPPEL: It happens in network television. It happens in professional sports. The name of the game is cut your losses. And that's what the Dodgers did.

I mean, I don't think they acted heroically, either. But when big professional sports organizations act like big professional sports organizations, I'm not surprised. They were covering their asses.

DAVEY LOPES: To this day, I don't agree with it. You wiped out a guy's life. Over one statement. All the good he did was thrown away.

Now, did he hurt a lot of people? Yes he did. But why is it that the people who seemed most hurt had never dealt with this man? I found it very ironic that Spike Lee and Jessie Jackson and all the other activists were coming down so hard on Al. They didn't know Al. They didn't know Al from a hole in the wall. If Al Campanis walked by them, not a single one of them would have known who he was.

BUD FURILLO: Peter had no choice. He was trying to figure out a way to avoid it. But he couldn't. He had to fire him. The black community was really pissed. It is also my belief that Rachel Robinson advised him to fire him.

I also believe he made the right decision. I said so at the time. I said, "I regard Al Campanis as my favorite uncle. But he deserved to get fired. He earned it."

BILL DWYRE: What else could Peter do? Any other way would have looked like a real cop-out. Remember, this is a team that brought up Jackie Robinson. And the irony of it is that Al Campanis was one of the biggest boosters of Jackie Robinson. But the legacy of the Dodgers and the legacy of the O'Malley family was bigger than Al Campanis. And Peter knew that.

GORDON VERRELL: I felt Peter did exactly what he had to. But I never felt that Peter abandoned Al. He made sure Al still had his tickets. He brought him to Vero Beach. He had him up in the box for subsequent games. I mean, Al pretty much went into hiding. He had a cabin up in Lake Arrowhead. But Peter O'Malley did not abandon him.

JIM CAMPANIS: The only thing that bothered me was when I took my dad to the airport after it happened. Peter was there. I said, "Peter, is this gonna cost my dad his job?" He said, "Jim, I promise you, this won't cost your dad his job." And Peter and I have been friends since we were kids.

Well, it ended up that my father resigned. But then I found out that it was his idea. Peter O'Malley was going to hang with him. But the NAACP said they were gonna picket the Dodgers' ballpark. They were going to hold protests. My father said, "Peter, don't fight it. I love the organization too much to put you all through this."

So I have no hard feelings toward Peter O'Malley. None whatsoever. If my dad said, "Let's fight this thing," I believe that Peter would have stood by him.

JOHN ROSEBORO: The Urban League, Jesse Jackson, everybody was jumping on the Dodgers. And everybody was jumping on Major League Baseball. In fact, Jesse Jackson was threatening to boycott baseball at that year's All-Star Game.

Then the Dodgers and the Phillies each hired a black for their front office. And that stopped the movement. Man, that really bothered me, because that was a good example of one of the problems that black people have in this country. Even when our so-called leaders get into positions of authority, they suddenly become tongue-tied and lack aggression.

This was a perfect example of that. A threat to boycott baseball was eliminated by hiring two people. Talk about a mediocre thing.

24

A FRAGILE TIME

1987

One week after the sudden exit of Al Campanis, the 1987 Dodgers were 0–5. They ended up 73–89, their same record as 1986, giving them back-to-back losing seasons for the first time in 19 years. To make matters worse, attendance dipped to 2.7 million after five consecutive years of three million plus.

Amid all the stories predicting the organization's demise, most of the questions centered on Peter O'Malley's succession plan for his front office. Why had he replaced Campanis with Fred Claire, a former sportswriter whose 18 years with the Dodgers had mostly been spent in marketing and public relations? Hadn't Lasorda longed for the GM job? And didn't Campanis plan for his protégé Lasorda to succeed him?

JIM CAMPANIS: There's no question about it. In fact, I'll tell you how it was supposed to go down. My dad was going to work another season. Then Tommy would take over as both GM and manager in '89. That's how my dad had it planned. I don't think Peter knew about it yet. But if everything had worked out how it was supposed to, my dad would have recommended it to Peter. Then *Nightline* came along, my father resigned, and he never had a say in who replaced him.

ROSS NEWHAN: That clearly changed the history of the organization. Had the timing been different, Peter might have made Tommy the GM.

JOE MCDONNELL: No doubt Tommy wanted the GM job. And I'll guarantee you that he was offered the job. The problem is O'Malley wanted him to quit managing. And Tommy didn't want to quit managing. He said, "I want to make sure we win another world championship."

But Tommy never stopped wanting to be the GM. And you know what? I don't blame him, because Tommy was the right guy for that job. He should have been general manager. Tommy really knew talent. And Fred Claire, although a nice man, was never qualified to do that job.

TOMMY LASORDA: When this thing happened to Al, Peter took me out three consecutive days to talk to me. And the first thing he said was, "Tommy, you cannot do both jobs. It's too much for one man, and I don't want to put that all on you."

So I could have been general manager or I could have been manager. And since I loved managing so much, that was the one I took. But if he said I could do both jobs, then it would have been a different story.

MARK HEISLER: I'm sure Al wanted Tommy to succeed him. But Peter was closer to Fred. Peter was buttoned-down. The son of Walter. He was a polite, drawing room kind of guy. So Fred Claire was very much his kind of guy. And Tommy wasn't.

Tommy was a brawler. Tommy was blue-collar. In fact, there was a lot of talk that Peter might fire Tommy if Tommy had another bad season or two. I mean, Peter appreciated that Tommy was this incredible Dodger Blue salesman. But at the same time, if things had gone badly for him another season, we thought Peter might do something drastic.

GORDON VERRELL: Was Tommy in trouble? Well, he was in the last year of his contract, and they just had two awful seasons. But when it got right down to it, I don't think Peter was close to making a move. Tommy brought too much excitement to that ballpark. Tommy had too many fans around the country. I think Peter was real sensitive to that.

TOMMY LASORDA: Well, you always think about it. You always hope that it won't happen. But I always said to them, "If at any time you feel that you've got somebody better for this job, you gotta do it." That's how I felt, because I loved the Dodgers very much. But I also didn't think there was anyone who could do a better job.

Still, it was a fragile time for this proud franchise. As the 1987 season ended with a second straight 73–89 record, the Al Campanis affair still hung over Chavez Ravine, Fred Claire's qualifications were being questioned, and Tommy Lasorda had one year left on his contract. Were these management issues beginning to weigh on the players?

MIKE SCIOSCIA: There was obviously a lot of media talk. But as players, you become immune to that. So I can't say the front office stuff really bothered us.

FRANKLIN STUBBS: Maybe a little bit, but the game is played on the field. And, there, what we lacked most was attitude. We needed that go-getter that you look for. We needed that guy who took charge. We found him the next season in Kirk Gibson.

25

GUNG-HO GIBSON

SPRING 1988

BY SPRING TRAINING OF 1988, THE SUDDENLY REBUILT DODGERS HAD SEVERAL other new faces to go with the unshaven Kirk Gibson. After two straight abysmal seasons of 73–89, Fred Claire had acquired proven closer Jay Howell, young starting pitcher Tim Belcher, smooth-fielding shortstop Alfredo Griffin, veteran catcher Rick Dempsey, kamikaze utility man Mickey Hatcher, and slugging free-agent outfielder Mike Davis.

Davis cost almost $2 million for two years, a hefty sum for a team that had sworn off buying free agents since getting burned on Dave Goltz and Don Stanhouse in 1980. But the Dodgers invested even more ($4.5 million for three years) on Gibson, the scowling left fielder and ex–college football player who brought power, speed, and reckless intensity to a team sometimes described as too laid back.

TOMMY LASORDA: What are you talking about? That was the wrong impression. We never got too laid back. They play for me, they don't get too laid back.

JAY HOWELL: It was a loose clubhouse when I got there. It was a fun clubhouse. But it lacked focus. There were some comedians there. Then Gibson came in and he changed everything.

FRED CLAIRE: We had dinner together when we signed him. Kirk said, "I want to win. And I just want you to know, I may have to bang some heads." I said, "Kirk, why do you think you're here?"

KIRK GIBSON: When I first got there, I didn't really have any preconceptions. The Dodger organization just carried an aroma with it, you know? It was a very classy organization. And the O'Malley name in baseball was very solid.

So when I went to spring training, I really didn't know what to expect. All I knew was the Tigers' way, and Sparky Anderson's way. Sparky's way was very "I am the ruler. My way or the highway." It was very serious, very structured.

When I came into the Dodger camp, it was just the opposite. Now, I'm not saying it was wrong. I'm just saying it was different for me. When we got out on the field during spring training, to practice our bunts and relays and stuff, it was just very, very loose.

And that's when I started to garner the opinion: They didn't have it right. They were screwing around too much. That's when the eyeblack thing happened.

It took place in March in Vero Beach, before what had been promoted as Gibson's first exhibition game with the Dodgers. But in a watershed moment for this miraculous season, the hotheaded Gibson never played that day.

TIM BELCHER: Jesse Orosco played a little joke on him. Jesse eyeblacked the inside rim of his hat. Kirk took off his hat to start running sprints, and he had this big black ring around his forehead.

CHRIS GWYNN: Then he rubs some of the black stuff into his hair. All the guys start laughing. Kirk starts getting pissed off.

MARK CRESSE: He said, "What are you laughing about?" I said, "What the hell have you got all over your forehead?" Then he wiped his forehead. He saw the black stuff. And he didn't say a word. He just started running toward the dugout.

The only coach there was Bill Russell. I saw Gibson ranting and raging, going nuts. He's throwing his hands in the air, he's so pissed off. And all I see Russell do is point to Lasorda. And poor Tommy, he's kissing babies and talking to these fans by the first-base dugout.

CHRIS GWYNN: Gibson told Tommy, "Look. You send in the SOB that did this to me. I'll be waiting in the clubhouse. I'm not playing today. This is bullshit."

TODD MOULDING: He yelled at Tommy in front of all the fans. Then he ran off. He was gone.

TOMMY LASORDA: He didn't yell at me. He just left the ballpark. And I fined him for leaving. But I never took his money. I just wanted him to know that he couldn't do that.

JAY HOWELL: I was in the clubhouse with some of the pitchers. He comes in and rips his uniform off. Buttons are flying everywhere, just flying. He says, "No wonder you fuckers were in last place last year. Bunch of fucking comedian motherfuckers. You're laughing all the way to fucking last place."

Then he showers and he leaves. We play the game. We're kind of laughing about it. I mean, we don't know this guy yet. There's some comments like, "We got a bad ass, but we'll break him."

TIM BELCHER: The next day Gibson came back. Gibson and Tommy had already talked by then. And Tommy says, "Gibson wants to make a statement." Then Gibson took the floor. And you could hear a pin drop in that clubhouse.

TODD MOULDING: It was pretty amazing. He tore the team a new ass.

MARK CRESSE: He said he didn't come to L.A. to be a clown. He came to L.A. to win a championship. And if anyone got in the way of that championship, they would have to answer to him.

KIRK GIBSON: The day it happened, I went nuts, okay? Then I came and stood up the next day and I basically told them what my makeup was. I said, "You wanna have fun? Winning is fun. You want to be a world champion? You might have to play hurt. You might have to play sick. And *don't* be screwing around when it's time to play."

But I also didn't want them to get the wrong idea, like I saw myself as being apart from my teammates. So I said, "I consider myself a total team guy. I will sacrifice for you. I will stick up for you. If you're a pitcher and you want to throw inside, and you happen to drill somebody, just run out to left field. I'll come right in and I'll kick their ass. I'm gonna be the best teammate you ever had."

JAY HOWELL: That was it. It was over. We broke for practice. There were some guys that snickered, but there were also some guys who seemed to have more focus during practice. And there were fewer guys fucking around during the games.

GORDON VERRELL: The chemistry took a turn that very day. He put the fear of hell in everybody. Especially Mike Marshall. He was terrified of Gibson.

Marshall had put up huge numbers in the minors. But if he wasn't 100 percent healthy, then Marshall wouldn't play. One time in the press box, they announced he was missing a game because of "general soreness."

This was a guy that just would not play hurt, and that drove people absolutely nuts. But Marshall played hard that year, and he played well. I really don't think that happens without Gibson.

JOE MCDONNELL: Gibson personified what they all wanted to be. They all wanted to be that tough competitor he was. And Gibson really unified that team. You had guys like John Shelby, who's very reserved, locking arms with Steve Sax and Mike Davis and singing the courage song from the *Wizard of Oz*.

So it was just a whole different world with Gibson there. And that's why that team was so much fun to cover. Because you expected nothing from them and got everything.

MICKEY HATCHER: That team came out of spring training with a bond. Everybody played hurt. Everybody played hard. That really set the tone for a magical season.

26

THE DESTINY BOYS

1988

IF THERE WAS CLEARLY PENNANT FEVER AT VERO BEACH, THE BASEBALL ANALYSTS were not impressed. In fact, as Steve Sax recalls it, most of them picked the 1988 Dodgers to finish fourth.

Instead they moved into first on May 26, and built an eight-game lead on July 18. Then, three disastrous weeks later, with their big lead nearly vanished, they lost again in St. Louis. That's when Gibson and Pedro Guerrero had their clubhouse showdown.

JAY HOWELL: Guerrero and Gibson had never hit it off. It was mostly locker room stuff. Like how to behave in the locker room after a loss. Guerrero used to like to play his music. He wouldn't play it too loud, but it was pissing off Gibson a little bit.

So then we lost in St. Louis and several Cardinals came into our locker room. Guerrero was standing with them. And Gibby says, "Watch this." Then he gets up and says, "If you fuckers want to be in our locker room, why don't you tell your agents to trade you here?"

Then Guerrero pops off. He says, "Who invited you into this conversation?" Gibson says, "Tell your buddies to get the fuck out of our locker room! And if they don't want to leave, I'll throw them out myself!"

Guerrero started after him a little bit, and somebody grabbed Guerrero, and Gibson was holding his ground, ready to roll. Then the Cardinals turned around and left. That was the incident.

KIRK GIBSON: Everyone handles losses differently. I was just a miserable bastard. So it's right after the game, and I'm sitting there reflecting. Because I want to dump everything there before I leave, so I can walk out of that locker room and be a person.

And then you're going to parade some guys from the other team in there? And you're all gonna start giggling? Not as long as I'm around. I mean, this is our war room. *Our* war room. Okay?

It wasn't anything personal. I liked Pete Guerrero. But you had to address it. And Pete was a very good player. He carried a lot of clout. So who's gonna do it? Me.

But maybe Gibson carried even more clout. Within a matter of days, Guerrero was sent to St. Louis for pitcher John Tudor.

FRED CLAIRE: No. There was no direct relationship. It wasn't a matter of wanting to move Pedro. We needed to have more pitching down the stretch. And Tudor, as it turned out, really helped us.

JAY HOWELL: It had everything to do with it. Gibson said, "One of us has to go." I think that's just how he put it. One of us has to go. Then Guerrero went, and he went quickly.

KIRK GIBSON: I didn't make that decision. You have to ask Fred. But I didn't hide anything. There wasn't anything secretive about it. My opinion was asked, and I gave it.

And we did get John Tudor for him. And I can tell you that John Tudor was a serious guy. Now, that's not to say we wouldn't have won it with Pete. But whoever made that decision, they knew there was a little bit of conflict there.

On August 30, two weeks after the Dodgers exiled Guerrero, Orel Hershiser began his remarkable pitching streak. He ended the regular season with a record 59 straight scoreless innings, including five consecutive shutouts in September. The old, supposedly unassailable record (58⅔ innings) had been held for 20 years by the Dodgers' Don Drysdale.

With Hershiser and Gibson leading the way, the Dodgers won their division with 94 wins and 67 losses. This pitted them against the favored Mets (100–62) in the National League playoffs, and some felt New York had maybe its best team ever, with Darryl Strawberry, Dwight Gooden, Keith Hernandez, Dave Cone, Ron Darling, and Kevin McReynolds. Moreover, the Mets had owned the Dodgers all season.

TOMMY LASORDA: They had beaten us 10 of 11 times that year. The 12th game was rained out. So nobody, and I mean nobody, gave us a chance.

FRANKLIN STUBBS: The Mets had more talent than any team in baseball. And that included Oakland.

MICKEY HATCHER: But you know what? We felt good. We felt good about ourselves.

A major reason for that was Hershiser, who entered the playoffs with those 59 consecutive scoreless innings. Then in Game 1 at Dodger Stadium, he ran his amazing string to 67. But with a 2–0 lead going into the ninth, the Dodgers lost, 3–2, on an agonizing bloop single with two outs and two strikes on Gary Carter.

BOB COSTAS: That was the very start of a thrilling postseason. Hershiser pitches great, and it looks like they can win Game 1 in New York. Then they lose it in the ninth because John Shelby's playing too deep and the ball falls in front of him.

Now, this would devastate almost any team. But if it devastated Lasorda, he would not let it show to his players. Lasorda always stayed up, and he always stayed on the lookout for an edge. Like that incident with me in the World Series. Lasorda used me to fire up his players.

We'll get to that entertaining moment soon. For now let's concentrate on David Cone, who became motivational fodder for Lasorda on the morning after the Dodgers lost Game 1. Cone made an ill-advised crack in the New York *Daily News* about Jay Howell, who Cone said reminded the Mets of a "high school pitcher." Cone's reasoning behind this? Howell threw too many curveballs when he relieved Hershiser in Game 1.

Of course, Lasorda found out, though the story was printed 3,000 miles away. And of course, Lasorda went right after Cone, who would be pitching Game 2 that night in Los Angeles.

TOMMY LASORDA: Boy, that was the ammunition I needed. Because we had just lost a very, very tough game. And when our guys showed up the next day, there was a copy of that story in each guy's locker.

CHRIS GWYNN: Tommy loved that stuff. He said, "These guys insulted you. They don't think you can play. We gotta show them. We gotta stand up for the city of Los Angeles."

JOE MCDONNELL: They tried to play it down when we came in. But they were really pissed. Gibson was ready to destroy somebody.

KIRK GIBSON: I know David very well now, and now it's all funny. But when Tommy taped up that story, we said, "Let's kill this guy."

JAY HOWELL: I had a good year. I had good stuff. So it certainly didn't bruise me. And there's plenty of other criticism out there. If you worry about that shit, it will eat you alive.

Then Cone went out to pitch. And the bench jockeys got going right away. I mean, guys were just making some beautiful comments. They wanted to whip his ass for what he said.

TIM BELCHER: Our entire bench was screaming at him. Rick Dempsey was on the top step of the dugout. Every time Dave threw a curve, Dempsey said, "Aw, that's high school."

And Dave heard it. It bothered him. He knew he screwed up.

TOMMY LASORDA: We called him every name in the book. We went after David Cone with a vengeance. And we managed to rattle a very good young pitcher.

Cone had gone 20–3 during the season. He lasted only two innings against the Dodgers, who defeated the Mets 6–3 to even the playoffs.

In Game 3 in New York, as if he needed any more controversy, Howell found himself awash in it in the eighth inning. The Dodgers led 4–3 and Howell was pitching when umpire Harry Wendelstedt ejected him for using pine tar on his glove. Then as millions watched on national television, the umpire gave the glove to National League President Bart Giamatti, who was watching the playoff game from his front row box.

While Giamatti inspected the glove and Howell fumed, the next three Dodger relievers gave up five runs. The Mets won 8–4 to lead the series, 2–1, which the Dodgers felt was punishment enough. But the next day Giammati announced that he was suspending Howell for three games.

CHRIS GWYNN: It was freezing in New York. It was rainy. The ball was slick. He used pine tar to get a better grip. Most pitchers do in those conditions.

KIRK GIBSON: There are things that go on in this game that everybody accepts. But Jay, they singled out. They made an example of him during the playoffs.

JAY HOWELL: Guys have been using it for a million years. Most hitters don't give a shit. They don't care about pine tar. They don't like spit-balls.

Anyway, I'm pitching to Kevin McReynolds. Then Davey Johnson comes walking out of their dugout. Davey says to Harry Wendelstedt, "Take a look at his glove." Harry comes out and touches the heel of my glove. He turns around and throws me out of the game. I said, "Harry, what the fuck are you doing? Why don't you just take the glove? I'll get another glove."

But it's too late. The fans are going bananas in New York. And I go into the dugout and I'm thinking: This is bullshit. David Cone is using a black glove. Gooden has a black glove. Are you kidding me? It's no mystery why guys use black gloves.

TODD MOULDING: You know how the Mets found out about Jay in the first place? They had a TV down in their bullpen. Which is illegal. So then they called down to the dugout and they ratted on him.

But you know what? I'm glad that episode happened. And the David Cone episode, too. If the Mets had just kept their mouths shut, they would have beat us. But they kept throwing matches on the fire.

TOMMY LASORDA: That was really a joke. All the pitchers use pine tar when it's cold. And this is what I said to Wendelstedt: "If you saw that on Gooden's glove, you would never have thrown him out. Because the fans in New York would have run you of town."

But they threw out Jay Howell, and they made a big show of it, and I was very disappointed. So you know what I did? I managed to get his suspension cut down. Because at the press conference, I told them a chemist had called me and said that pine tar was a liquid form of rosin.

They believed it, but no chemist had ever called me. I just made it up. And I got him suspended down from three games to two. Then I told our guys, "We're gonna beat the Mets with or without Jay."

And yet, with the Dodgers now trailing the series 2–1, the prospects looked grim for them late in Game 4. Then, losing 4–2 in the ninth against the commanding Dwight Gooden, they suddenly tied the game on Scioscia's two-run homer. Gibson won it 5–4 in the 12th with a tremendous blast off the right field scoreboard.

That dramatic victory evened the series. The Dodgers won it back in Los Angeles when Hershiser shut out the Mets 6–0 with everything riding on Game 7.

STEVE SAX: But you know what we kept hearing? That the best team didn't win. That's a bunch of bullshit. The best team won. We may not have had as much talent as the Mets. But we were unbelievably determined.

The Dodgers would have to be, because the mighty Oakland A's were overwhelming favorites to win the 1988 World Series. Well managed by Tony La Russa, Oakland had won 104 games before sweeping the Red Sox four straight in their playoff series. The "Bash Brothers," Jose Canseco and Mark McGwire, had hit 74 home runs by themselves. The entire Dodger roster hit 99, and 25 of those belonged to the hobbling Gibson, who had just sprained his right knee and reinjured a torn left hamstring against the Mets.

The dream was about to end, in other words.

JAY HOWELL: We got four or five regulars hurt besides Kirk Gibson. We're just sticking together with bubble gum. We got no chance of winning. That's the perception.

MIKE DAVIS: I played in Oakland before I played for the Dodgers. Well, on paper, it was a slam dunk. They were the powerhouse. And they were just going to walk on us lowly Dodgers.

MARK CRESSE: Don Baylor made a statement before that series. He said Oakland wanted to play the Mets, because they wanted to play the best team in the National League. That quote was even more hated than David Cone's. And it also went right up on our bulletin board.

MICKEY HATCHER: The Mets *did* have the best team. And we had just beat the Mets. So we came into the World Series pretty relaxed.

The Series opened at Dodger Stadium, where Hatcher, starting in place of an injured Gibson, hit a two-run homer in the first inning. Then the muscular Canseco upstaged Hatcher with a screaming line-drive grand slam that put a dent into a center-field camera.

The Dodgers trailed 4–2 after two innings, and Howell remembers thinking, "Wow, guys, what have we got ourselves into?" But in the Oakland dugout, Tony La Russa had a different reaction.

TONY LA RUSSA: We just had an unbelievable season. We had won 104 regular season games, and then swept a very good Boston team with Roger

Clemens. So I believe, deep down, we felt that it was our destiny that year.

Then when Jose hit that grand slam in Game I, I could almost sense our club feeling, hey, this Series is over. Whatever we need, it's going to be there for us. Which is a mistake. You're never safe until you get the last out. Which Kirk Gibson proved when he hit that home run.

He is referring, of course, to Gibson's game-winning blast in the ninth inning—the most epic home run in Dodger history and a World Series moment for the ages.

TOMMY LASORDA: Yeah, I've seen many home runs. But I never saw one with that much drama attached. Here's a guy who was on the rubbing table the entire game. Here's a guy that never even came out for the introductions!

MARK CRESSE: The last time I saw Kirk Gibson before the game, he was in his underpants, eating spaghetti, back in Tommy's room. I had to get him a fork, because he couldn't walk ten feet to get it.

CHRIS GWYNN: He was hurt and miserable and getting his legs packed in ice when the game started. He didn't even get dressed. So everybody knew he wouldn't play.

Everybody was wrong, including broadcaster Vin Scully, who told millions of NBC viewers that Gibson would not be swinging a bat that night.

KIRK GIBSON: I was getting wrapped in ice, and getting a couple cortisone injections. So I was watching the game from the clubhouse, and they kept scanning our dugout with their cameras. They said, "No, there's still no Kirk Gibson. He's unable to play." I said, "My ass."

When Gibson finally got dressed, he still stayed out of sight, hitting balls off a tee into a net. That's where Bob Costas heard Gibson when the A's came up in the ninth with a 4–3 lead.

BOB COSTAS: I was doing the postgame for NBC. And they wanted me to interview Lasorda. So I'm standing in the corner of their dugout. And I think I'll be talking to the guy who's lost the game.

Well, you could hear Gibson taking his swings off the tee. And you could hear his grunts of pain and discomfort. Then Ben Hines, the batting coach, came walking up the tunnel and turned into the dugout where I was standing. Hines said to Lasorda, "Kirk says he's got one good swing in him."

This is really like something out of a B movie. So I'm kind of thinking, "Wow, how wild would this be?"

In the bottom of the ninth, with Los Angeles still losing 4–3, Dennis Eckersley took the mound for Oakland. Eckersley, the top reliever in baseball, retired the first two batters before Mike Davis came up. That's when Lasorda pulled a slick move on the A's.

TOMMY LASORDA: I knew Gibson was gonna hit for the pitcher, but I didn't let him go in the on-deck circle. I put Dave Anderson out there. I was using him as a decoy, because I knew if they saw Gibson, they'd pitch differently to Mike Davis.

Davis played for Oakland the year before. He hit 20-some homers. So they pitched too carefully and walked Mike Davis, because they wanted Dave Anderson to hit. What's Anderson gonna do? He's just coming off the disabled list.

BOB COSTAS: That was a nice decoy by Lasorda, who had a terrific World Series. Because if you think Kirk Gibson is going to hit, you don't fool around with Mike Davis. You go right at him.

TOMMY LASORDA: After they walked Davis, then I said to Gibson, "*Now* get out there!" And, God, I got goosebumps when I heard the reaction.

FRANKLIN STUBBS: Oh, man, what a moment. Gibson limps out of the dugout. The crowd is going crazy. But he can barely walk to home plate.

JAY HOWELL: Gibson is so lame he almost falls down on his first swing. We're thinking, "This is a joke. Why is he even up there? He's gonna strike out and we lose."

TODD MOULDING: I was mad at Tommy. I thought, "Is Tommy just throwing in the towel? Just so Gibson can have a cameo?" I mean, in the heat of the moment, you're thinking, "I want the money. I want the ring."

Gibson, on crippled legs, simply could not get around on Eckersley's fastball, which he kept fouling off. But after Davis stole second, and the count reached 3–2, Eckersley made a monumental error. Instead of another fastball—his best pitch—he threw Gibson a slider.

JAY HOWELL: I'm warming up in the bullpen. Gibson hits this rocket. But it doesn't look like it's out. It looks like it's a gapper. Then the crowd goes bananas. You can almost feel the stadium shaking. The hair on the back of your neck is standing up.

STEVE SAX: The dugout's going crazy. Tommy's kissing and hugging everybody.

BOB COSTAS: It wasn't this chest bumping stuff that you see now. They were jumping up and down like Little Leaguers.

MICKEY HATCHER: It was just plain magic. We send a cripple up there in a wheelchair, and he hits a home run to win a World Series game. I mean, come on.

TOT HOLMES: I was in the stands, and nobody went home. It was like a block party. Everybody just milled around and hugged people they didn't know.

And what was Gibson thinking, as he staggered around the bases, pumping his fists? Remember, this is Gibson. So don't expect vanilla.

KIRK GIBSON: A lot of things go through your mind really quickly. Obviously, you're happy. You're taking in the scene, the response to the game-winning home run. You're thinking about your parents, and about the people who supported you, and about what other people motherfucked you. Because baseball is a very humbling game. It's a game of failure. And it's one where a lot of expectations are laid upon people. I was the next Mickey Mantle. That was the label they gave me. And if you don't live up to that . . .

So this was like vindication, when you tell all those people, "Thanks for your support. And don't worry about those idiots all over me. I knew our day would come. And now it has."

JOE McDONNELL: Gibson was through for the Series. That was his only at bat. But he'd already won the Series for his team. Because Oakland was done after that. They were toast.

BOB COSTAS: Not only do you lose this game in shocking fashion, but their untouchable reliever gets taken out by a guy limping up to the plate. And now they're looking the next night at Hershiser, a guy who can shove the bats up their rear ends. So the whole momentum and psychology of the Series shifted completely on one pitch.

TONY LA RUSSA: Well, that was a stinger. You got two outs and nobody on, and all of a sudden, a few pitches later, you're walking off as a loser in the first game of the World Series.

But let me add something. It is never a great memory to see that Gibson home run. But the fact that it was Gibson has really taken some of the hurt out of it. If he was a marginal player, and he hit that home run off a marginal pitcher, that would be one thing. But this was Gibson and Eckersley. A classic confrontation between two great players. So that helps ease the pain a little bit.

In Game 2 the gracious La Russa was beaten by yet another premier player. Hershiser not only shut out Oakland 6–0, allowing just three singles, he also hit two doubles and a single. The A's won Game 3, 2–1, when

McGwire homered off Howell in the ninth inning. Then, the following evening, Bob Costas joined David Cone as grist for Tommy Lasorda.

It started in the pregame show when Costas called the Dodgers' lineup for Game 4 one of the weakest in World Series history. Considering their depleted batting order—Steve Sax, Franklin Stubbs, Mickey Hatcher, Mike Davis, John Shelby, Mike Scioscia, Danny Heep, Jeff Hamilton, and Alfredo Griffin—Costas was probably right. But no matter, the fuse was lit.

TOMMY LASORDA: We just finished a meeting in the clubhouse, which we weren't even gonna have, but then Bill Russell came to me and said that Mike Marshall didn't want to play because he had a headache. I was furious. How the hell can a guy not play in the World Series with a headache?

So I got really mad and very demonstrative. For some reason then I reached up and turned on the TV. And there's Bob Costas saying, "This may be the worst team ever put on the field in World Series history."

And I took it and ran with it. I mean, Bob was a very good friend. But I had to use it. I had to use it as a stimulator right then and there.

BOB COSTAS: I never said they were one of the weakest *teams*. What I said was, "Pitching aside, and pitching may carry them through, this Dodger lineup, absent Gibson and absent Mike Marshall, is one of the weakest *lineups* ever to take the field for a World Series game."

And I didn't say that lightly. I ran it through my head. I was thinking of teams like the 1959 White Sox. I was thinking of the Koufax-Drysdale Dodgers, but even they had Tommy Davis and Frank Howard. I wasn't so sure about the 1906 White Sox, who were called "the Hitless Wonders." But certainly in my own lifetime, I'd never seen a lineup like this take the field in a World Series game.

CHRIS GWYNN: The guys were still milling around inside the clubhouse. Then Costas makes his statement and Tommy goes, "WHAT?"

MICKEY HATCHER: Tommy went on a rampage. He said, "Can you guys believe that? Listen to what this guy says! Listen to this bullshit!"

JAY HOWELL: Tommy was going bananas. Then everybody started screaming, "Kill Costas!"

BOB COSTAS: So, anyway, now the game is about to start. I'm down on the field, and there's no way to get off before the national anthem. So while the anthem is playing, Hershiser whispers, "Boy, Tommy really got the guys jumping over what you said."

So now I'm kind of tipped off. But I didn't know the full extent of it, how Tommy had done a real Knute Rockne pep talk. Now, according to what I heard later, there was a chant that went up. And I've heard it was one of two things. It was either "Kill Costas" or "Fuck Costas." I'm honored in either case.

STEVE SAX: Costas basically said that we didn't belong on the same baseball field with Oakland. So we were pissed off when we came out to play. We wanted to stick it up their ass. And we did.

The Dodgers won 4–3 as the badly beleaguered Howell found redemption by popping up McGwire with the bases loaded to end the seventh inning. Then, with a man on base in the ninth, Howell put down Canseco and big Dave Parker. "That was one really tough save," La Russa said afterward.

JAY HOWELL: Now we go to the fifth game. And Orel just puts on his Superman suit. He shuts them out, 2–0, and we win the Series. And when it was finally over, it was really a David-and-Goliath feeling. How did we just knock that fucker down?

That was pretty much the question. Given the strengths and weaknesses of the two teams, how did the Dodgers pull off a World Series upset of stunning proportions?

The conventional wisdom said the A's had vastly more talent. In fact, they had a better team. But the 1988 Dodgers had bigger hearts.

STEVE SAX: I don't totally agree with that. They had a chance to beat us. They had seven games in which to do it. But talent doesn't mean shit if you don't apply it.

TONY LA RUSSA: Execution. The Dodgers did a lot of the baseball things right. They hit the cutoff men, they played hit-and-run, and made it work. It was just a clinic in really good baseball.

TIM BELCHER: The biggest key was our pitching. What did Canseco and McGwire do that World Series? They had two hits between them. We closed them down.

As for having more heart, I don't know about that. But we may have been more determined. I mean, you can call us the underdogs. You can say we're inferior. But you still gotta take the field. You gotta earn it. That year, the Dodgers earned it.

KIRK GIBSON: We busted our ass. Okay?

27

LIGHTNING STRIKES ONCE

1989

AFTER THEIR SHINING SEASON, THE ACCOLADES KEPT COMING FOR THE DODGERS. Gibson won Most Valuable Player for his .290 average, 25 home runs, 76 RBIs, and hard-ass attitude. The Cy Young Award went to Hershiser, whose 23–8 record and 2.26 ERA included his record streak of 59 scoreless innings. Claire was widely praised—and he also secured his job as general manager—for assembling a world champion just one year after replacing Al Campanis.

Finally there was Lasorda, dissipating the ghost of Jack Clark's homer, signing another three-year contract extension, and earning the recognition that had sometimes been withheld by his detractors. "Lasorda beat the mighty A's in 1988 with a team that didn't belong anywhere near October," wrote Mike Lupica in *Esquire.* "It was one of the finest managing jobs ever."

TONY LA RUSSA: I have always felt—and so do a lot of other baseball men—that he's such a great ambassador for the game that it sometimes overshadows his knowledge of the game. He's a very shrewd and experienced baseball man. And he managed very skillfully that World Series.

BOB COSTAS: Everything Lasorda did worked. Everything. It was like a managing clinic. But as any manager will tell you, you can push all the right buttons and it doesn't mean the players will execute. Well, Lasorda made all the right moves and they executed virtually 100 percent of the time.

TOMMY LASORDA: Let me tell you something. I can be in Los Angeles and put the hit-and-run on. Sparky Anderson can be in Detroit and put the hit-and-run on. And Whitey Herzog can be in St. Louis and put the hit-and-run on. All at the same time.

Whitey's guy swings and misses, and they throw the guy out at second. Sparky's guy hits a line drive, they double the guy at first. My guy hits a little looper over first base, and we got runners at first and third. What did we do different? Huh?

We didn't do anything different. So you can put all the moves on, and if the players don't come through, then what the hell good is it?

So whatever credit I got in 1988, I owe to those players. Those guys loved each other. They were proud to wear the Dodger uniform. It was a great ballclub and a great season.

So what happened to destiny's boys in 1989? Gibson's injured hamstring made him a part-time player. Sax left as a free agent, taking his hitting and hustle to the Yankees. Hershiser went only 15–15, although his ERA was 2.31. And he wasn't alone in lacking offensive support. Both Howell and Belcher recall night after night of 0–0 games in the sixth inning.

Thus, the team's anemic fourth-place finish (77–83) just one year after destroying the A's in five games. Still, it had been a strong decade for one of baseball's elite organizations. In the 1980s, Los Angeles had won four division titles, two pennants, and the 1981 and 1988 World Series. Which meant since moving out west in 1957, the Dodgers had won five world championships.

Surely, in the 1990s, they would bring home grand prize number six?

PART V

THE NINETIES

28

STRAWBERRY COMES HOME

1990-91

In 1990 Iraq invaded Kuwait and U.S. President George Bush launched Operation Desert Storm against the Iraqis. The mayor of Washington, D.C., Marion Barry, was arrested for smoking crack in a hotel room. The NBC comedy *Seinfeld* debuted to meager ratings while Fox's *The Simpsons* became an immediate hit.

In baseball that year, Pete Rose began serving a federal prison sentence for tax evasion. Commissioner Fay Vincent suspended Yankees owner George Steinbrenner because of his association with gambler Howard Spira. In October, Oakland swept Boston again in the playoffs, only to get swept itself by underdog Cincinnati in the World Series.

As the 1990s progressed, baseball still found itself plagued by the skirmishes between its billionaire owners and millionaire players. In 1994–95, in fact, the most destructive strike in baseball history wiped out the 1994 World Series and tested the faith of even the staunchest of fans.

Some of those wounds were salved by the great home run race between Mark McGwire and Sammy Sosa in 1998, but even that brilliant performance could not obscure baseball's deep problems in the nineties. The ever-increasing salaries paid to players resulted in vastly higher ticket prices. As the economic gap between small- and large-market teams kept widening, the 1997 Pittsburgh Pirates paid their entire roster $9 million, while the 1997 Chicago White Sox paid $11 million just to Albert Belle. That same year, the Florida Marlins spent $89 million in free-agent contracts. The newly formed Marlins won the World Series, but even before their fans could get to know them, they were sold off by management after the season.

Back in Los Angeles in 1990, the Dodgers (86–76) finished second, a fairly impressive showing for a team that was plagued by injuries. Still, with Gibson leaving via free agency, Hershiser's career at risk after shoulder surgery, and attendance flattening out at Chavez Ravine, the Dodgers whipped out their checkbook and signed $37 million worth of free agents that winter.

The biggest catch was Darryl Strawberry, who left the New York Mets for a five-year, $20.25 million contract. Another team had reportedly offered him more, but Strawberry grew up in South Los Angeles, starred at Crenshaw High School, and even while still a Met, openly spoke of wanting to play for the Dodgers.

Strawberry, 28, was the youngest player to ever hit 200 homers, and he was coming off one of his best seasons (37 home runs and 108 RBIs). But in his eight stormy years in New York, he had also filled the tabloids with reports of excessive drinking, violent skirmishes with his wife, Lisa, a fistfight with teammate Keith Hernandez, and his criticism of manager Davey Johnson.

In November 1990 when he joined the Dodgers, Strawberry said his problems were behind him. He was a born-again Christian, he announced, and he was entirely done with alcohol. Of course, some people doubted him on both counts. Others, like Tom Verducci, the national baseball writer for *Sports Illustrated*, were surprised the Dodgers had signed the gifted but troubled slugger in the first place.

TOM VERDUCCI: Like a lot of other people, I always thought of the Dodgers as being the absolute masters of public relations. A player's image was just as important as his on-base percentage. So that surprised me when they went after Darryl.

But Darryl was always a charmer, and I think he probably charmed the Dodgers by convincing them that the best thing for him was to go home. In fact, it was the worst thing to go home.

FRED CLAIRE: I knew it would generate interest in the Dodgers. And Darryl grew up in South Central. I thought he could make a tremendous impact on the city.

BOB COSTAS: He still had a huge upside when he arrived. It would not have been out of the question for this guy to string together five years for them where he averaged 35 homers and 100 RBIs.

GORDON VERRELL: Anyone who says that they never should have signed him is full of crap. It was seen as a great acquisition at the time.

Bill Plaschke and Eric Young give their perspectives. Plaschke covered Strawberry for the *Los Angeles Times*, where he is a talented and sometimes controversial sports columnist. Young played with Strawberry in 1991, spent the next five seasons with the Rockies, then returned to the Dodgers in 1997 as their top base stealer and second baseman. He was traded again, to Chicago, following the 1999 season.

BILL PLASCHKE: I'll never forget when he signed. After a long year, I had finally gone on vacation to Hawaii. But the week before I left, I had written that the Dodgers were very interested in Strawberry.

And nobody believed it. My own editors didn't believe me, because the Dodgers had never done that before. They had never paid huge money for some hotshot free agent. Now remember, they got Kirk Gibson, but he didn't cost nearly as much as Strawberry.

So Darryl Strawberry was almost like the Dodgers' first modern ballplayer. With all the problems and all the hype that went with it.

ERIC YOUNG: Kirk Gibson was history, and they needed a marquee player to replace him. And Strawberry was a very exciting hitter. Even the other players liked to watch him. They knew, every at bat, he could go deep.

TOT HOLMES: The fans went crazy for him at Vero Beach. I remember one batting practice. I saw him hit six balls over the flagpoles in center field, and they were 20 feet behind the fence, and the fence was 400 feet.

It was almost like he was hitting golf balls. Just that sweet swing of his, *click*, and it would be gone. *Click* and it would be gone. And everyone in the stands would be in awe.

This guy was absolutely a superstar, and had he stayed clean, he would have been among the best Dodgers ever.

TIM BELCHER: There was *such* a media crush, I actually moved my locker away from his. Darryl was just such great copy, even if he did nothing in the game. He was always going to say something off-color, controversial, or just plain strange.

TODD MOULDING: There's always been a lot of media here. But we were used to Kirk Gibson. He would protect us when the media got too close. Then Strawberry came aboard, and he seemed to enjoy the media circus.

So the expectations were high. The pressure on him was high. Darryl was gonna take us to the promised land.

In 1991 Strawberry struggled mightily in the first half. He had just eight homers at midseason, and his .230 batting average seemed etched in stone. But in his only productive season as a Dodger, he wound up with 28 homers and 99 RBIs. Moreover, says infielder Lenny Harris, Strawberry showed himself to be a team player.

LENNY HARRIS: We kept battling Atlanta for the division, and Darryl carried our team that final month. Then in our last game, after the Braves already won the division, we had the bases loaded with no outs. Then Tommy asked Darryl if he wanted to pinch-hit, so Darryl could get a chance at 100 RBIs.

Darryl told him, "No, that really doesn't mean anything to me." That's the type of ballplayer he was. And if we didn't have Darryl, no way we come that close in '91.

TODD MOULDING: The Braves beat us by one game. But the story that year was not the Dodgers failing. The story that year was the Braves. That was the beginning of the Braves.

And we knew we were in trouble after they won it. Ten years later, we're still in trouble with them. The Braves are still in the forefront. Who knows what would have happened had they not caught up with us in '91.

Moulding makes an interesting point. In 1991, after finishing last the previous season, the Braves went all the way to the World Series—one of the biggest turnarounds in baseball history. Subsequently, in the 1990s, Atlanta dominated the National League, winning eight straight division titles and playing in five World Series.

BILL PLASCHKE: In 1991, I felt the Dodgers could have won the World Series. I thought they were that good. But they lost out to the Braves that final weekend.

I think that began their downward spiral. Because that was their best team. They haven't had as good a team since then. And they still haven't found an answer for the Braves.

29

STRAWBERRY BLUES

1992-94

UNAWARE OF THE FIASCO THAT AWAITED, THE 1992 DODGERS HAD GREAT expectations. As in championship expectations. But then, why shouldn't they? With a then large payroll of $43 million, a veteran team that had finished just a scant game behind Atlanta one year ago, the addition of Strawberry's boyhood friend Eric Davis, and Strawberry coming off his strong second half, Los Angeles had every right to think World Series.

Then it became apparent: This was another Dodger team that couldn't field. As Ron Fimrite pointed out in *Sports Illustrated,* they not only led the major leagues in errors (169), but also "bonehead plays."

JAY HOWELL: Yeah, we didn't play sound baseball. We made a lot of errors. Tremendous amount of errors. We made a shitload of errors!

Jose Offerman made 42 himself. The third-year player was such an awful shortstop—and his teammates were not much smoother—that Lasorda told *Sports Illustrated*'s Fimrite, "I guess I've been wrong about this game all these years. I thought the easiest thing about it was catching the damn ball."

TOMMY LASORDA: I didn't dislike Jose Offerman. And he's still a very good offensive player. But I just never felt he was a good shortstop.

Neither did many other prominent Dodgers. So why did they keep Offerman at such a key position for so long?

Lasorda says "no comment," but this is what Bill James wrote in his absorbing book on managers: "There is reason to believe that Lasorda, left to his own devices, would never have played Offerman at shortstop . . . The Dodgers sometimes make those decisions in the front office and tell the manager to live with them."

This view is supported by reliever Roger McDowell, another former Met who joined the club in 1991.

ROGER MCDOWELL: That one came from Fred Claire. He insisted on Offerman as the everyday shortstop. Lasorda had to play the hand he was dealt.

GORDON VERRELL: But Fred wasn't just relying on his own instincts. He was listening to the scouts, who told him this Offerman kid could do everything. And he *could* do everything. He could go into the hole. He had a great arm. He just couldn't pick up a routine ground ball.

So in 1992, one year after the Dodgers finished a close second, just how pitiful a season was it?

TOMMY LASORDA: Let me put it this way. I was the first Dodger manager to finish in last place since 1905.

Eighty-seven years later, when the Dodgers went an unthinkable 63–99, their bats were nearly as useless as their gloves. They scored the fewest runs in the league as Strawberry and Davis both struggled with chronic injuries. In fact, Strawberry hit a paltry five home runs in only 43 games. Davis hit five homers in 76 games.

Troubled by his poor play and ailing back, Strawberry also struggled off the field. He had serious drug and alcohol problems, and though the public didn't know that yet, there were already some Dodgers who suspected he was living life too hard.

JAY HOWELL: Darryl was well liked. But then he started showing up late. He would get there five minutes before batting practice. And guys would grumble about that. I never really noticed him partying, because I never saw him out. But showing up at the ballpark late, always having a bunch of people hanging around him, that became noticeable.

ERIC YOUNG: I always figure when you bring a guy to his hometown, all the old friends, all the cousins, that you might not have seen for ten years, come out of the woodwork. When I say friends, I'm talking about your boyhood pals. So naturally you're gonna get with them. And, you know, Strawberry coming from South Central, there's a lot of activity going on there.

FRED CLAIRE: He would be late to the park or miss something. And I hammered him pretty good. Because I cared about Darryl. So I screamed at him. I yelled at him. I challenged him every step of the way. I recall one day at Dodger Stadium. He didn't show up until late in the game. I went right down and told the press. Because I never tried to look the other way.

However, when you are dealing with someone who has a substance abuse problem, denial is so strong. Deception is so strong. So I tried to the best of my ability. But, boy, when it was happening? And you were trying to get the evidence, and nail him for his own good? That was pretty tough to do.

In 1993 the Dodgers improved from a wretched 63–99 to a pedestrian 81–81 as catcher Mike Piazza won Rookie of the Year for his 35 homers, 118 RBIs, and .318 average. First baseman Eric Karros, showing glimmers of the big bat that he would provide all decade, hit 23 homers with 88 RBIs. Strawberry, however, played in just 32 games after a slow recovery from back surgery. He hit only five homers, giving him but 10 the past two seasons.

His personal life was an even bigger mess. In September, he was arrested for allegedly striking his live-in girlfriend. Later in September, he discussed suicide in a *Los Angeles Times* interview. Then, during the city's November wildfires, he flippantly said on the radio, "Let it burn. I don't live there anymore."

In May 1994, with two years still remaining on his contract, Strawberry's days as a Dodger abruptly ended. First, on Saturday evening, April 2, he homered his last time up in an exhibition game in Anaheim. But after an all-night drug and alcohol binge, Strawberry never showed up for Sunday's game. That's when a concerned and furious Claire tried locating his troubled outfielder.

FRED CLAIRE: I was absolutely worried about him. This is a big game. The last exhibition game. Darryl wasn't there. Where was he?

He called me that night at home. He said, "Fred, I'm fine. Everything is all right." I said, "Everything is not all right. Everything is not fine. Be in my office tomorrow morning. Be there with your attorney. Because I will not tolerate what is happening."

Then the meeting was switched to a law office in downtown Los Angeles. I met with Darryl and Robert Shapiro, his attorney. Before the conversation even started, Robert said, "Darryl has a substance abuse problem." Darryl, tears in his eyes, said, "Fred, I just want you to know I'm sorry I let you down."

That's a moment I'll never forget, because he meant it. He knew that he had lost a tremendous opportunity here. He knew that he had disappointed a lot of people, including himself.

On April 4, the eve of the regular season opener, the Dodgers announced Strawberry had a substance abuse problem and placed him on the disabled list. Strawberry then began a drug treatment program at the Betty Ford Center in Rancho Mirage.

ROGER MCDOWELL: I was not surprised. And, honestly, I felt he let us down. Here we are going into a new season and he's gone. I mean, we're supposed to care about him, but he doesn't give a shit about us.

Of course, on opening day, Lasorda was pressed by reporters for a comment on Strawberry's drug abuse. "First of all," Lasorda said, feeling himself getting angry, "it's against the law. Number two, it's harmful to your body. Number three, all it will do is lead you down the path of destruction. How anyone can be dumb enough or weak enough to take (drugs) is something I cannot comprehend."

Then Lasorda repeated what he said ten years before regarding Steve Howe. "This is not a disease, like leukemia or cancer. This is a weakness."

ROGER MCDOWELL: There was a public lambasting after that. Tommy really got beat up by some people. But that's how Tommy felt. And he was fed up with Strawberry by then.

MARK CRESSE: Tommy has strong opinions about drugs. He's always been very adamant about that. It's old school. And that's good. Drugs have no place in society or baseball.

TOMMY LASORDA: I never had a bad word for Strawberry. I was pulling for the guy. But I was sick and tired of people saying it was a sickness. And I got a ton of mail. I've still got a lot of the letters that I've saved. I've received probably a thousand, and every one of them was in my favor.

TOM VERDUCCI: I don't think Tommy and Darryl ever really got close. It sort of reminded me of Darryl's relationship with Frank Cashen. Frank had drafted him No. 1 for the Mets. But Darryl, as much as he respected Frank Cashen, just never related to the man. Never got close to him.

I think the same thing happened with Tommy. I think it's hard for Darryl to relate to that kind of older, white authority figure. It just didn't click. But I do know Tommy tried hard to make Darryl feel welcome. I know he tried to make him feel like part of the Dodgers.

So I think that's really why Tommy said some of those things. I'm sure it hurt Tommy, personally, that Darryl's life in L.A. was basically a lie.

TOMMY LASORDA: Darryl never had a mean bone in his body. My wife took him to church. I still love the guy.

But he could not resist the temptation. And he hurt the team, he hurt himself, he hurt the fans. That was wrong for him to do. And I told him so. He was a good man, he was a good friend, but he let everybody down and that's what hurt me.

On May 4, one month after confessing his drug habit, Strawberry completed his treatment at Betty Ford. His star-crossed homecoming saga ended on May 24 when he was released by the Dodgers, who were surprisingly in first place after failing to contend the past two seasons.

How hard a decision was this for Fred Claire, the man most responsible for bringing back Strawberry to L.A.?

FRED CLAIRE: Well, it really wasn't hard. Because the course had been run. We had given him every chance. We had given him all our support. We had done everything, in my judgment, that was humanly possible for an organization to do.

Dodger pitcher Tom Candiotti, one of baseball's best knuckleballers in the 1990s, calls Strawberry a "great guy with a big heart." And yet, he agrees with Claire's assessment.

TOM CANDIOTTI: It didn't work out for Darryl. It didn't work out for the Dodgers. It was probably best for everyone that he move on.

30

THE MIKE BUSCH
CONTROVERSY

1994–95

IN MAY 1994, *SPORTS ILLUSTRATED*'S RICHARD HOFFER WROTE A COLUMN entitled "Dark Days in La-La Land." Lamenting the collapse of professional sports in Los Angeles, Hoffer presented the Raiders, Rams, Lakers, Clippers, and Kings as teams that had lost their past glory or never had much glory to begin with. As for the Dodgers, wrote Hoffer, they "have not only been mediocre in recent seasons but have also now been tainted by scandal."

Hoffer was referring to a team that had gone five years without a playoff berth, and to Darryl Strawberry, whose series of personal problems had created far more headlines than his bat.

And yet, led by Piazza and Karros, 37-year-old center fielder Brett Butler, rookie right fielder Raul Mondesi, and a youthful pitching staff anchored by Ramon Martinez, the Dodgers led the National League West on the night of August 11, 1994.

At midnight, unfortunately, all major league players went out on strike.

ROGER MCDOWELL: We never thought it would wipe out the World Series. In the past the owners had always buckled. There'd always been cracks in their armor. A guy like Steinbrenner would go in and say, "Hey, listen, enough's enough. I'm losing a lot of money and maybe Seattle can afford to do it, but I can't."

But in 1994 the owners didn't buckle. They had just enough guys with heavy hands. And they basically shut the whole thing down.

Of course, *both* sides were hostile and bullheaded. When the owners claimed 19 of the 28 teams would lose money in 1994, the players said the owners were being dishonest. When the owners proposed a salary cap, saying this would help erase the financial disparities between large-market teams and small-market teams, the players flatly rejected the salary cap as a ploy to roll back their salaries and bust their union.

The bitter labor war lasted all fall and winter, scotching the 1994 World Series and angering millions of loyal baseball fans. Then in February 1995, not a single big leaguer broke ranks and came to spring training. Thus at Vero Beach, Lasorda and his staff worked with little-known players such as Mike Busch, a minor league third baseman whom the Dodger front office had asked to be a replacement player.

Busch, 27, knew there could be repercussions if he were to play in regular season games. But the six-foot five-inch Busch, a former All-American football player at Iowa State, says he was told spring training games were fine.

MIKE BUSCH: Before the spring training games started, I went to a lot of union meetings. The majority of the spokesmen said, "We don't really care about spring training. It's the regular season we're worried about."

And I explained to them, too. I had only committed to playing in the spring, because I wanted the exposure. And then I was going back to Albuquerque. I was not gonna play in L.A. if the strike still carried into the regular season.

GORDON VERRELL: Here's what another Triple-A player told me. Donald Fehr, head of the union, told these guys directly, or in some cases indirectly, that they could play in exhibition games. But if the season began and they still were playing, then, yeah, they would be considered scabs.

So now you take Mike Busch. In just one month during spring training, he's got a chance to earn what he'd probably earn all year in Triple A. And he got called a scab, and he got ostracized by major league players making $2 million a year!

MIKE BUSCH: Yes, that was a factor. We had a baby girl, my wife and I, and you don't make a whole lot of money in the minor leagues. So that was a major issue. I took care of my family first and went from there.

JOE McDONNELL: He was a scab. That's the bottom line. I know he came up with "I've got a family to feed." But you know what? There were a lot of people with families to feed who didn't cross the picket line.

The owners were trying to break the players union. They were trying to break the strike. And by these other guys taking jobs—whether it be in spring training or regular season—they were being used by the owners as tools to break the union and the strike.

I think you either support the union or you don't. And if you don't, you gotta figure on some consequences.

Those consequences would come the last week of August. First, after seven months of acrimony, the baseball strike finally ended the week before opening day. The players then went through a brief "spring training" before the strike-delayed season began on April 26.

Four months later, on August 29, the 1995 Dodgers had a tenuous one-game lead in the National League West. That's when general manager Fred Claire threw his clubhouse into an uproar by calling up Mike Busch from Triple A.

The Sporting News called this a "silly mistake." *Sports Illustrated* took a harder line, pointing out that "Claire decided to risk the chemistry of his first-place team to add a platoon third baseman who hit .269 in the minors."

But Claire says he made the move simply because he needed another third baseman after starter Tim Wallach injured his knee. And since he couldn't pull off a favorable trade, Claire looked to Albuquerque, where Busch had 18 homers and 62 RBIs to accompany his .269 average.

This made Busch the most qualified candidate, Claire says. Furthermore,

Claire says, he had promised the replacement players that appearing in spring training games would not have any bearing on their future.

FRED CLAIRE: So then the '95 season comes. And I called up Mike Busch. Well, I knew the players would not be happy. But my obligation was to bring up the best player that we had to help us win games. And that's exactly what I did.

Of course, this required some prior debate, and Lasorda says he warned Claire that he was making a big miscalculation.

TOMMY LASORDA: I told him not to bring him up. And I told him why. We were playing Cincinnati and they brought up a guy named Reed, and the players on our bench went crazy when they saw this guy pitching. They were screaming at him, calling him every name you could think of.

I said, "What are they gonna do when they have one of these guys on their own team? You're gonna have a problem with this thing."

TOM VERDUCCI: This was also on the heels of a real ugly situation in Houston. They brought up Craig McMurtry, another replacement player, and the other Astro players raised holy hell. So unless Claire was naive, totally naive, he must have known he was playing with dynamite.

CHRIS GWYNN: I was scratching my head. I didn't understand it. We were in first place, and we had other guys who could play third base.

But this was during the time when the management and players were still not on good terms. And they were gonna send a message to us. I mean, there's no way they thought that Mike Busch was gonna make that much of a difference.

JOE MCDONNELL: The feeling at the time was that Dodger management did this to stick it to the players. "Okay, you walked out on us last year. Screw you. We're doing this now."

I don't doubt that for a second. They're gonna tell you, "Oh, we brought

him up because we needed help. And we thought he could help us win."
Bull. They were using Mike Busch to stick it to the players.

BILL PLASCHKE: I think Fred was doing what Fred always subtly did.
He was telling the players that it was not their clubhouse. He was telling the
players the Dodgers were bigger than them. And this was not their team. It
belonged to the city of L.A., and it belonged to the Dodgers, and they were
the ones who ran it.

GORDON VERRELL: What the players maintained was that Fred should
have run this by them in the clubhouse. But Fred maintains, "Who's running the club?" Well, he almost found out. I mean, there was a rebellion.

It began on August 29 when Busch arrived at Dodger Stadium. After the
players told him to leave the clubhouse, voted to return him to the minors,
and failed in their attempt to convince Claire, they refused to play catch
with Busch before the game. They would not take batting practice with him.
When he took infield practice, there was nobody standing at first to take
his throws from third.

The shunning of Mike Busch was done in plain view. Any fan at Dodger
Stadium could see it. And when the papers came out the next morning with
quotes from Butler calling Busch a scab—and a photograph of Busch sitting alone in the dugout during the game—the Dodgers had their biggest
controversy since Al Campanis had self-destructed on *Nightline*.

ERIC KARROS: No one had forced him to cross the picket line. He
chose to cross. And that was very shortsighted. So there were some rami-
fications.

But as far as being hard on him, I wouldn't say we were hard on him. We
did not harass him or abuse him. We just didn't deal with him.

MITCH WEBSTER: I did it, too. I gave him the silent treatment. It was a
bad deal for everyone. It was not fun. But as major league players, we knew
there were guys before us who fought for our rights. There were guys like

Curt Flood, who basically got crucified, back in the days when players had no rights. They were basically just a piece of meat. So to see any of that work undercut by your own ranks is just terribly disturbing.

JOE MCDONNELL: Well, they should have shunned him. He was a scab. Of course the fans took his side. They felt, "Oh, this poor guy is getting trashed."

MIKE BUSCH: I knew there'd be a situation when I got there. But I didn't care. This was my first time in the big leagues. And since I was a little kid, that was my dream.

So I put up a hard shield before I got there. Then I went about my business. I went out and did my job.

MARK CRESSE: The good thing about Busch is that Busch is like six foot five, 220 pounds. And he was a great football player at Iowa State. So he wasn't going to be intimidated or pushed around. Here's a guy who could pinch their heads off if they said too much. That's why there wasn't a whole lot of face-to-face. They weren't cocky at all face-to-face. But they did do real good in the newspaper.

BOB COSTAS: I think it's an indication of how totally lacking in perspective the Players Association has become and the players as a group are. If your team acquires a felon, here are guys who, literally, say, "Hey, it's okay with us. Everyone deserves a second chance. As long as he can help us, we're happy to have him in the clubhouse."

These are guys who happily dress next to multiple-time drug offenders. Next to some of the biggest horse's asses who've ever walked the earth in any walk of life. Next to guys who have beaten their wives, showed up late, and tanked on their team in big games. I'm not saying these guys are universally popular, but you don't hear anyone publicly condemning them.

But the single greatest pariah is a replacement player. "We couldn't possibly play catch before a game with a replacement player. We'd sooner come in proximity with Typhoid Mary." I mean, this is so intellectually bankrupt that it's a joke. My God, a replacement player! Oh, the most odious of individuals. And hey, you know, we'd love to have Albert Belle. We have no problem with Albert Belle. But, my God, do we have to hang around with Mike Busch?

Dodger fans agreed overwhelmingly with Costas. On August 30, they gave Busch standing ovations before and after his first big-league at bat (a strikeout on three pitches). Meanwhile, the fans booed Butler, a staunch union supporter, like few Dodgers had ever been booed at Chavez Ravine.

TOM CANDIOTTI: Butler was really upset. Karros was upset. I was upset. I mean, it was really tough to hear all those people cheering for Mike Busch.

JOE MCDONNELL: Butler got killed on that. The fans just went berserk. But Butler was 100 percent right. The only thing Butler did wrong was talk about it. It would have been better for him if he kept his mouth shut.

BRETT BUTLER: It was just the American underdog type of thing. He was the underdog. I was the bad guy. I was the player rep, who was supposedly the ringleader, who told everybody not to talk to Mike Busch. Which was not true. That was just the way it was portrayed, because I was the one speaking on behalf of the union. So, yes, those days were tough. They were tough on Mike Busch and tough on me. He got shunned for a number of days. I got booed by 50,000 people.

MIKE BUSCH: Brett was the one being quoted in the paper. And then, of course, the majority of the L.A. fans didn't really respect his views. They swallowed it really hard. Then they let Brett know about it during the games.

BILL DWYRE: In letters to the *L.A. Times*, we received more letters on the Mike Busch thing than on anything we've ever had. The only thing that has brought up more hate and anger over the years is every USC-UCLA game.

The huge majority of the letters were pro–Mike Busch. The fans saw the players as fat cats. They saw Busch as just a guy trying to take advantage of this Rocky-like shot that he had.

See, the fans cannot relate to million-dollar players as union guys. A union guy ought to carry a lunch bucket, or go down into the mines. They should not carry briefcases into the locker room and talk to their stockbroker before the game, and get in their limos and Porsches afterward. That isn't a union member to the fans.

After Mike Busch's arrival, the first-place Dodgers had lost two games to the Mets. Moreover, says Derrick Hall, the franchise now had a public relations nightmare.

Hall was their PR director from 1994 to 1998—one of the most tempestuous times in club history. Then he left to host a popular radio show before returning to the Dodgers as their senior vice president.

Here he recalls what happened on the third day of the Mike Busch episode.

DERRICK HALL: Brett was a smart guy, and he knew that he was getting killed publicly. So he came to me and Fred and said, "I'd like to hold a press conference. And I'd like Mike Busch to be there." And Mike Busch, to his credit, said he would do it.

TOM VERDUCCI: I was at that press conference. Butler kind of kissed and made up with Busch. I think Piazza and Karros went up there, too. But I got the sense their hearts weren't into it. Those guys were standing up there because they had to. I think they were blown away by the backlash from the fans. But I think, deep in their hearts, they hadn't forgiven Mike Busch.

MIKE BUSCH: There was still electricity in the locker room. So they wanted to have a meeting, in front of the cameras, to let everybody know that things were fine now, we were getting on with the season, that kind of thing. I mean, just try and whitewash everything.

Of course, that didn't take care of anything. Everybody could tell just by looking at the TV screen. What a bunch of crap.

DERRICK HALL: *Nobody* was relaxed. It looked tense and almost staged. But because they went through with it, publicly, it was too late to go back. They could no longer treat him that way.

TOMMY LASORDA: Well, let me tell you about how that thing ended. See, I did not want him called up, because I knew there would be problems. And there were some problems. Big ones.

So then I told Butler to call that press conference. And then I told the players, "I don't care whether you don't like Mike Busch. I don't care if you don't ever want to talk to Mike Busch. But I'm gonna tell you something. Mike Busch is wearing a Dodger uniform. And when I put Mike Busch up to hit and he gets a base hit, when he comes back in the dugout, you better shake his hand. Because when he walks through that clubhouse door, Mike Busch is a Dodger. And you better do everything to help him." It ended the whole situation.

Of course, as Lasorda, Busch, and Claire point out, it also didn't hurt when Busch had several key hits during September, including a pinch-hit homer that helped Los Angeles clinch its first division title since 1988.

Busch didn't make the postseason roster, however. He watched on TV as the Dodgers got swept (0–3) by the Reds in the first round of the play-offs. Afterward they were labeled underachievers, a team with sufficient talent but too many cliques. Some critics said, in fact, the only time the Dodgers seemed truly united was in their anger toward Mike Busch and Fred Claire.

As for Major League Baseball, it would take three more years and the great home run race between Mark McGwire and Sammy Sosa to heal most of the wounds from the destructive players strike of 1994–95.

CHRIS GWYNN: Well, I still think it was worth taking a stand against the owners. But it wasn't worth blowing up the World Series. The World Series and playoffs are sacred, you know?

TOT HOLMES: That was as black a time in American baseball as the 1919 Chicago White Sox scandal. I'm talking about the strike, *and* the reaction to the replacement players.

That whole thing really turned off a lot of my friends. And it put me to the test. Had I not been as strong a baseball fan, I would have dumped the game like a whole lot of other people that I know.

ERIC KARROS: I remember there was a strike when I was in high school. I said, "How can these guys go on strike? How can there be a labor stoppage? I mean, I play this game for nothing!"

So I had the same kind of views. But unless you're involved in this game, understand the business aspects of it, you can't say what you would or wouldn't do. Because I completely support what happened in '94.

But you can't explain that to people outside of baseball. And you spend your time spinning your wheels if you even try. Because you know what? Nobody cares. Nobody gives a rat's ass. They just want to see baseball.

31

A LEGEND STEPS DOWN

1996

BRETT BUTLER AND MIKE BUSCH, TWO MEN WITH LITTLE IN COMMON THE PREvious summer, had similar reactions to the news of Tommy Lasorda's heart attack on June 24, 1996.

BRETT BUTLER: Tommy was like a father figure to me. He·was wonderful to my family, my wife, my children. When he had his heart attack, my son Blake was in the pool. I said, "Blake, I wanted to let you know that Uncle Tommy had a heart attack."

My mother had just died. And Blake thought Tommy had died. And it just crushed him. That's how close Tommy was to me and my family.

MIKE BUSCH: Tommy and I had a good relationship. He was very professional toward me. Tommy treated me like I was just another guy under his command. He is such a good baseball man, such a good human being, it was really hard on us when he got sick.

After Lasorda, at the age of 68, underwent an angioplasty on June 26, he was replaced on an interim basis by his top bench coach Bill Russell.

And immediately the industry started talking. Would Lasorda return to the dugout that summer? If he did make it back, would the Dodgers retain him for his 21st season in 1997?

"I recognize that there's going to be a certain amount of speculation, but anyone looking to next season is way beyond where we are right now," said Fred Claire. "The No. 1 issue is Tommy's health. Nothing is a close second."

The 1996 Dodgers were 41–35 and had a two-game lead in their division when Lasorda was hospitalized. Over the next five weeks, they went a mundane 14–16 under Russell. Then, on July 29, at his emotional news conference at Dodger Stadium, Lasorda announced his retirement as manager. Russell would run the club the rest of the season, and Lasorda would move upstairs as a vice president.

Lasorda stressed that this decision was his. He was quitting, he said, fighting back tears, because he was concerned about his heart. "For me to get into uniform again, as excitable as I am . . . I decided that it's best for me and the organization to step down as manager of the Dodgers."

Still, his resignation raised a number of questions. In the aftermath of his heart attack, hadn't Lasorda vowed to keep managing? Didn't he still love the job? Did he truly volunteer to leave the dugout, or was Lasorda pressured by the front office?

Tim Kurkjian and Dave Wallace give their perspectives. Kurkjian is a senior baseball writer for *ESPN the Magazine* and an on-camera reporter for *ESPN* television. Wallace is the New York Mets' pitching coach, and held the same job with the Dodgers from 1995 to 1997.

TIM KURKJIAN: There were all sorts of rumors that Tommy was adamant about coming back and that he was absolutely angry when he didn't come back. I personally don't think he wanted to step down. I think Tommy was forced, to a degree.

But it wasn't anything malicious. The travel was getting harder. The job was stressful. And Tommy was up there in years.

DAVE WALLACE: Tommy *never* wanted to retire. That's just the way Tommy is. But I don't think the front office pushed the issue.

My take on it was—and I was pretty close to the situation—that Mr. O'Malley feared that Tommy's health was at risk if he managed again. And

I distinctly remember Tommy coming back, and he did not look good. It wasn't the Tommy of old, and it made you wonder.

FRED CLAIRE: Peter and I expressed to Tommy that we were concerned about his health. It's a very high-pressure job. This is a man who's had a heart attack. And Tommy had talked about the death of Don Drysdale. He had talked about the death of Don McMahon—right on the mound at Dodger Stadium.

But we still concluded that the job was his. What we said to Tommy was, "If you want to continue to manage, your uniform is in your locker downstairs. It's totally your decision."

So the thought that Tommy was forced out is 100 percent wrong. The decision he made was totally his own.

DERRICK HALL: Peter still had confidence in Tommy. He had just extended Tommy's contract. But I think after this hit, everybody stepped back and said, "Wait a minute. We think of Tommy as Superman, and he's not."

Then there was a meeting at Dodger Stadium. And Tommy had the option. Peter said, "Tommy, you can go back on the field. We'll let you manage. However, I don't think you should. Dr. Mellman doesn't think you should. Your heart specialist, Dr. Reid, doesn't think you should. So here's what I propose. You and Jo decide on this together. You can still manage this team if you want to. But regardless, you're a Dodger for life. I'll give you a vice presidency, which you have definitely earned, and we'll take care of you."

And Tommy and Jo thought about it, talked about it, and I remember Jo crying and bawling and saying, "Tommy, this is the right thing to do." And Tommy made the decision. He said, "I think it's probably time."

Several people close to Lasorda have weighed in, and now the question is put directly to him. Did the front office push him into retirement?

TOMMY LASORDA: That's wrong. That's radically wrong. Peter O'Malley told me, "Whatever decision you make, we'll all be happy about it."

Now, at first, I wanted to come back. I wanted to come back really bad. Then what happened to me was I got scared. Because I thought about Don

Drysdale. Don Drsydale and I went up the elevator together in Montreal and I said, "Hey, Big D, let's have breakfast." He said, "Call me." He was dead the next day.

I thought about Don McMahon dying in my arms down there after throwing batting practice. I thought about John McSherry walking off the field and dropping dead. I said, "What the hell am I gonna do, go down there to die?" I said, "No way."

Then I really got scared because the team was out of town, and I was coming to the ballpark and I felt tired. I said to myself: "If I'm tired coming in here at one in the afternoon, how am I gonna feel when I leave at midnight? And if I can't go down there and manage the way I manage—I scream, I jump up, I holler at the umpire, I holler at the opposition—then I'm not going back down there. Because then I'm not the same guy."

So I said at the meeting, "Peter, would you excuse me? I want to take my wife out and talk to her." My wife and I walked out and I said, "Honey, what do you think?" She said, "Tommy, you're the only one that can make that decision." And I said, "Something is telling me not to go down there." And she said, "You just found your answer."

I went back in and told Peter that I just didn't think I could go down there. Peter looked at me and he said, "I'll accept that. And you are now a vice president of the Dodgers." And I got up and hugged him.

Now, for the people who said that I was forced out, let me give you a little picture. If I were forced out, do you think I would still be working for the Dodgers? Do you think that I wouldn't have raised some kind of hell about that? *Say, hey, wait a minute, I had a heart attack and now I've lost my job? What did I do wrong? The team was in first place.*

So if they had said to me, "You can't manage the Dodgers anymore," I'll guarantee you one thing. The whole world would have known about it, and I would have walked out of there and never walked back in. I would have been really, really upset, because no player who ever played for me lost his job because of an injury. *Nobody.*

So, yeah, I've heard the skeptics. But all I say to them is, "Hey, I don't care what you believe, or what you don't believe. Because I *know.*"

In 1996, when Tommy Lasorda resigned after 20 seasons at the helm of the Dodgers, he had had more victories (1,559) than any active manager in baseball. He had produced nine Rookies of the Year, more than any manager in baseball history. Lasorda had won seven division titles, four pennants, two world championships, and secured himself a place in the Hall of Fame. Above all, there was his bottomless passion for baseball.

BUD FURILLO: Ted Williams told me in 1985, "Tommy Lasorda is the best ambassador baseball ever had." I think Ted Williams would know.

BILL DWYRE: Any business, any sport, any pursuit in life, needs personality. You can have the most qualified person running your business, being your CEO, being your manager, and if that person has no charisma, it just won't work. Particularly in a public entity like the Dodgers.

Tommy Lasorda was always interesting. He always made the Dodgers interesting. It was a huge loss for baseball when he stepped down. A huge loss.

GEOFF WITCHER: I've never seen anyone in baseball, including Ernie Banks, who got famous for the expression "Let's play two," who had more energy, more enthusiasm for the game than Tommy Lasorda.

But because he had so much personality, because of the Hollywood stuff and bleeding Dodger Blue, he may never have gotten the credit he deserved. Lasorda was a very good manager. In 1988 he outmanaged Tony La Russa in the World Series. In fact, he was magnificent all year.

BILL PLASCHKE: Was he a great manager? He had some great years. And 1988 was the greatest year I've ever seen of any manager. He won the World Series with a team that had nothing. Bob Costas was right. That was the worst team I've ever seen in the World Series.

KIRK GIBSON: Tommy was a character. He was intense like me. He was a pretty goddamn good manager, too.

In the summer of 1996, while Lasorda moved into his vice presidency, the Dodgers finished the season under Russell, a much more stoic leader who had played 18 seasons for the Dodgers and had managed for two years at Albuquerque before returning to Los Angeles as Lasorda's top bench lieutenant in 1994.

With his status beyond that season still uncertain, Russell went 49–40 after replacing Lasorda. That secured second place and a wild-card spot, but Los Angeles would have won its division if not for a total collapse the season's last week. The Dodgers had a 2½-game lead with only four games to play. They lost all four games, including the last three at home to San Diego.

Then for the second straight season, the Dodgers were swept in the first round of the playoffs. This time Atlanta beat them in three games, and out came the charges again of underachieving. After all, said their critics, how could a team with Piazza, Karros, Mondesi, Ramon Martinez, and Hideo Nomo not win a single playoff game in two years?

But was the underachiever label valid? Were these Dodgers teams of the mid-nineties truly that gifted? Or were they average teams saddled with unreal expectations?

TOM VERDUCCI: I thought they had pretty good talent. Maybe not '98 Yankees talent. But I thought there was enough talent to do better. So I definitely think they underachieved. And a lot of that had to do with the chemistry there.

MARK CRESSE: There was no fire in the belly. There was no fiery leader. There was no Kirk Gibson, who would get right into a guy's face if he was doggin' it. I don't know why that was. But some players play cool, and some players play balls-out. We just didn't have those balls-out players.

TOM CANDIOTTI: The Braves were tough to beat in '96. Talentwise, they were better than us. But the tough thing to swallow was how we just choked off against the Padres. All we gotta do is win one game at home? And we lose all three?

I still don't understand it. There just wasn't that intensity. That feeling if you lose this game, you're going home.

JOE MCDONNELL: To be swept by the Atlanta Braves is not an embarrassment. But that San Diego series was a joke. And that's when I knew this team had some problems, because they didn't seem to care if they won the division or not. All they cared about was making the playoffs.

Let me qualify that. There were some guys who cared. I know Karros cared. But there were other guys who I don't think it mattered to.

ERIC KARROS: Well, I'm not saying those things aren't important. But when people start talking about chemistry or desire or intensity, I think that's the easy way out.

Because you have to be realistic. And the reality is, sure we had a good team, but we didn't have a deep team. We had weaknesses. We weren't solid one through 25.

So while we definitely had talent, we were not a team that would just steamroll. We had very good teams, but were we World Series teams? Well, a lot of things would have needed to go right for us.

BILL RUSSELL: I think they played as hard as they could every day. But it comes down to pitching, too. You look at the Dodger teams I played on. You look at the Yankees. You look at Atlanta. The name of the game is pitching.

Now look at the Dodger pitching when I was there. They had some good young arms, but sometimes it takes a little while for them to develop. That's the bottom line.

ROSS NEWHAN: The Dodgers had a weak bench. They lacked balance in their batting order. They particularly lacked left-handed power, which made them real vulnerable to right-handed pitching.

So in 1997 I finally wrote that the Dodgers had not underachieved. They had probably gone as far as they could talentwise.

TIM KURKJIAN: I know the Texas Ranger teams were like that. They'd have four or five really big-name guys, but then everybody else was ordinary. And I'm convinced now in baseball that the way to win is having all the pieces. They don't all have to be great pieces, but the pieces must be assembled. And I'm not sure the Dodgers ever had all the pieces.

So maybe, myself included, this is what people missed throughout the nineties. We all overestimated the Dodgers. We all overrated a little bit. Maybe they just weren't that good, but we expected more, because they always had some big-name guys.

32

THE O'MALLEYS SAY
FAREWELL

1996

THE NEWS OUT OF DODGER STADIUM CAME WITHOUT WARNING. PETER O'Malley, the patriarch of baseball's oldest family dynasty, was putting up a FOR SALE sign on the Dodgers.

O'Malley made the stunning announcement on January 6, 1997— 47 years after his father, Walter, bought a majority interest in the Brooklyn Dodgers. Peter O'Malley was 11 then. Now, at age 58, he was relinquishing control of one of the most respected and stable organizations in baseball.

Many longtime Dodger watchers were shocked, and then a bit skeptical when he said his main reason for selling was family estate planning. If O'Malley died while still owning the Dodgers, his beneficiaries would have to pay an estate tax of 55 percent on all assets after the first $5 million. If O'Malley sold the team, however, he would only be liable for a 28 percent capital gains tax on his profits from the sale. "Call this a preemptive strike," O'Malley said.

But as Bill Madden observed in the *New York Post*, "Estate taxes are something you worry about when your health starts failing or you reach retirement age. Peter O'Malley is 58 years old, trim, and so far as anyone knows, in the best of health. He has hardly been acting like a man getting ready to retire."

Another important factor, O'Malley said, was baseball's radically chang-ing economics. "Professional sports is as high risk as the oil business," he said. "You need a broader base than an individual family to carry you through the storms. Groups or corporations are probably the way of the future."

Since he was always loath to plaster Dodger Stadium with advertising, or to stick it to fans by raising ticket prices, this notion seemed more credible than his professed concern about estate taxes. Some people, however, felt that O'Malley downplayed or kept private at least three other key reasons why he was selling:

- His diminished role in baseball's policy making.
- His contentious relationship with then acting commissioner Bud Selig.
- His anger at Los Angeles politicians for not supporting his effort to land a National Football League franchise and build a new sta-dium for it at Chavez Ravine.

BUD FURILLO: People used to say that Walter O'Malley ran baseball. They said Walter told Bowie Kuhn what to do. But that was actually Peter. When Bowie Kuhn was still commissioner, Peter was Bowie's boss.

GORDON VERRELL: Peter used to wield a lot of power. But then Bowie Kuhn got ousted against his wishes. And with the owners like Ted Turner coming in, the Steinbrenners, and more recently the Reinsdorfs, they just kind of shoved him out. He was no longer in the inner circle.

TOT HOLMES: Walter O'Malley would eat those guys for lunch. And if Peter has a fault, it's the fact that he isn't aggressive. He doesn't have a mean streak.

But Peter, in my opinion, was also trying to do what he thought was best for baseball. He kept saying, "We have too many labor problems. We've got to form an alliance with the players union. We can't remain adversaries, where every three years they strike and baseball suffers."

I think the owners were saying, "Wait a minute. This isn't the way I run U.S. Steel. This isn't the way I run Chrysler Motors. *I* tell *them* what to do."

And Peter tried to explain that you can't hire a shortstop the way you hire another rear end man.

TOM VERDUCCI: I think things might have been different had there been another commissioner. If Peter was somehow able to get another commissioner in there, maybe Peter might have hung on. But by the time he sold, it was clear that Bud Selig wasn't going anywhere.

DERRICK HALL: When the O'Malleys started discussing the future, I don't think his kids had much interest in taking over. And I think Peter just saw, "Hey, I'm the end of the line here. My kids aren't gonna take over the Dodgers."

Number two, he lost complete power among baseball owners when Bud Selig took over. It became small-market owners versus large-market owners. They said, "Peter is not on our side," and they forced him out.

He was off every executive committee at that point. And I think he felt very bitter toward the Major League Baseball owners.

BILL PLASCHKE: I do think it had to do with his estate taxes. Peter saw what happened to Joe Robbie's family. When he died, they had to sell the Dolphins in order to pay the taxes. So Peter worried about that.

I think he was also tired. He and Bud Selig were jousting. He and Selig were rivals when Selig still owned the Brewers. It was Bud Selig, small-market, and Peter O'Malley, big-market. They were battling, and Bud won. Bud became the commissioner. So, yes, he lost some clout inside of baseball.

The third thing is, I really think Peter thought that he'd move right into football as an owner. He wanted to build a new football stadium next to Dodger Stadium. And it turns out it wasn't there. At least not yet.

So he lost the political battles in L.A. for that stadium. He lost the battles in the boardrooms with Selig and the other owners. In the end, Peter was tired of all the jousting.

Plaschke's boss, Bill Dwyre, the well-connected sports editor of the *Los Angeles Times* and a close friend of Peter O'Malley, says, "There's no question why he sold the Dodgers. I can tell you exactly why he sold them."

BILL DWYRE: He fell in love with the idea of having an NFL team. He spent lots of time meeting with NFL owners. They fell in love with him. NFL owners like to have in their club people they're comfortable with at their cocktail parties. Peter is it. He may be the only guy in L.A. who they're comfortable with to this day.

Now, at this point, Peter still plans on owning the Dodgers. Or maybe he'll sell part of them to investors, but he would still keep 51 percent. Because Peter correctly sees that now he has a way to diversify his investments and make it viable to still run a baseball team. Because now you got a pro football team, which starts every year with $79 million in cash from TV before you sell a ticket. Pretty good deal.

So Peter starts working with Bob Graziano on this. This is where Bob Graziano comes to the forefront. Very bright guy. Legal things and real estate. And so then Mayor Riordan comes to Peter. Riordan says, "We need the National Football League. We need this in this city. You're the man. You got to do this."

Well, then things get complicated. Councilman Mark Ridley Thomas starts seeing that if the NFL goes to Dodger Stadium, the Coliseum won't get the NFL, the Coliseum is dead, and that's his constituency. And Mark is a very bright guy and a very strong politician, and he and some others in that area impose upon Riordan that the Coliseum can't just sit there and die. It has to stay viable.

So Peter O'Malley gets a note to call the mayor's office. And Peter still keeps the little pink slip of paper. He keeps the message to call the mayor's office, because he remembers it. It sticks in his craw. And according to Peter, it wasn't Riordan who said, "Could you back off?" It was one of his aides. He said, "We need you to back off, because we need to get the whole community behind the Coliseum deal."

Now Peter's pissed off. He needed this, financially, to stay viable in baseball. And he also wanted a new project. The Dodgers were still Walter O'Malley in many people's minds. And so Peter really wanted this football stadium. He wanted to be the guy who brought the NFL back to Los Angeles. He wanted his own legacy, which he had every right to. And the politicians took all that away from him. And look what the politicians ended up with. Nothing! There is no NFL team in Los Angeles!

So Peter got pissed off. Then he put the Dodgers up for sale. And you can talk about the economics of baseball, and the labor negotiations, and the fact that Peter thinks Bud Selig is not a strong commissioner. And all of those things played into it, but the straw that broke the camel's back is here comes Riordan and the city saying, "Well, thanks, but no thanks, we'll go a different direction. And it was nice that we could use you for a year, while you spent $1.5 million on your plan, but now we're gonna look elsewhere, because of politics."

The money was not an issue. But Peter understood fully what had happened. And there was a lot of anger. That's when he said, "We're going to sell the Dodgers."

As for Peter O'Malley's legacy? In 26 of the 28 years he served as team president, the Dodgers attracted more than two million fans. They hit the three million mark in 13 seasons, more than any team in baseball history. In 1997, *Fortune* magazine picked the Dodgers as one of the best 100 companies to work for. No other sports franchise made the coveted list.

On the field under O'Malley's aegis, the Dodgers finished either first or second 19 times. They won five pennants and two world championships. But their ledger also showed a recent decline. They did not win a single playoff game during the 1990s.

TOM VERDUCCI: If you're going to pass blame, certainly it has to go upstairs, too. You can't just lay that on Fred Claire or Bill Russell or Tommy Lasorda or Mike Piazza. I think in some respects Peter got complacent.

But when people start to look back, I think they will also remember the stability. That was such a remarkable run, with just Alston and Lasorda there for so many years. The way managers change today, people will probably look back and not believe it.

TIM KURKJIAN: It's one of the great franchises of all time. You can make a case for it being, after the Yankees, the most historic franchise in the history of baseball.

So I think Peter's legacy will be a good one. He took over from Walter, who set up the franchise perfectly when he went west, and then Peter was very successful in his own right.

NEIL SULLIVAN: Both O'Malleys should be in the Hall of Fame. Walter should be there now for what he did to nationalize the game. Peter should be there later for what he's done to promote the game internationally.

There are enormous opportunities in Asia. In Latin America. If baseball does things right, it could become like soccer internationally. And Peter O'Malley has been right at the forefront. He was an absolute pioneer of international baseball.

In late 1996, as Peter O'Malley sized up prospective buyers, he wanted one who shared his vision for the promotion of baseball internationally. He wanted a buyer who would keep the Dodgers in Los Angeles. And to withstand baseball's changing economics, he wanted a major corporation "with broad shoulders."

It wasn't made public yet, but O'Malley's choice was Rupert Murdoch's Fox Group, a subsidiary of the News Corporation, the global media empire that included the Twentieth Century Fox movie studio, the Fox TV network, Fox Sports Net, the *New York Post*, the *Times* of London, *TV Guide*, and HarperCollins book publishers among its more high-profile properties.

The Australian-born Murdoch was not a baseball fan. In fact, he had not seen a game at Dodger Stadium since moving to Los Angeles in 1986. Murdoch was, however, a staunch believer in the value of sports programming. He made that plain in 1994 when Fox spent an astonishing $1.58 billion for the right to broadcast NFL games. His critics said that Murdoch overpaid, but the purchase helped cement Fox as the nation's fourth TV network.

Since then, Murdoch had gained control of a number of regional cable sports channels. One of them, Fox Sports West, would now televise the Dodgers. Thus Fox wouldn't have to pay those expensive TV rights, and it couldn't lose the rights when they expired (the way CBS lost the NFL to Fox).

Murdoch bought the Dodgers for $311 million, which was then the most ever paid for a sports franchise. Thus it was said again that Murdoch bid too high, but in addition to the Dodgers, he also received Dodger Stadium, the prime real estate it sits on, and the Dodgertown facility in Vero Beach.

Moreover, like Peter O'Malley, Murdoch saw the huge potential of promoting baseball internationally. In fact, Murdoch owned international satellite systems, and one day he envisioned televising Dodger games around the world. As he told stockholders in 1996, "We intend to use sports as a battering ram and a lead offering in all our pay-television operations."

Of course Murdoch's deep, deep pockets and his aggressive nature made some Major League Baseball owners anxious. There was even speculation that the owners would marshal together and block the transaction. But in March 1998, when the exhaustive approval process finally ended, only two of 30 owners cast negative votes, and one was Murdoch's longtime foe, Ted Turner.

In April 1997, with the Dodgers already for sale, but Murdoch not yet announced as the chosen buyer, the team began its last season under O'Malley. The manager was still the quiet Bill Russell, who had experienced difficulties after replacing the emotional Lasorda the previous summer.

MARK CRESSE: Tommy spent three seconds a day not talking. Billy spent three seconds a day talking. So the players were used to more communication. It wasn't like Billy was a bad manager, but there wasn't a lot of fire there.

DAVE WALLACE: Billy Russell was a Dodger all his life. Billy knows the game. But any time there's a change after that long-term a manager, an icon and a Hall of Famer, there's going to be rumblings and unsettled waters.

BILL RUSSELL: I followed a guy who was there for 20 years. But Tommy followed a guy who did 20 years, too. And Tommy did a great job when he took over. But he also inherited a lot of talent.

So, yes, it was a challenge to come after Tommy. There was no question about it. But you've heard it said many times: You're only as good as your players. Well, it's as simple as that.

DERRICK HALL: I wouldn't say every player turned on him. Not at all. But, yeah, some players had their problems with him.

BILL PLASCHKE: Tommy's biggest strength was his longevity. His players knew Tommy would be there longer than they would.

Suddenly, in Russell, they had a guy on thinner ice than they were. So they started talking about him off the record. Second-guessing him. Taking a little bit more advantage of him.

TOM CANDIOTTI: Things started popping up in his second season. He had that incident with Valdez. Then he had that incident with Astacio.

Candiotti is referring to pitchers Ismael Valdes and Pedro Astacio, who each confronted Russell in the dugout during the same turbulent week in early June. Though Valdes stuck around after his outburst, Astacio soon got traded for ex–Dodger second baseman Eric Young.

ERIC YOUNG: Those pitchers were upset that Russell was taking them out of games too soon. That's what I heard when I got there.

And you got to remember, players got to respect their manager. And if you don't respect him, you're gonna challenge his leadership. And that's what happened there.

MARK CRESSE: They didn't want to be taken out. He took them out. They showed him up. They went into the dugout, ranting and raving. That should not be done. The manager makes the decision, and you gotta live with that.

Now if you still got something to say, you can go in the clubhouse and say it. But you don't do it in public. You know that with modern-day coverage, as soon as a pitcher gets pulled, one camera follows the pitcher, just hoping he'll show up the manager. That's a fun thing for those camera guys. They live for that. Then they show it every ten seconds on TV.

DERRICK HALL: Yeah, those cameras hurt. Those cameras killed him. Especially with Valdes, because it started on the mound and went back to the dugout. And Russell actually pushed Valdes.

With the Astacio incident, Astacio just snapped. Then he came after Russell in the dugout, and Russell moved his hand, like "Get outta here. Let's do this up in the tunnel."

FRED CLAIRE: They exploded publicly, and Billy looked confrontational with them. But I think both players acknowledged that they didn't handle the situation well.

BILL RUSSELL: They're tough competitors. They weren't pitching well at the time, and I got into their face to motivate them. And they just both reacted.

I wouldn't want it any other way. I wouldn't want them to hang their head and walk into the clubhouse like they're defeated. I want them to fight back, and that's what they did, and there's nothing wrong with that. Unfortunately, it happened with all the cameras watching.

TIM KURKJIAN: When players and managers yell at one another—right in the dugout, on national TV—that becomes a story anywhere. But when you're mild-mannered Bill Russell, managing the Dodgers, following Tommy Lasorda, and anything goes wrong, it's bound to be bigger than if it happens in Minnesota or Detroit. It's always magnified in Los Angeles.

No argument here. Yet after a shaky first half, Los Angeles led its division by two games on September 16. Then, during two crucial season-ending series, the Dodgers lost five straight games to the Giants and Rockies. Which meant dating back to 1995, they had gone 0–3 against Cincinnati, 0–3 against San Diego, 0–3 against Atlanta, 0–2 against San Francisco, and 0–3 against Colorado in their five most important series. Their combined record in these key games: 0–14.

In 1997 the team's late swoon cost it a playoff spot. That's when Russell was questioned publicly by reporters, off the record by players, and face-to-face by Claire for some debatable tactics down the stretch.

FRED CLAIRE: We let that season get away from us. We should have been in the playoffs. There were some game situations . . . there was one game against Colorado that very frankly we never should have lost.

I realize it probably sounds like a second-guess. But I said so at the time. I wasn't pleased with how '97 ended. Billy knew it. I wasn't a happy camper.

Meanwhile, the Dodgers were tagged as underachievers again—this time for not only failing to win their division, but for yielding it to the makeshift Giants, a team with only one star, left fielder Bobby Bonds.

As *Sports Illustrated* wrote in late September: "In a matchup with L.A., the Giants have a clear edge not only in heart but also in left field. The Dodgers get the nod just about everywhere else."

The *Los Angeles Times* asked later, "Is this a team that simply can't handle pressure, a team that chokes?"

ESPN the Magazine took a broader view: "The recent travails of the Dodgers—no postseason wins the past ten years, no postseason at all last year, outclassed in '97 by a Giants team with nowhere near the talent but ten times the heart—clearly have hardened their laidback following."

ESPN the Magazine was right. Even the Dodger faithful were ready for change.

33

THE BUTLER–PIAZZA–*L.A. TIMES* EPISODE

SPRING 1998

IN 1998, A YEAR OF TURBULENCE, TO SAY THE LEAST, THE VERY FIRST ERUPTION came on March 1. In that morning's *Los Angeles Times*, retired Dodger Brett Butler called Mike Piazza a "moody, self-centered '90s player." Butler also said, "Mike Piazza is the greatest hitter I've ever been around. But you can't build around Piazza because he's not a leader."

After slamming Piazza to the *Times'* Bill Plaschke, Butler was promptly ripped by several Dodgers who rallied around Piazza at spring training. Then Derrick Hall did, again, what all good publicity men do. He tried to stop the bleeding.

DERRICK HALL: I remember calling him up. I said, "Brett, Plaschke really got you there." He said, "I didn't say that." I said, "Brett, don't do that. Don't say I was misquoted. That doesn't work. Just be prepared because these players aren't happy with it."

And they weren't. They came to me and said, "Hey, we want to get a quote out." And I said, "Great." So I got some of the writers together and Todd Zeile and Eric Karros and Eric Young, and they all went to Mike's defense. They said, "This is so untrue. This guy just wants to win."

Butler heeded Hall's advice and never disputed the accuracy of his quotes. He did, however, issue a press release criticizing the *Times'* story as "a senseless display of journalism."

BRETT BUTLER: I'll probably regret this, but I'll tell you exactly what happened. The guy comes to my house. Is here for two days. Sees my son play roller hockey. Comes and watches my son play basketball. And we're in my office and he says this to me: "So what do you think about Mike making a hundred million dollars?" And I said, "Mike's probably the best hitter I've ever played with. You know what? He'll probably get it."

And then his response was: "Well, would you build your club around him?" And I said, "Well, probably not. There are times when Mike can get moody and self-centered. We all get like that, but it's more prevalent today in the '90s player."

So what I basically said was a general statement about today's '90s player. That's how I said it. And the headlines in the papers the next day were: "Butler says that Piazza's a moody, self-centered '90s player."

Well, that's not what I said. I made a comment, which was obviously left out, that there are times when Mike's moody, and we all get like that, but it's more prevalent today in the '90s player.

So I made a general statement. And because there was nothing going on in spring training, he put a personal touch on it. He put Mike Piazza out there. Because why? Because Mike was getting ready to try to sign this contract. Well, then the headlines came out. And I was shocked.

BILL PLASCHKE: He never said that I misquoted him. If he says that in your book, then it's the first time.

I absolutely did not misquote him. We were sitting around and I asked him about Piazza, and he just started talking about Piazza, and talking and talking. And then I'm writing this down, and Butler *stops* talking so I can catch up writing.

So then I wrote some more and more and more. And I thought Brett was purposely sending a message from the grave to his teammates, who didn't have the power to say this stuff.

I mean, Brett Butler was right. Since then, Mike Piazza has matured. Mike has changed and grown up quite a bit. But at the time, Brett Butler was right. And in a little while, after that season started, everybody was saying Butler was right.

Of course, the ethical argument is—and I've discussed this in several journalism classes—"You went to to his house to do a story about him as a retired gentleman farmer. Why are you writing about this as well?"

Well, this is what he *said* while I was down there. And my company is paying me to report about his life. And that was part of it. What he said. So I ended up doing two stories—a gentleman farmer story and also this.

Plaschke's boss at the *Times* gives his perspective.

BILL DWYRE: Plaschke was at spring training with me, and he went to see Butler. He was going to do a column on how Brett Butler was doing with the cancer that he had and everything. And in the course of the conversation Butler went off on Piazza.

Then Plaschke called me up. He said, "I went to get a feature and a news story broke out." And Butler never did say he was misquoted. He just thought that we stressed the wrong thing. Well, you can't tell us that. We're the journalists.

So it was just a situation where a guy got caught. And the sad thing is, there are some lesser reporters who would have let him get away with that. Some guys would have said, "Well, he didn't mean it."

But Plaschke's a newspaperman, and when a guy says that in a newspaper situation, it's fair game. So, again, it's just a guy who got caught with his guard down. And I'm afraid that's the news biz.

Piazza has repeatedly declined to comment on his experiences with the Dodgers since leaving the organization. But others are willing to discuss the Butler-Piazza episode, as well as the question raised throughout Piazza's career in Los Angeles. Did he in fact lack leadership qualities?

LENNY HARRIS: Piazza isn't rah-rah, if that's what you mean. He lets his bat do the talking.

FRED CLAIRE: You judge a player on the total scope of what he is all about. There wasn't anybody contributing any more to our team than Mike Piazza.

ERIC KARROS: I don't think that Plaschke went looking for this. But when he got a little taste, he decided to run with it. It really didn't benefit anybody. It's just a nice way to create some controversy.

As for some of the comments, I don't know exactly what Brett said. But what defines a leader anyway? Mike is not the type who's going to be a leader in the clubhouse. But isn't hitting .330, driving in 100 runs, and hitting 35 homers good enough?

ROSS NEWHAN: His remarks about Piazza strike me as the kind of things we're hearing now about Sammy Sosa and Mark McGwire. These guys are hitting 60 home runs and driving in 140 runs, and suddenly they're not team players. Well, these guys are already doing their parts. Now put a good team around them.

TOM VERDUCCI: Butler probably spoke words that other people in that clubhouse were thinking all along. But I think that happens often with star players. There was a blowup years back with Tony Gwynn and the Padres. Jack Clark and Mike Pagliarulo contended that Gwynn was selfish. And I heard a lot about Wade Boggs being selfish.

My take on it was that Piazza definitely is very aware of his offensive statistics. Piazza wants to be known as the best hitting catcher of all time, and I think that's why he's stubborn about playing another position.

As for Butler, I always thought he was a great team player. Then about '95 or '96, people started telling me that the guy just cared about himself. That's a time when the Dodger clubhouse was notorious for having no team chemistry in there at all. And Butler was definitely one of those people that they pointed to.

TIM KURKJIAN: A lot of people felt like Butler was a '90s player also. So they thought it was a little out of line for a guy who wasn't particularly well liked to come out and take a shot like that at Piazza.

As for Piazza, the rap on him's always been that maybe he takes his offense behind the plate with him. If he's stumbling at the plate, if he's upset he hasn't gotten his hits, he takes it behind the plate and he isn't nearly the defensive catcher that he should be.

I can live with all of that, however, given the offensive numbers he throws up there.

MITCH WEBSTER: I would say that Mike was hot and cold. If he didn't perform, he could go into a shell.

MARK CRESSE: I don't know what Brett's purpose was there, rapping on Mike Piazza, but it wasn't real smart, because Mike was pretty popular in L.A.

Mike did get moody, though. If I had one knock on Mike Piazza, that would be it. When things were going good, he was a great guy. When things would go bad, he would turn into a monster.

He would go into these moods where he'd be completely irate if he didn't get a hit. We would win, and if he went 0–4, he'd be pissed off. And that's when he would get his criticism. When you win, everybody's supposed to be happy.

So some things Brett Butler said about him were true. But at the same time, all in all, Mike Piazza's the kind of guy you want on your ballclub.

34

———— • ————

PIAZZA'S STORMY EXIT

1998

By THE 1998 SEASON, IF HIS DEFENSE AND LEADERSHIP WERE STILL GRIST FOR debate, Mike Piazza had proven to be a fabulous hitter. Further, he'd done it against remarkable odds. A 62nd-round draft choice, he was selected as a favor to Tommy Lasorda, who grew up in Norristown, Pennsylvania, with Piazza's father, Vince, the son of an immigrant who became a millionaire in the auto industry.

Demie Mainieri explains how being a "courtesy pick" shaped Piazza's early years in professional baseball. Mainieri coached Piazza at Miami–Dade North Community College, where Piazza hit .364, but still would have been passed over if not for Lasorda.

DEMIE MAINIERI: Tommy talked the Dodgers into picking him. Then on top of that, here's a kid who comes from a very rich family. So he must be spoiled, right? He must be a stereotypical, spoiled rich kid.

But Vince is a hard worker. Vince is a self-made guy. And he instilled that in Mike. You know how many hours Mike spent lifting weights? You know how many hours he spent in the batting cage?

One night I called him and I got his mother. I said, "This is Coach

Mainieri. Can I talk to Mike?" She said, "Oh, I'll go get him. He's down-stairs hitting in the batting cage."

Now this was Christmas Eve. He's been in the league four years and he's taking batting practice off a pitching machine in the basement. That's a kid who's willing to work hard.

In 1993 the determined Piazza won Rookie of the Year after batting .318 with 35 home runs and 112 RBIs. Another three big offensive seasons followed, and then Piazza was due for a hefty new contract. In January 1997 he and his agent, Dan Lozano, wanted $60 million for six years.

In retrospect it would have been a bargain, while possibly making Piazza a Dodger for life. But the Dodgers, who had just gone up for sale, rejected Piazza's demands on the grounds that such an investment should only be made by the new owners. When a compromise could not be reached, Piazza ended up filing for arbitration before signing for two years at $15 million.

DERRICK HALL: At $60 million for six years, it would have been a lot less than what he got offered later. It also would have ended the problems right there.

ROSS NEWHAN: There were a lot of things, pre-Fox, that grated on Piazza. That negotiation was one of them. He was their best player and he had two years before his free agency. So that was the time to give him a multi-year contract.

But it turned into a difficult negotiation, and he signed for only two years. That was a big mistake on the part of the Dodgers.

In 1997, beginning his two-year deal, Piazza batted .362 with 40 home runs and 120 RBIs. It was his biggest season thus far, and now he wanted a long-term contract extension. In fact, he and Lozano gave the Dodgers a February 15 deadline. Without a new contract by then, Lozano said, "Mike will play out the year (1998) and test the free agent market."

How much did Piazza-Lozano seek this time? Most reports put the figures at $100 million for seven years. This would make Piazza the highest-paid player in baseball, and the game's first $100 million man.

TOM VERDUCCI: There were a couple factors going on there. One of the big things was that this was the first big deal for Piazza's agent. Dennis Gilbert had always run that agency, but Gilbert had just left. So this was their first opportunity to make a really big signing on their own, and what better way than to crack the $100 million barrier?

So they figured that Piazza was the guy—and that the Dodgers had the money. But it was a total miscalculation on their part, because they weren't dealing with Peter O'Malley anymore. They were starting to deal now with the Fox people, who every day had negotiated contracts much bigger than this. And they basically made it clear that they had dealt with bigger fish than Dan Lozano, and that they weren't going to be bullied by him.

The other thing happening was that Piazza and Lozano are really close friends. So it wasn't like Lozano was just his advisor. It was like two friends trying to get a deal done together.

But I always say, ultimately, the player must make the choice. Piazza has to step in. If it's really true he wants to stay in L.A., then that was the deal to get done. In fact, the deal he wound up signing with the Mets is for less money per year than what the Dodgers offered him. So obviously the Dodgers had nothing to apologize about.

On February 15, 1998, though Lozano's deadline passed without a contract extension, the negotiations continued. On March 19 the baseball owners approved Peter O'Malley's sale to Fox. On March 31, opening day, the Dodgers lost 6–0 at St. Louis as Mark McGwire launched his record-breaking season with a grand slam.

That's when Piazza made a serious blunder. After the season opener, he complained to reporters about his stalled negotiations. Piazza, who would be paid a team-record $8 million that year, said he felt "underappreciated" by the Dodgers. He also felt "disappointed and confused," which a lot of Dodger fans took to mean *distracted.*

ROSS NEWHAN: Here it is opening day. You're trying to establish a good feeling for the new season. And you've got your primary player popping off about his contract situation.

BILL PLASCHKE: Mark McGwire hits a grand slam, the first of his 70 home runs that season. It was a great baseball day, a tough Dodger loss, and all Piazza wanted to talk about was his contract and how unhappy he was. That struck a sour note with the L.A. fans.

TOM VERDUCCI: That was the turning point. That's when Dodger fans started to turn on Piazza.

DERRICK HALL: I knew he was frustrated, but I didn't know he was that frustrated. Then the writers came to me and told me what he said. Then I talked to Fred Claire and it came to a head.

We all came back the next day and I pulled Mike aside. I said, "Look, there's a couple ways you can go about this. You can either take back everything you said in a nice way, or just say this is how you feel and go forward as you were doing." He said, "Well, it is how I feel, and I'm just not gonna say anything else about it."

Then Fred came over and took him in the back room. Fred said, "If you want out of here, I'll trade you." I mean, Fred loved Mike, but Fred was very upset. The situation had gotten very nasty.

And personally, yeah, you're right, it was a PR nightmare for me because here is the star player, the biggest thing in L.A.—it's him and Shaq—and he's saying on opening day, "I want out of here."

ERIC KARROS: Bad timing. It was bad timing on his part. I mean, he brought that on himself. But does that mean people should start booing? I mean, shouldn't his contract situation be irrelevant to the fans? That's between Mike and the Dodgers. The fans don't have anything to do with it. Whether they think they do or not.

Karros and Piazza came up through the minor leagues together. When they became Dodgers, they shared a bachelor pad in Manhattan

Beach. Thus, Karros should not be faulted for defending a close friend.

Still, Karros may be missing the point. Piazza made his contract the fans' business when he chose opening day to gripe about it.

ERIC KARROS: Yeah, well, you still have to understand Mike's history with this organization, and what was done that off-season. I mean, the Dodgers went out and gave Raul Mondessi a six-year deal. It was a four-year deal with a two-year option.

Yet they can't make a commitment to Piazza? They're screwing around with him and they're signing somebody else? I mean, come on. Their numbers were night and day.

This time Karros makes a better argument. According to several sources, Mondessi's new and lucrative multi-year contract signed in January 1998 was one of the crucial factors in Piazza's bitterness toward the pre-Fox Dodgers.

On April 7, 1998, exactly one week after his ill-timed comments on opening day, Piazza was booed mightily at the Dodger home opener. On April 8, the Dodgers made Piazza their final offer of six years at $80 million. It wasn't the seven years Piazza wanted. It wasn't the $100 million. But at more than $13 million per season, it was the biggest offer in baseball history. And when it got rejected by Piazza, the two sides agreed to terminate negotiations until after the current season ended.

BOB COSTAS: My impression from a distance was that the Dodgers felt they had made him the most generous possible offer, and it still wasn't good enough. So they decided, at least at that time, that they would draw a line. Obviously the line moved a year later with Kevin Brown.

TIM KURKJIAN: If I were Mike Piazza, I may not have accepted that money, either. As greedy as that sounds, that is what free agency is there for. It was built for guys like Mike Piazza to go out on the open market and see what they're actually worth.

But I also don't think Piazza was very happy being a Dodger by then. If he was, he would have been thrilled to take that deal.

So I think he was ready to move on. I don't blame him for that. I don't blame the Dodgers, either. It was time for some new chemistry on that club.

It certainly seemed that way on May 15 with Piazza's free agency looming and the Dodgers a listless 19–21. Still, L.A. fans were shocked when a blockbuster trade was announced with the Florida Marlins. Piazza and third baseman Todd Zeile were exchanged for All-Stars Gary Sheffield, Charles Johnson, and Bobby Bonilla, along with Jim Eisenreich and Manuel Barrios. Only one week later, the Marlins shipped Piazza to the Mets.

Oddly enough, the Piazza deal wasn't made by veteran general manager Fred Claire. It was brokered by Chase Carey, chairman of Fox Television and one of Murdoch's most trusted advisors, and also by Bob Graziano, Peter O'Malley's handpicked successor as Dodger president.

So where did that leave Claire, who had recently discussed a possible Piazza trade with Florida? So far out of the loop he nearly resigned.

FRED CLAIRE: I had been talking to the Marlins about acquiring Johnson and Sheffield. But I had never mentioned Bobby Bonilla. Well, then I got a call from Bob Graziano. He said, "Chase has completed the trade and it needs to be announced tonight." I said, "Well, there will be two announcements tonight. I'll announce the trade, then I'll announce my status. Clearly you don't need me if somebody else is going to be making the trades."

So I was not happy with that. Said I wasn't happy. That was that.

DERRICK HALL: Fred didn't resign, but he called a press conference. That's when he told the media, "I am the man." He said, "I'm the general manager of this team. I make the decisions, and I'm gonna make the decisions. From now on, no one ever does that again."

That was the big "I am the man" day. There were big headlines: I AM THE MAN. So he kind of took on his bosses at Fox, and that was disastrous.

By now you may be wondering: Where was Tommy Lasorda during all this? Since becoming a Dodger vice president in 1996, he had rarely been utilized by general manager Claire and manager Bill Russell. In fact, Lasorda felt stung and cast aside.

As for the Piazza trade? Lasorda first heard about it from a radio station asking him to comment.

In less than two months, Lasorda would reemerge as a powerful figure in the organization. But for now his role was ceremonial, and with Claire's position tenuous at best, Graziano moved to center stage.

"I recommended the deal to the people at Fox," he told reporters. "I think this helps improve our chemistry, helps improve our hitting, and helps improve our defense. I think the team is markedly improved."

Everyone under the sun, including Graziano, now knows the Piazza trade was a huge bust. In fact, in September 1999 there were published reports that said the Dodgers wanted to reacquire Piazza, but the New York Mets were having none of that.

BILL CAPLAN: Like I told you before, I was a Dodger fan since I was seven years old. And for me the saddest departure was Piazza's. That was devastating. Still is, and always will be as long as Piazza is playing ball.

Trading him was an absolutely huge mistake. This is not to say anything bad about Kevin Brown, but if they didn't have $90 million for Piazza, how can they turn around and give $105 million the next year to Brown? Brown is a guy who pitches every fifth day, and he was 34 years old when he pitched his first game. Piazza's an everyday player who was the best hitter in the history of the L.A. Dodger franchise.

I still love the Dodgers, and I always will. But they should have figured a way to keep Piazza. In a sense, it was like Boston letting Babe Ruth go.

Okay, the trade was bad. It was very bad, even though Sheffield would prove to be a valuable addition. But now let's take away hindsight. How was the blockbuster deal perceived at the time?

ERIC YOUNG: Shocked. Shocked. Shocked. I just didn't think it would happen right when it did.

But it didn't look to me like a bad trade. We were getting three All-Stars and giving up one All-Star. I thought it might help the team.

DERRICK HALL: I remember thinking: "Wow. If we're gonna lose Piazza anyway, why not get Sheffield, Johnson, Eisenrich, Bonilla. Yeah, that's a heck of a trade."

BILL PLASCHKE: I thought it was a good trade. I thought Chase Carey had guts. The Dodgers were stagnant.

TOM VERDUCCI: At the moment he left, it wasn't like people looked back on the Mike Piazza era very fondly. They never went to the World Series with him. They never even won a playoff game.

On the other hand, I'm still blown away to this day that the biggest trade of the century was consummated by a TV guy. And I also thought what they got for Piazza was just okay. I remember the Dodgers saying they needed to move quickly. That once the word got out that they were trading Piazza, it would have been a nightmare.

And I understood that. One morning the story is in the *L.A. Times*—the Dodgers are shopping Piazza—and then all hell would break loose. Every day the players would come to the ballpark wanting to know what the latest rumor was.

But I say, so what? Live with the nightmare. Make everybody know that Mike Piazza is available and try to get a bidding war going on. But they basically dealt only with the Marlins. So I'm not sure they got the best deal that was out there. And I'm not sure how many teams would have taken Bobby Bonilla.

BILL PLASCHKE: I was worried about Bonilla. But I thought Charles Johnson would be a stud.

MARK CRESSE: Defensively, Mike Piazza is average at best. He may be a little below average. So everyone was excited about Charles Johnson, especially when it came to stopping the running game, because other teams were running wild on Mike.

BOB COSTAS: Charles Johnson was coming off a great World Series, where he got some national attention. A lot of people thought that he was the best defensive catcher in baseball. So he was expected to help their pitching staff.

And even though the Dodgers may have been criticized *since* then for this trade, things were different at the time. Piazza was getting his share of criticism and booing.

Still, Piazza was definitely their best player. He was their marquee player. Well spoken. Nice looking. Good guy to have as the centerpiece of your team. The greatest hitting catcher, at least by the numbers, in baseball history. So he was a tough guy to lose.

MARK CRESSE: Overall, I didn't like the trade because I had known Piazza since he was a kid. But they offered Piazza $80 million, and when he turned it down, they said, "We're gonna lose this guy at the end of the season. He'll become a free agent and we'll get nothing. So let's see if we can get something for him."

That's really all it was. I don't think they had any big problems with Mike. Plus this was the first major move for the Fox Group. They wanted to hit the news with a blockbuster. They didn't want to come in with a little bang. So they came in with a boom. They came in and rocked it.

35

UPHEAVAL AT CHAVEZ RAVINE

1998

On June 21, 1998, five weeks after the Mike Piazza trade, how were the reconstructed Dodgers faring? Well, this is how the *Los Angeles Times'* Ross Newhan started his national baseball column that day:

> Hard to believe that the Dodgers and Colorado Rockies are conducting a four-game series in mid-June—with their summers seemingly over. Face it. The Rockies are dead in the National League West, and the Dodgers are close to it, struggling to keep their wild-card hopes alive.

Newhan's column came out on Sunday morning. That afternoon in Denver, where the Dodgers fell to a lifeless 36–38 after losing their third of four games to the lowly Rockies, general manager Fred Claire got a phone call from team president Bob Graziano. When Graziano wanted Claire to meet him at Dodger Stadium later that Sunday, after the team got back, Claire was not entirely surprised. He thought Graziano was going to fire manager Bill Russell.

FRED CLAIRE: Bob had continually wanted to talk about Bill, as far as making a move. I was urging patience. We'd gone through the Piazza trade.

We'd gone through the Nomo trade. We'd gone through the Randy Johnson trade discussions.

So I felt: "This is June. Let's give our team a chance to get its feet on the ground. Then let's see where we are and go from there."

The denouement came that fateful Sunday night at Dodger Stadium, where Claire's earlier suspicions were confirmed. Russell, in fact, was getting his pink slip. And Graziano had other big news, too.

FRED CLAIRE: Bob said he couldn't recommend me on a go-forward basis. He said I was being replaced by Tommy Lasorda.

BUD FURILLO: I can tell you how that all came down. At the end of '97, when they didn't make the playoffs, Peter O'Malley had everyone on their toes. So they knew they needed a good start in '98. Otherwise it looks terrible for the new owner. They buy a team and suddenly it's collapsing.

So then as '98 started, all the attention was focused right on Bill Russell. But then they quickly traded Piazza and Nomo. So Fred's contention was: Let them settle down. Let them just play.

Well, they didn't settle down. They got worse. So, fed up and remembering what Peter said, Graziano made the double switch. He dismissed Claire, too.

Russell and Claire were replaced on an interim basis by Albuquerque manager Glenn Hoffman and vice president Tommy Lasorda, respectively. And according to Graziano, who announced the dramatic makeover on June 22, he had done more than "remember" O'Malley's edict. Graziano said that he had spent "countless hours" with O'Malley, still the team's board chairman after the sale, getting O'Malley's "advice on the best way to right this team."

Thus at the same June 22 news conference, a reporter asked O'Malley if he supported firing Claire and Russell, who had worked a combined 63 years for the Dodgers.

"I've been asked probably 100 times the hypothetical question—'Peter, if your family still owned the club, would you have done the same thing?'—

and the honest answer is yes," O'Malley said. "I've been disappointed in the team's performance, felt we were flat and have been for some time. I think it's time for a change."

Of course, this provoked some skepticism. "Right," wrote Murray Chass in the *New York Times.* "And he would have become a middle-aged hippie, too." Thomas Boswell asked in the *Washington Post,* "Is that right, Peter? Is that why, when you and your family really were in charge, no Dodgers manager had been fired in the last 45 years?"

What went unremarked upon, however, by these two great columnists and possibly every columnist east of Los Angeles is that the O'Malley Dodgers were never all that benevolent behind the scenes. As early as 1958, and then again in 1962, Walter O'Malley wanted to fire Walt Alston, but in each case Buzzie Bavasi saved Alston's job. In 1976, according to several top players from that era, Alston was forced into retirement by Peter O'Malley. In 1996, although Lasorda says it isn't true, some longtime Dodger observers think Lasorda was pressured by Peter O'Malley into stepping down as manager.

On the other hand, there was the timing of the Fox-owned Dodgers: Claire and Russell got canned before the All-Star break even arrived.

BOB COSTAS: What made this remarkable was not that a manager or general manager was fired in midseason, but that it was the Dodgers. If they were gonna make any move at all, their past history would have indicated that you make it cleanly—at the end of one season and prior to the other.

So I think it was just out of character for the Dodgers. If it was another organization, it's not historic. It's just that week's story.

TOT HOLMES: It was definitely un-Dodgerlike. Maybe they should have been relieved of their duties, but not in the middle of the year like that. I thought the whole purge was just too quick.

ERIC YOUNG: I don't think they gave Russell enough time. His whole lineup changed when they made the Piazza trade. I thought he would get more time for us to mesh.

ERIC KARROS: I don't know if Russell really ever got a fair shake here. I don't want to say fair shake, but I don't know if he ever felt comfortable. I think he was always looking over his shoulder. Like if he didn't win today, then *oh, man.*

Fred—I was shocked. I could not believe that. I thought for sure he would be given the year. Then they would make their evaluations afterwards.

BILL PLASCHKE: Do it at the end of the year, and I don't think anybody would have any problems with it. I mean, I was one of the ones writing that they hadn't won a playoff game in ten years. And I was Russell's biggest critic the year before. But Russell was learning the job, and the team was learning him, and I think he deserved the rest of the year. I think Fred Claire deserved the rest of the year.

TIM KURKJIAN: If you look at Fred's whole stay, it obviously was not a successful one. They didn't win a whole lot after 1988. And Fred did make some bad trades. He traded Pedro Martinez for Delino DeShields.

JAY HOWELL: Fred hit some home runs and he made some big mistakes. He brought in Kirk Gibson. But he also traded Pedro Martinez. Can you imagine how much better the Dodgers would have been during the '90s if they had kept Pedro Martinez?

TIM KURKJIAN: Now, when that trade was first made, everybody, including myself, rated that as a pretty good trade for both teams. So that should be pointed out in fairness to Fred.

FRED CLAIRE: I liked Pedro a lot. But we felt we needed a second baseman. Delino was a young second baseman with superstar ability. So it looked like it would be an outstanding trade.

Of course, it didn't work out. Pedro has become one of the game's top pitchers. And Delino has never reached the levels that I felt—and a heck of a lot of other people felt—that he was capable of.

TOM VERDUCCI: I had more of a problem with the way Fred Claire got fired than with the timing. I thought they essentially fired him when they made the Mike Piazza trade. I thought they publicly embarrassed him by keeping him completely out of the loop on such a big deal. So I knew this guy was not long for the job.

Claire also wasn't a Fox guy. He just moved way too slowly for them. They like to fly by the seat of their pants, make a decision and move on, and Fred is just the opposite. So I think his firing was inevitable.

As far as Russell goes, he had serious problems in the clubhouse. He had a fractured team that seemed to be getting worse. I don't think he was a great game-manager. I thought the Dodgers were underachieving, especially the pitching staff.

So on a purely baseball level, there were reasons to fire the manager in that case. I think it's easy if you're a columnist to paint the Fox people as the bad guys. These guys come in and start bloodletting immediately, and everybody calls to mind the Dodger history and how long their managers have stayed on and they never fire a manager in the middle of the season. But that doesn't mean it should be run that way forever. Times change, and if you think you need to make a change, then make it. Why wait until after the season?

ROSS NEWHAN: Fred's situation was clearly tenuous, so that was not a shocker. And the club wasn't performing under Russell. So he was vulnerable, too.

But coming off the road? And being told to come to Dodger Stadium that night? Maybe that wasn't the best way it could have been handled.

FRED CLAIRE: I think it could have been handled differently. I think it could have been done in a better fashion. But ownership has the right to do what it feels is best. I don't argue with that. I don't debate that at all. Ownership always has the right to make changes.

BILL RUSSELL: No one likes to get fired, especially three months into the season. So obviously I think we should have been given more time. At least finish out the year before you decide if you should make changes.

But I also understand the situation. New ownership, big investment, the team's not playing the way they thought it should. They thought they could bring in some people and make a big impact. They thought they could make a big statement, real quickly.

If they had to do it over again, would they do the same thing? Who knows? But I thought they should have given it more time.

DERRICK HALL: The team wasn't performing, and everyone liked Glenn Hoffman. I mean, the reports were glowing on Glenn. He's a super guy, his players love him, he knows baseball, and he's your Triple-A manager. So you think, "All right, let's give him a shot."

In Fred's case, I really think Fox tried to give him a chance. After Piazza got traded, they said, "Embrace the trade and it was yours. You made the trade."

I think if Fred had done that, maybe he would still be working for the Dodgers. But Fred wanted it to be known that he didn't make that trade. And that's when he told the media, "I am the man."

So it was a matter of time. And Fred was very classy when it happened. He called a press conference at the Ritz Carlton in Pasadena. All of his friends in the media were there, and I went there, too, on behalf of the Dodgers, to sit back and listen and sort of take notes.

Fred said, "They're entitled. That's their prerogative. New ownership, they can make changes." Then he ended it by saying, "I want to work in baseball again." And that was smart. That was Fred.

As for the deposed Russell? He went out in a burst of controversy (although as we mentioned in the Alston years, and as we will get to again, he now blames this controversy on someone else).

First, a little more background. Since 1996, when Russell replaced Lasorda as manager, both Russell and Claire had rarely consulted Lasorda in his new role as team vice president. Moreover, most of the local media knew it, including the *Times'* Bill Plaschke and Jason Reid. Plaschke called it "strange" that management had decided "to cut him (Lasorda) out of major league decisions." Reid pointed out that Lasorda felt "cast aside" during the final years of former general manager Fred Claire's reign.

Which leads us back to June 23, 1998—one day after Claire and Russell got fired and Lasorda returned to power when he was appointed interim general manager. That morning in the Long Beach *Press-Telegram*, Russell was quoted as saying by Doug Krikorian, "Tommy's just vicious when he wants something. He did the same sort of thing when he was a coach under Walter Alston and wanted Alston's job. Tommy's been second-guessing me ever since I took over for him. Why? I don't know. All I know is that we haven't spoken for months."

Responded Lasorda, "That's ridiculous, a lie, and you can tell Russell that. I haven't been in town this much that season, and no way I've been campaigning for any job."

Now, before the principals respond, several observers give their views on the Russell-Lasorda rift that still finds them not talking to this day.

JOE MCDONNELL: Tommy and Russell were really close at one time. And when Tommy stopped managing, Tommy was the guy who handpicked Russell. Then I think Tommy felt slighted, because Russell didn't consult him, didn't keep him close, didn't ask him for any advice. So their relationship became very strained. And it was a bit ironic, because it was Tommy who wanted Russell as manager.

BUD FURILLO: I talked to Tommy about it. I said, "Why the hell didn't you talk to Bill Russell? The way you avoided him in training camp and never talked to him."

He said, "Why did he get the job? Because I picked him to get the job. Then Bill Russell never called and thanked me."

That was Tommy talking. And he was miffed.

BILL PLASCHKE: Tommy is too smart to organize any kind of campaign. But Tommy is loud and emotional. And when he was mad at somebody or disagreed with somebody, people around him would hear it.

So did he start a campaign to undermine Russell? I was never aware of that. But would Tommy get mad and say stuff? Yes. And because he was Tommy, people would listen.

TOM VERDUCCI: Do you remember when Russell had those blowups in the dugout with his pitchers? The story I heard is that Lasorda told some friends—and he might have gone on the radio with this, too—that he was mad at Russell for not calling him for his advice on how he would have handled those situations.

And when Russell heard that, he just blew up, and he just started killing Tommy to the writers, mostly off the record. The way I understood it, that was the turning point: when Tommy criticized Russell, and Russell turned around and criticized Tommy.

Russell's televised clashes with Ismael Valdes and Pedro Astacio both occurred in June 1997. Then in August 1997, at his Hall of Fame induction in Cooperstown, Lasorda was asked a loaded question: If he was starting a team from scratch, who would be his first choice as manager?

ROSS NEWHAN: Lasorda said Bobby Valentine, the manager of the Mets. Which I considered to be a slap at Bill Russell. I think Tommy was saying, nationally, that I'm not high on this guy.

BUD FURILLO: Yeah, I think it was a swipe at Russell. But the truth is, Tommy and Bobby Valentine go way, way back. Tommy managed Bobby in the minor leagues. And they became and stayed extremely close.

Then Bobby was ticketed to be the starting shortstop with the Dodgers. But because he smiled all the time, Walt Alston didn't like him. He got rid of him. That's how Russell got the shortstop job.

TOM VERDUCCI: By his Hall of Fame induction, Lasorda and Russell were not on speaking terms. But that obviously pushed it over the edge.

BILL RUSSELL: It really hurt for him to make a statement like that. Because even if he felt it, there's no reason for him to say it in that situation. I know Bobby's his friend, but I've been with him longer than Bobby has. So it just tells you what Tommy's thinking is.

TOMMY LASORDA: Somebody asked me a question. I thought the guy meant outside of Billy Russell. I thought he meant *other* than Russell, because he was already managing the Dodgers. So I felt it was a compliment to Bobby, and it wasn't even regarding Billy Russell.

BOBBY VALENTINE: Tommy took a lot of heat for that statement. And I don't think it was a slap at all at Russell. Tommy wasn't asked who the best manager was, or who he would like to see manage the Dodgers. They said if he had the opportunity to be a general manager, who would he like to work with?

Well, that was the day that Tommy went into the Hall of Fame. And I happened to be on his mind when this off-the-wall question was presented to him. So he answered it honestly, rather than politically correctly. And I think it's a darn shame that when a guy speaks the truth he has to catch grief for it.

As for Tommy's feelings about Russell, I don't really have that insight. But I did see Bill Russell as a minor league player, a major league player, a coach for Tommy, and then as a big league manager. And I've never seen anybody change as much as he did. When Bill Russell was a coach, everything Tommy said got Bill's attention. And when he became manager, he never even mentioned Tommy's name. I mean, how do you go from "Tommy said this" and "Tommy said that" to "Tommy who?"

I thought it was really weird. Especially because I always heard Tommy praise him. I was with Tommy a lot, and I *never* heard him criticize Bill Russell. Even if I said, "Hey, did you see the game the other night?" Tommy would always say, "Well, that's the way you play it in that situation," or "Billy knows what he's doing," or "Billy's learning and he's gonna get better with every move."

Let me say one more thing. I know you won't print it, but if you want you can. I always felt that if Tommy was going to criticize Billy to anyone, it would be to me. And I never had the joy of hearing Tommy do that.

So it's just an easy little cop-out to say, "Hey, I shouldn't have been fired. If it wasn't for Tommy, I'd be managing the rest of my life." Because Fox had just bought that team. And it's very uncommon in the sports industry that someone spends hundreds of millions of dollars and doesn't change upper management. It's very uncommon. It's the exception rather than the rule.

TOM VERDUCCI: We heard all those Machiavellian rumors about Tommy doing things behind the scenes. But now that I've seen the Fox people in action for a year or so, I think it was inevitable that Russell would go. Russell was not a great manager. He had no star quality, which the Fox people like.

So maybe Tommy convinced them and maybe he didn't. Either way, I think Russell would have been gone.

BUD FURILLO: Everybody knew that Tommy hadn't spoken to Russell in over a year. So immediately Tommy was under suspicion. But Tommy Lasorda didn't fire Bill Russell. Bob Graziano stepped forward and said he fired Bill Russell. And Bob Graziano did fire Bill Russell. Tommy Lasorda had nothing to do with it.

TOMMY LASORDA: I nurtured Bill Russell. I made him a coach—when certain people didn't want me to make him a coach! I made him a coach because he was like a son to me, and that's why I wanted him to be the manager of the Dodgers! I told Russell, "Hey, I'm not gonna make this decision. It's gonna be Peter O'Malley and Fred Claire who make the decision. But if they ask me, I want you to be the guy to replace me." And that's the way it happened.

Then I stayed away from the guy, just so I would not be a distraction, just so I wouldn't be in his way. But I told him every time, "If you ever need me, I'm there to help you."

He never once invited me to lunch, never once invited me to dinner, never once asked me what I should do, which is fine, that's okay with me. He's got to survive on his own ability. But if he needed me, I was always ready to help him.

So when he made that statement, it was like somebody stuck a knife in me. Hurt? I was unbelievably hurt. What I did for that guy? Because I loved him and I believed in him? And for him to make that statement was terrible. Terrible!

There's no way! Why would I want him out of there if I'm the guy that wanted him in there? Why would I say anything bad about him? I loved him like a son! And for him to do that to me, I will never, ever forgive him! Never! I feel that he hurt me so bad, and Doug Krikorian, too! And you can put all that in there!

BILL RUSSELL: As a manager I wanted to stand on my own. I learned a lot of things from Tommy, and we talked occasionally, but it was my job, and I wanted to do it the way I was taught, the way I learned from Walter Alston and Tommy. So if he took it the wrong way, it wasn't meant to be that way. I did it like Tommy did when he took over. He didn't consult Walt Alston. He wanted to do it his way. I wanted to do it my way. That's basically the point.

So I don't know what really happened. I will mention that Tommy and I haven't talked since the firing. But basically there's no use getting into it again. It's over and done with, and we had a long relationship, and it's too bad it came down to something like this. Because we were like father and son at one time, and no more. But there's no use getting into it and saying a lot of things. It's just not a good friendship anymore. That's basically all I want to say about it.

And as for the explosive statements attributed to him in the Long Beach *Press-Telegram?* As was noted in the Alston years, Russell now denies ever making them.

BILL RUSSELL: That basically came from Doug Krikorian. He came into my office and he made a lot of statements to me. A lot of statements that I didn't deny, but I didn't say anything. Doug's the one who made all the statements, and he wrote that I said it, which is not right. I didn't. Doug's the guy who did all that.

TOMMY LASORDA: Why wouldn't he call me up and tell me he didn't say it? If he didn't say it, then he should have immediately called me and told me, "Hey, I didn't say it."

But he didn't. So that made me believe that he did say it.

Doug Krikorian has not responded to numerous requests for an interview. So, on to the final subject of *As the Dodgers Turn:* What about the published rumors that Lasorda undermined Claire in order to get his job as general manager?

TOMMY LASORDA: It's a joke! Why in the hell are they blaming me? Who would I go to to get Claire fired? Who? Claire got himself fired! He got himself fired when he called that press conference and told everybody, "Hey, I didn't make that Piazza deal." He was talking about the people who employed him!

Why would I want to get him fired? I had reached the top of the mountain, I had become a Hall of Famer, I had nothing else to gain. I didn't want anybody's job. All I wanted was to help the Dodgers become a successful organization. That was my every intention, to help in every way that I could, and I *do* help in every way. If they need me to go talk to somebody, I go. They need me to do this, I do it.

And I will do it till the day I die. I will never work for anybody else. This is my 50th year with them. And let me tell you something: You don't last that long if you talk about other people in the organization! You don't last if you try and step on somebody's toes! You don't last if you try and get people fired! I outlasted them all, Russell and Fred Claire and everyone else!

FRED CLAIRE: The decision to fire me wasn't made by Tommy. So Tommy didn't fire me. So I don't hold him responsible.

It's that basic and it's that clear to me. I was told by Bob Graziano. Bob said it was his recommendation. So I take him at his word. That's my view of it.

When this strange and tempestuous season had finally ended, the 1998 Dodgers had played baseball better under Hoffman-Lasorda (47–41) than under Russell-Claire (36–38). But they couldn't overcome their sluggish start and a summer crammed with so much change and distraction. They finished 83–79, 15 games behind the first-place Padres, and failed to make the playoffs for a second straight October.

Thus ended the Dodgers' 41st year in Los Angeles, and their first topsy-turvy season under Fox.

36

GREAT EXPECTATIONS

1999–2000

A<small>FTER A BUSTLING BUT FOCUSED OFF-SEASON, THE</small> 1999 D<small>ODGERS SEEMED LIKE</small> a team on its way to restoring its former glory. They started by putting three big pieces in place: general manager, manager, No. I starter.

The new general manager was 41-year-old Kevin Malone, a respected baseball man, picked jointly by Graziano and Lasorda, who at age 70 moved back into a senior vice presidency. Malone came to Los Angeles via Baltimore, where he became known for his aggressive deals, and before that from Montreal, where he helped build one of the game's best minor league systems.

The new manager was the equally confident and even more accomplished Davey Johnson, who had replaced the promising but inexperienced Glenn Hoffman. Johnson, 51, had never finished lower than second place in his ten full seasons as manager of the Mets, Reds, and Orioles. He won four division titles, one National League pennant, and one World Series championship with the young and raucous Mets in 1986.

The new ace of the pitching staff was 34-year-old right-hander Kevin Brown. Armed with a nasty slider and a 95-mile-per-hour fastball, he was coming off three dominant seasons and two straight World Series appearances, which had vaulted him to the top of the free-agent market. More-over, in the tradition of Don Drysdale, Brown was a snarling enforcer who didn't hesitate to throw inside.

But in December 1998, when the Dodgers made him the highest-paid player in baseball history with a seven-year, $105 million contract, the news touched off a round of industry sniping. The other clubs complained that by breaking the $100 million barrier, the Murdoch Dodgers had widened the gap between the small-market and large-market teams. To which the brash Malone promptly replied, "To me, it's just sour grapes. Everyone is jealous of the Dodgers." Then the hard-nosed Brown said, "If they don't like it because you're trying to win, too bad."

Including Brown's $15 million per year, the Dodgers' payroll soared from $48 million in 1998 to $80 million in 1999. It was the second-highest payroll in the majors, and it brought along the burden of great expectations. Some analysts picked the Dodgers to win their division, their first postseason game since 1988, and possibly even World Series rings.

Then, even before spring training, Malone cranked up the volume even louder when he said he was the "new sheriff in town" and to look for the Dodgers and Yankees in the World Series. Even if he was kidding, as he said later, his comments got wide play and all but painted targets on L.A. uniforms.

Of course, that wouldn't matter if the Dodgers could back up Malone out on the field. But after starting a so-so 26–24 in April and May, the Dodgers went a disastrous 8–17 in June.

Just how bad did it get for the Dodgers that month? On June 26 their pitcher Carlos Perez got tagged out near first base when San Francisco first baseman J. T. Snow pulled off the hidden-ball trick. Yes, the hidden-ball trick, which rarely even works in Pony League.

Then on the following day, June 27, the Dodgers (34–39) moved into last place in the National League West. That's when the columnists *really* had their fun.

On August 11 the gifted but immature Raul Mondesi demanded to be traded. But Mondesi didn't stop there. He blasted Malone and Johnson in a shocking, foulmouthed tirade that made its way into the morning papers. When Mondesi issued the standard apology, he was still booed for weeks by skeptical Dodger fans.

Meanwhile, the critics still banged on the Mike Piazza trade the previous season. Even though Kevin Brown was racking up wins, many Piazza supporters could not quite understand why the Dodgers had paid an excellent pitcher $105 million after refusing to pay an excellent everyday player $100 million. Furthermore, said those who missed Piazza, he had been dealt to the Marlins for five players, and only one (Sheffield) remained in L.A.

Of course, Sheffield had a different view.

"It's time people move on with that issue," Sheffield told the *Los Angeles Times*. "If Mike Piazza wanted to be a Dodger, he would have been a Dodger. All he had to do was sign the contract, and he didn't. He would have signed if he had wanted to be here, and it (the trade) would never have happened."

By October 3, the regular season finale, Los Angeles had some positives to point at. Brown went 18–9 with only 59 walks and 221 strikeouts. Karros had a career year with 34 homers, 112 RBIs, and a .304 batting average. Sheffield hit .301 with 34 home runs and 101 RBIs. And two of the players acquired by Lasorda in his brief stint as interim GM—reliever Jeff Shaw (34 saves) and shortstop Mark Grudzielanek (.326 average)—also produced strong individual seasons.

As a unit, however, the 1999 Dodgers were a bust. With their $80 million payroll, they still went 77–85, finished third in the NL West, and spent their third straight postseason on the sidelines.

On October 28, one day after the Yankees won their second consecutive World Series, the Fox Group made yet another dramatic shakeup when it turned over control of the storied but struggling franchise to former Warner Bros. chairman and lifetime Dodger fan Robert Daly. Although Fox remained the majority owner, Daly purchased five percent of the team, and as its new board chairman and CEO, he would be running the club on a day-to-day basis.

"Not only is my heart in this, so is my wallet. I will do everything to bring the Dodgers back to the position they should be at," said Daly, a 62-year-old native of Brooklyn who had seen his first Dodger game at Ebbets Field when he was in first grade.

Of course, as a studio head for nearly 20 years, Daly had no track record in baseball. But he was smart and successful, and enormously popular even in screw-your-buddy Hollywood. As for the local reaction to Daly becoming the new boss of the Dodgers, the headline on Bill Plaschke's column in the October 29 *Los Angeles Times* seemed to capture the sentiment of the city: GOOD TO HAVE A FAN IN THE OWNER'S SEAT.

Moving quickly but shrewdly, Daly made two good moves in one major transaction on November 8. He shipped out the unhappy Mondesi for Toronto's multitalented Shawn Green, who in 1999 hit 42 homers, drove in 123 runs, stole 20 bases, and made one error all season in right field.

The 27-year-old Green would hopefully provide the left-handed power that the Dodger lineup had lacked for so many years. He also grew up in Orange County, just 40 miles south of Chavez Ravine. Finally, Green was Jewish in a city that still worshipped Sandy Koufax, a city with nearly 600,000 Jews.

Unfortunately for the hardworking Green, even he was somewhat disappointing as the Dodgers began the twenty-first century with moderate improvement on the field and even more upheaval in the front office. Then again, what else is new? Since Fox bought the Dodgers in 1998, all they've consistently done is change directions.

The 2000 Dodgers went 86–76, giving them one less regular-season win than the world champion Yankees, and nine more victories than the Dodgers had produced the previous season. Sheffield hit a career-best 43 homers, tying the franchise record set by Duke Snider in 1956. Kevin Brown led the National League with a 2.58 ERA, and Chan Ho Park (18–10, 3.27 ERA) emerged as one of the game's most dominant young pitchers.

On the other hand, more was expected from a team with the third-highest payroll ($98 million) in the majors. A significant chunk of that went to Sean Green (.269 and 24 homers), who clearly started pressing after signing his new six-year, $84 million contract. Meanwhile, the defense was awful (135 errors, second-most in the majors), the starting pitching atrocious in the number 4 and 5 spots (11–26, 6.28 ERA), and the offense far too dependent on home runs. The result was a fourth straight year of watching the playoffs on television, and a second-place finish 11 games behind the surging Giants.

Nearly as aggravating to the fans were Kevin Malone's self-serving public statements. In August, Malone blamed Johnson for the team's failures while also absolving himself of responsibility. "We did the things we needed to

do with our moves in the off-season and we added talent before the trading deadline," Malone told the *Los Angeles Times.*

In reality, Malone had made a series of dubious personnel moves, including bringing back Ismael Valdez, trading Charles Johnson for Todd
Hundley, and the $15.6 million that Malone gave to inept Carlos Perez.
And yet, in Malone's estimation, the Dodgers had not played better because
of Johnson's poor game strategy and laid-back leadership style.

By then everyone knew the Malone-Johnson partnership was doomed.
The only question was Who will be the fall guy? Daly made that pretty
clear when he criticized Johnson at the All-Star break. "You'd hope we
could manufacture a few more runs and win some of those closer games
when we don't have the two- or three-run home run," Daly told the *Times.*

Johnson knew he was through after reading Daly's pointed comments.
Then the Dodgers made it official in early October, firing baseball's win-
ningest active manager after his two seasons in Los Angeles.

Later that October, while Roger Clemens was making an ass of himself
by throwing a splintered bat at Mike Piazza, and the otherwise classy
Yankees were winning their third consecutive World Series, the Dodgers
were looking to hire their fourth manager since the middle of the 1996 season. In the 42 years before that, only Alston and Lasorda had managed the
ballclub.

On November 1, the Dodgers named bench coach Jim Tracy as their new
manager. They chose the low-key Tracy over their more emotional batting
coach Rick Down, who had the clubhouse support of Kevin Brown, Sean
Green, and Eric Karros. Tracy, 44, had never managed in the major leagues.
His seven-year minor league record was an ordinary 501–486. Thus his
biggest selling point appeared to be his good standing with Malone.

But for all the "Jim who?" remarks heard in Los Angeles after his hiring, Tracy may turn out to be successful. Alston and Lasorda are Hall of
Famers and neither of them had managed in the majors before the Dodgers
gave them their big break. Tracy better prove himself quickly, however.
He only received a two-year contract and the era of Dodger patience is a
memory.

Which brings up the paramount question for this franchise: Will it
regain its stability, repair its tattered image, and resume winning World
Series rings?

Nobody can predict the future, of course. At least not with any certainty. But that didn't faze Tommy Lasorda, the irrepressible Dodger since 1949, who showed he still had the touch by leading the U.S. baseball team to an unexpected gold medal in the 2000 Sydney Olympics.

TOMMY LASORDA: We're talking about the Dodgers. This organization has a great tradition. And if we can all gather around, and pull *together,* we can bring this club back to where it belongs. There is no doubt in my mind we can come back. No doubt at all.

AUTHOR'S NOTE

I was seven years old when Sandy Koufax refused to pitch in Game I of the 1965 World Series because it fell on Yom Kippur. As a Jewish kid who loved baseball, I took pride in Koufax's decision. In fact, he became one of my idols.

Aside from Koufax, however, I don't recall giving much thought to the Dodgers back then. I grew up on the North Side of Chicago, where I pledged my allegiance to Mike Royko, Mayor Daley, and for some cruel and twisted reason the Cubs.

It wasn't until 1984, when I moved to Los Angeles for a new job, that my long-standing indifference to the Dodgers changed into healthy curiosity. First I met a woman named Mary Kay, an attractive Angeleno who happened to be a lifelong Dodger fan. Then we ended up getting married on October 15, 1988—and if you're any kind of Dodger fan at all, you not only know what that date means, you remember where you were that giddy evening.

We were at my sister-in-law's house in Palos Verdes, watching the World Series opener on television. There were seven or eight of us, still tipsy, the only ones left at the after-wedding party, when Kirk Gibson limped out of the clubhouse to pinch-hit for the Dodgers. They had one man on base, but there were two outs in the ninth, and the mighty Oakland A's led 4–3.

Gibson, on two injured legs that had been packed in ice most of the game, could not get around on Dennis Eckersley's fastball. Gibson kept fouling off pitches, looking feeble. Then Eckersley threw a slider and Gibson crushed it, and Chavez Ravine was bedlam as the Dodgers won 5–4 on Gibson's implausible World Series homer.

And at that very moment, as I literally jumped out of my seat, I felt a connection to the Los Angeles Dodgers. Now, 13 years later, with a wife and three children all born in Southern California, I still find myself rooting for the home team . . . except when they play the Cubs.

As a journalist and an author, somebody always looking for good book ideas, I found the Dodgers intriguing for their success on the field (nine pennants and five World Series victories), their box office appeal (they have drawn three million fans in a record 15 seasons), their engaging blend of personalities (Walter O'Malley, Koufax, Wills, Garvey, Lopes, Sutton, Lasorda, Gibson . . .), and their fair share of major controversies (O'Malley's stunning move to California, Koufax's shocking retirement, the Garvey-Sutton scuffle, Steve Howe's cocaine troubles, the Al Campanis–*Nightline* episode, the trading of Mike Piazza, the firings of Bill Russell and Fred Claire . . .).

To bring this rich story to life, I have interviewed 124 people spanning six decades, including mostly past and present Dodgers, but also a lively group of longtime fans, key opponents, and well-informed writers and broadcasters. Fortunately, I was able to speak with most of the principal characters. The most notable exceptions were Koufax, Peter O'Malley, and Piazza, who all declined my interview requests.

As for the form I chose—oral history—I have employed it twice before in books on firefighters and Notre Dame football. In each case I liked the candor and intimacy that resulted from hearing the stories of people who *lived* them. I hope I have created the same unvarnished feeling in *True Blue*.

LIST OF INTERVIEWS

Sparky Anderson: former manager of Cincinnati Reds
Denis Anthony: longtime Dodger fan
Dusty Baker: Dodger outfielder (1976–83)
Buzzie Bavasi: Dodger general manager (1951–68)
Tim Belcher: Dodger pitcher (1987–91)
Milton Berle: TV star and longtime Dodger fan
Carroll Beringer: Dodger bullpen coach (1961–72)
Steve Brenner: Dodger public relations director (1975–87)
Greg Brock: Dodger first baseman (1982–86)
Bill Buckner: Dodger outfielder–first baseman (1969–76)
Mike Busch: Dodger third baseman (1995–97)
Brett Butler: Dodger center fielder (1991–97)
Jim Campanis: son of late general manager Al Campanis and Dodger
    catcher (1966–68)
Tom Candiotti: Dodger pitcher (1992–97)
Bill Caplan: longtime Dodger fan
Orlando Cepeda: former outfielder with San Francisco Giants
Ron Cey: Dodger third baseman (1971–82)
Fred Claire: Dodger general manager (1987–97)
Jack Clark: former outfielder with St. Louis Cardinals
Bob Costas: broadcaster for NBC
Warren Cowan: prominent Hollywood publicist
Roger Craig: Dodger pitcher (1955–61)

Robert Creamer: author and former *Sports Illustrated* writer

Mark Cresse: Dodger coach and bullpen catcher (1975–98)

Mike Davis: Dodger outfielder (1988–89)

Tommy Davis: Dodger outfielder (1959–66)

Don Demeter: Dodger outfielder (1956, 1958–61)

Rick Dempsey: Dodger coach and former catcher (1988–90)

Al Downing: Dodger pitcher (1971–77)

Mel Durslag: former *Herald Examiner* columnist

Bill Dwyre: *Los Angeles Times* sports editor

Carl Erskine: Dodger pitcher (1948–59)

Ron Fairly: Dodger outfielder–first baseman (1958–69)

Ron Fimrite: *Sports Illustrated* writer

Bud Furillo: former *Herald Examiner* sports editor

Steve Garvey: Dodger infielder (1969–82)

Kirk Gibson: Dodger outfielder (1988–90)

Dick Gray: Dodger third baseman (1958–59)

Chris Gwynn: Dodger outfielder (1987–91, 1994–95)

Derrick Hall: Dodger senior vice president

Tom Haller: Dodger catcher (1968–71)

Pete Hamill: Brooklyn-born author and newspaperman

Lenny Harris: Dodger infielder (1989–93)

Mickey Hatcher: Dodger utility man (1979–80, 1987–90)

Mark Heisler: *Los Angeles Times* writer

Richard Hoffer: *Sports Illustrated* writer

Tot Holmes: Dodger historian

Jerome Holtzman: former columnist for *Chicago Tribune* and *Sun-Times*

Burt Hooton: Dodger pitcher (1975–84)

Frank Howard: Dodger outfielder (1958–64)

Steve Howe: Dodger pitcher (1980–85)

Jay Howell: Dodger pitcher (1988–92)

Jaime Jarrin: Dodger broadcaster

Dr. Frank Jobe: Dodger team doctor

Tommy John: Dodger pitcher (1972–78)

Lou Johnson: Dodger outfielder (1965–67)

Jay Johnstone: Dodger outfielder (1980–82, 1985)

Roger Kahn: Brooklyn-born author

Paul Kalil: former Dodger marketing executive

Eric Karros: Dodger first baseman (1991–)

Kevin Kennedy: Fox baseball analyst and former minor-league manager for Dodgers

Ted Koppel: host of ABC's *Nightline*

Tim Kurkjian: writer for *ESPN the Magazine*

Clem Labine: Dodger pitcher (1950–60)

Tony La Russa: manager of Oakland A's in 1988 World Series

Tommy Lasorda: Dodger senior vice president and former manager (1977–96)

Jim Lefebvre: Dodger infielder (1965–72)

Mike Littwin: *Rocky Mountain News* writer and former *Los Angeles Times* writer

Davey Lopes: Milwaukee Brewers manager and former Dodger infielder (1971–81)

Demie Mainieri: Mike Piazza's coach at Miami–Dade North Community College

Mike Marshall: Dodger pitcher (1974–76)

Willie Mays: former outfielder for San Francisco Giants

Tim McCarver: Fox baseball analyst and former catcher for St. Louis Cardinals

Joe McDonnell: Los Angeles radio reporter

Roger McDowell: Dodger pitcher (1991–94)

Ken McMullen: Dodger infielder (1962–64, 1973–75)·

Joe Moeller: Dodger pitcher (1962, 1964, 1966–71)

Rick Monday: Dodger radio broadcaster and former Dodger center fielder (1977–84)

Chris Mortensen: correspondent for ESPN TV and former writer for *Herald Examiner*

Todd Moulding: Dodger bullpen catcher (1983–94)

Ross Newhan: *Los Angeles Times* columnist

Roger Owens: the famous Peanut Man

Claude Osteen: Dodger coach and former Dodger pitcher (1965–73)

Scott Ostler: *San Francisco Chronicle* columnist and former *Los Angeles Times* columnist

Danny Ozark: Dodger coach (1965–72, 1980–82)

Jim Palmer: former pitcher for Baltimore Orioles

Bill Plaschke: *Los Angeles Times* columnist

Johnny Podres: Dodger pitcher (1953–55, 1957–66)

Doug Rau: Dodger pitcher (1972–79)

Mark Reese: son of the late Pee Wee Reese and film producer

Phil Regan: Dodger pitcher (1966–68)

Jerry Reuss: Dodger pitcher (1979–87)

Bobby Richardson: former second baseman for New York Yankees

Ed Roebuck: Dodger pitcher (1955–58, 1960–63)

John Roseboro: Dodger catcher (1957–67)

Joe Rudi: former outfielder for Oakland A's

Harry Rudolph: bat boy for Brooklyn Dodgers

Bill Russell: Dodger shortstop (1969–86) and manager (1996–98)

Steve Sax: Dodger second baseman (1981–88)

Mike Scioscia: Anaheim Angels manager and former Dodger catcher
   (1980–92)

Larry Sherry: Dodger pitcher (1958–63)

Norm Sherry: Dodger catcher (1959–62)

Joseph Siegman: coorganizer of Hollywood Stars Game

Rabbi Hillel Silverman: prominent Los Angeles rabbi during Sandy
   Koufax era

Bill Singer: Dodger pitcher (1964–72)

Reggie Smith: Dodger outfielder (1976–81)

Duke Snider: Dodger outfielder (1947–62)

Dave Stewart: Dodger pitcher (1978, 1981–83)

Franklin Stubbs: Dodger outfielder–first baseman (1984–89)

Neil Sullivan: Los Angeles–born author

Don Sutton: Dodger pitcher (1966–80, 1988)

Jeff Torborg: Dodger catcher (1964–70)

Dick Tracewski: Dodger infielder (1962–65)

Bobby Valentine: New York Mets manager and former Dodger infielder
   (1969, 1971–72)

George Vecsey: columnist for *New York Times*

Tom Verducci: writer for *Sports Illustrated*

Gordon Verrell: writer for Long Beach *Press-Telegram*

Dave Wallace: Dodger pitching coach (1995–97)

Mitch Webster: Dodger outfielder (1991–95)

Stan Williams: Dodger pitcher (1958–62)
Maury Wills: Dodger shortstop (1959–66, 1969–72)
Geoff Witcher: Los Angeles radio reporter
Steve Yeager: Dodger catcher (1972–85)
Eric Young: Dodger second baseman (1992, 1997–99)

ACKNOWLEDGMENTS

There are many good people to thank. Above all, I thank the Los Angeles Dodgers who were kind enough to be interviewed for this book. It could not have been written without their cooperation.

I am deeply indebted to David Black, one of my close friends and the best literary agent in the business. My gifted and gracious editor, Mauro DiPreta, provided sharp thinking and honest criticisms. Mauro's assistant, Joelle Yudin, was never less than wonderful to work with. Thanks also to Lou Aronica and Patricia Lande Grader for nurturing the book in its early stages.

I am especially grateful to Ruth Ruiz, Brent Shyer, and Derrick Hall from the Dodgers front office. They were remarkably helpful, no matter how many times I dialed their numbers. I'd also like to express my gratitude to Donna Carter, Barbara Conway, and Dave Tuttle of the Dodgers.

Thanks to these talented print and broadcast journalists for their generosity and expertise: Bob Costas, Robert Creamer, Mel Durslag, Bill Dwyre, Ron Fimrite, Bud Furillo, Pete Hamill, Mark Heisler, Rick Hoffer, Tot Holmes, Jerome Holtzman, Jaime Jarrin, Roger Kahn, Kevin Kennedy, Ted Koppel, Tim Kurkjian, Mike Littwin, Tim McCarver, Joe McDonnell,

Chris Mortensen, Ross Newhan, Scott Ostler, Bill Plaschke, Neil Sullivan, George Vecsey, Tom Verducci, Gordon Verrell, and Geoff Witcher.

For their various contributions, I'd also like to say thank you to Sparky Anderson, Denis Anthony, Jennifer Anthony, Kathleen Anthony, Larry Babcock, Dusty Baker, Brian Bartow, Mark Becker, Milton Berle, Sarah Boss, Steve Brener, Dr. Andrew Cameron, Bill Caplan, John Carlin, Eric Carrington, Orlando Cepeda, Jack Clark, Warren Cowan, Gary Delsohn, Eilene Delsohn, Penny Delsohn, Sharon Delsohn, Jonathan Diamond, David Eisenstein, Steve Fink, Matt Goldfield, Paul Gomez, Sheldon Gottlieb, Tim Hevley, Brad Horn, Jay Horowitz, Dr. Frank Jobe, Dennis Johnson, Paul Kalil, Sandy Kempa, Tony La Russa, Demie Mainieri, Willie Mays, Mary McPherson, Phil McPherson, Gary Morris, Lyly Novis, John Olguin, Roger Owens, Jim Palmer, Susan Raihofer, Mark Reese, Bobby Richardson, David Rubenstein, Joe Rudi, Harry Rudolph, Dick Russell, Michael Salmon, Dr. Kenneth Saul, Peter Schivarelli, Jim Schultz, Joseph Siegman, Rabbi Hillel Silverman, Joy Tutela, Rick Vaughn, Bart Wylie, and Nick Zaccagnino.

Special thanks to my amazing daughters, Emma, Hannah, and Grace. Their love and tenderness have blessed my life.

Finally, my deepest thanks to Mary Kay Delsohn, my wife and best friend, who helped me at every stage of this work, listening to my stories about baseball, patiently reading each draft, suggesting ideas and changes.

She is everything to me, always.